PARADISE AND BEYOND

CONTENTS

To Sam, Frankie, Oliver, George, James and Harry

First published 2011
by Black & White Publishing Ltd
29 Ocean Drive, Edinburgh EH6 6JL

1 3 5 7 9 10 8 6 4 2 11 12 13 14

ISBN: 978 1 84502 349 2

The publisher has made every reasonable effort to contact
copyright holders of images in the picture section. Any errors
are inadvertent and anyone who, for any reason, has not been contacted
is invited to write to the publisher so that a full acknowledgment
can be made in subsequent editions of this work.

A CIP catalogue record for this book is available
from the British Library.

Typeset by Ellipsis Digital Ltd, Glasgow
Printed and bound by ScandBook AB, Sweden

PARADISE AND BEYOND

MY AUTOBIOGRAPHY

CHRIS SUTTON

WITH MARK GUIDI

BLACK & WHITE PUBLISHING

ACKNOWLEDGEMENTS

There are many people I would like to thank. My wife Sam for her continuous love and support throughout. My parents, Mike and Josie, for their patience, love and guidance, which led to me having a career in football.

Mark Guidi, a man of incredible patience and humour, whose help and input in this book has been exceptional. The work he has put in and the time he has given me are something I will always be grateful for.

Campbell Brown and Alison McBride at Black & White Publishing for giving me the platform to tell my story. John Richardson and Rachel Kuck for their work on the book. Janne Moller for her research on the pictures.

I would like to thank Mike Walker, Kenny Dalglish, Roy Hodgson, Gianluca Vialli and Martin O'Neill for taking the time to contribute to my book. I may not have always been straight-forward to manage, so I appreciate their time in giving their thoughts.

Henrik Larsson and Ian Pearce for their contributions. These are two people who I have the utmost respect for on and off the pitch.

John Robertson and Steve Walford for their guidance and mentoring through my happiest period in football. I owe them so much. Dave McGhie and Billy Mckinlay for their advice and friendship.

To all football fans, especially the clubs I played for – Norwich City, Blackburn Rovers, Chelsea, Celtic, Birmingham City and Aston Villa.

Chris Sutton

Dave 'Springsteen' McGhie – many thanks for getting the ball rolling on this.

To Campbell, Alison, John, Rachel and Janne at Black & White Publishing, especially John and Rachel for their patience and understanding. To Gavin Berry for his excellent research. Brian McSweeney for his advice and technical wizardry. And thanks to Jim Duffy and David McKie.

Sam and the boys for making me welcome in their home.

To Chris, many thanks for choosing me to collaborate with you on your book. Your attention to detail and high standards were superb. Whether it was Glasgow or Norfolk, Birmingham or Barcelona, it was always a pleasure.

Mark Guidi

FOREWORD
BY HENRIK LARSSON

I was introduced to Chris Sutton on a beautiful, sunny day in Copenhagen in July 2000 at Celtic's pre-season training camp. Martin O'Neill had just been appointed manager, my fifth boss in my three years at the club. As a player, you are always interested in what way the new man will go about it. You always want to know what kind of players he will bring to the club.

Martin signed Chris from Chelsea and he joined up with the squad in Denmark. I was aware of Chris from seeing him play for Blackburn Rovers. I felt he was a quality player. Chris had had a hard time at Stamford Bridge the previous season and admits later in this book he arrived in a fragile state of mind. Well, I would never have known he was short of confidence after our first training session together. We clicked immediately. I knew he was a striker of the highest calibre.

The way he played the ball into my path was first class, perfectly weighted. And he never stood still. He was on the move and gave me options. I could fake a pass in his direction, take the ball on myself or give it back to him. He gave defenders a problem, used space well to receive a pass or leave a gap for a team-mate.

At the end of that session, I felt great and optimistic about the season ahead. I knew we could play together. It brightened up even further what was already a lovely day.

If there was one little doubt in my mind it was what Martin had planned for the team. I had never worked with Martin before and when a new striker arrives, especially someone as good as Chris, it brings a little bit of apprehension into your mind because with him playing in the same position as me, you wonder about your own self-interest, first and foremost. Thoughts such as 'where does this leave me?' and 'will the manager want to play a lone striker or a partnership?' are in your head. But as things shaped up in the days and weeks ahead I could see the manager wanted myself and Chris to play together.

Our first game in the SPL was away to Dundee United and we won 2–1. We both scored to give the team a perfect start and our partnership a platform to build on. Chris then opened the scoring in the 6–2 win over Rangers at Parkhead. We both scored twice that day. That was an important victory.

Our partnership was getting better and it was a case of we didn't even need to speak on the pitch, it all came naturally to us. The game that summed it up for me was away to Dunfermline in our first season. A ball was played up and I stepped over it. Chris was behind me and he played a one-touch pass through as I continued my run. I scored. It felt as though our partnership was telepathic.

I really enjoyed my football that season. I had broken my leg the previous season and it was good for me to come back into the team with someone as talented as Chris beside me. He had a great physical presence and was a great shield for me. Our partnership blossomed and the team won the treble in 2001. I only wish we played more often together but Chris was so versatile that he was used as a midfielder in a number of games.

Off the park, we were very friendly. We socialised together with the families. In terms of football, it's not vital to have a good relationship away from the pitch, but it certainly doesn't do any harm if you do. I got to know Chris as a person and appreciate his sense of humour. He isn't too bothered what people think about him and you only find that about him once you get to know him.

For some reason he used to love to say to people, 'Your grasp of the English language is absolutely atrocious.' I smile when I think about that. It was a little saying that was a part of his humour. Of course, he never said that to me. He knew better!

He is also a fine family man and nothing else is more important to him than that. I think he is trying to build his own football team, the amount of sons he has. He has taught his sons to play cricket, or rounders as I call it! I'm not sure why he wants them to play that sport!

We had four great years together at Celtic. It was a very special time for both of us in our careers. I missed Chris when I joined Barcelona in 2004. When you leave someone behind, it's natural that you feel a little bit empty for a period of time. Even though I had a fantastic time at Barcelona and played in a brilliant team, I think it would have been even better for me if Chris was beside me. But that just wasn't possible.

During my career, I was fortunate to play with many good strikers but Chris was undoubtedly the best strike partner I ever had. The best out of all of them. Of that I'm absolutely certain.

INTRODUCTION

I thought long and hard about whether to write a book or not. Part of me felt I should but I did have reservations. But after talking with my family, and people in and out of the game, I decided it was definitely worthwhile.

I'm not doing this to settle any scores or to put anyone down. Likewise, I'm not out to criticise any football club. But I felt strongly about clearing certain things up. If I am critical, it is only me expressing my opinion, being as truthful I can be about any incidents or situations during my career. That is what a book is all about.

I'm delighted several of my former managers agreed to be interviewed for the book. They were given freedom of speech and encouraged to be open about what they felt about me as a footballer and a person. Some of them have left a bit on me and I don't have a problem with that.

Unfortunately, Glenn Hoddle refused my invitation to be interviewed. I refused to play for his England B team in 1998 and it caused a stir around the country. In these pages, I've given my opinion on him and have been reflective about the decision I made back then. I really wanted him to be honest about what he thought about me back then and, thirteen years on, what he now thinks. But he politely declined to speak.

In the pages ahead, you will get a candid account of my career

– the good, the bad and the ugly. As a player, I was probably my harshest critic and was rarely, if ever, satisfied with my performances. But this is a piece of work I'm satisfied with and, crucially, I'm completely comfortable with everything I've written in *Paradise and Beyond*.

I hope you find it enjoyable reading.

Chris Sutton

1

IT'S NOT MORE IMPORTANT
THAN LIFE OR DEATH

DECISIONS. As a footballer, I had to make countless decisions on the park in every game with only a split second to decide on most of them. Do I make a front-post run or peel off the back? Do I play in my team-mate or do I shoot? Do I foul my opponent or let him run on with the ball? Do I complain to the referee or keep my mouth shut? I called some decisions correctly and got others horribly wrong.

But that was nothing compared to the decision my wife Sam was faced with on the day of Wednesday, 21 November 2001. Her quick thinking and mother's intuition saved the life of our son, James.

She had just dropped our other three sons, Frankie, Ollie and George, at school and nursery and then had some dry-cleaning to hand in. James was in the back of the car, in his car seat. James was born on 15 September 2001, at just twenty-eight weeks. He weighed just 3lbs 1oz. He was so tiny I could hold him in the palm of my hand. He was kept in intensive care at the Queen Mother Maternity Hospital in Glasgow for weeks. He had only been out for ten days at this point.

In the early days, James was placed in the intensive care unit due to how premature he was at birth. This wasn't unusual for a baby born so early. He needed help with his breathing via a ventilator and was monitored twenty-four hours a day for several weeks. During this period, he had four blood transfusions and suffered from jaundice, but that was quite common for premature babies. He was moved to the high dependency unit when he could breathe on his own with oxygen. He was then taught how to feed and when he was feeding properly after about seven weeks, he was allowed home. It had been a huge relief to finally have him home and feel that we could start getting life back to normal.

After dropping off the dry-cleaning, Sam could hear James choking and he then stopped breathing at times. Sam didn't take any chances and phoned the hospital to tell them of her concerns. They told her to bring James in immediately.

I was in Spain that day, preparing for a UEFA Cup tie between Celtic and Valencia. I was more than 1,000 miles away in the Sidi Soler Hotel. For me, it was a normal build-up to a big game, thinking over how the game might work out, the challenges the opposition presented and getting focused on this really important European tie. Valencia isn't an easy place to play, even with our fantastic travelling support, but we were there to do a job and determined to get a result. For me, it was business as usual but for Sam, it was the start of a nightmare as she headed for Yorkhill Children's Hospital in Glasgow, worried sick about James and with the added pressure of trying to hold the family together. Had Sam not been so decisive, I could be here telling a totally different story about our son, one of tragedy and heartbreak.

Sam: I had been concerned about James the previous couple of days. I just knew something wasn't right with him. The midwife came to the house to make a routine check on James on the Tuesday morning, the day before I rushed him into Yorkhill. I told her I was a bit worried, that he had a cold and was bringing stuff up. But she said that he was

2

fine. I took her word for it. I was to go to a Tupperware party at Emma Gould's house, wife of Celtic keeper Jonathan, the following morning and was excited at taking James with me, to show him off.

But I knew he wasn't right. I said to my good friend Magdalena Larsson, Henrik's wife, early on the Wednesday morning that I was probably going to call off going to Emma's as I felt James wasn't quite right. But she said that he'd be fine and to come along, that he probably just had a little cold. So, I thought maybe I was being paranoid. But I knew deep down my son wasn't the way he should have been.

I dropped off Frankie, Ollie and George. I went to the dry-cleaners and then could hear James was choking and losing his breath. I stopped the car to look at James and his face was starting to change colour. So, I phoned the hospital immediately and they told me to bring him straight in. I panicked. I was worried. I was scared. I went through red lights, the lot, to get there as fast as I could. Chris was in Valencia and I phoned him to tell him what was happening. He told me to be as calm as possible and not to worry, that James would be fine.

When Sam phoned me from the car she was anxious. She told me James was choking and then losing his breath. She was scared. I told her to calm down, drive safely and to get off the phone and concentrate on her driving. I didn't hear from her again for close to three hours. During that period I had mixed feelings. A small part of my stomach was churning but the main part of me felt Sam was probably over-reacting, being over-protective, as mothers normally are.

I thought back to when James was born and how small he was. He was almost three months premature but was still a healthy weight for a baby born so early.

3

I wasn't overly concerned when I put the phone down. Deep down, I honestly thought he may just have had a bit of congestion. James was our fourth baby. His elder brother Frankie was six then, Ollie five and George was three. By the time James came along I was much more relaxed about coughs and wheezes and grazed knees. It was all part of your kids growing up. But I was helpless this time. I couldn't kiss and cuddle Sam or the boys, offer them reassurances, the way I would have had I been at home. But this was much more serious than I was aware of.

Sam: I got to the hospital, sat in the waiting area and then James went a funny colour, sort of blue and purple around his mouth. He stopped breathing so I shook him a couple of times, which made him breathe again. Seconds later his whole face went purple. I ran to reception and asked to see a nurse. I was told one was on the way and then I screamed that my baby had stopped breathing. Within seconds about six or eight nurses ran towards me, grabbed James and took him into a side room. I was left standing there, completely helpless. It was a horrible moment. It didn't seem real. I didn't know what was happening and I didn't know if I was going to see my son alive again or not. I was taken to a room and the recollection of that time and events after this are quite hazy. I was in a state of shock. I just wanted my son to come through this horrendous ordeal.

The midwife who'd been out at the house earlier that week and told me there was nothing to worry about sat with me at the hospital. We didn't exchange any words.

A Dr Coutts looked after James. He knew James from when he was in intensive care after he was born. He was the respiratory doctor, a top consultant, an amazing man. He came to see me a few minutes later and told me he'd brought James back again. James had died and come back to life again. Dr Coutts said James' heart and lungs had stopped working and had to be fully resuscitated. He had been checked for brain damage and was fine on that front. He was also having his heart checked. He said he would keep me informed as to what was happening. We owe Dr Coutts and the nurses everything.

I couldn't get hold of Chris at this point, so I phoned the Celtic club doctor, Roddy McDonald, who was also in Valencia. I handed my phone to this midwife and asked her to explain what had happened to James and what tests he was now going through. I was shaking but remember her words to Roddy: 'Don't worry, Chris doesn't need to come home. It'd only be for Sam he'd need to come home. James will be fine.' Her words left me confused. Why was she saying this?

I then got to see James and he was all blown up. He was on a ventilator and had been given all sorts of drugs and medicines. Magdalena came to the hospital that evening to give me support and she apologised for not believing me when I had told her James was really poorly. I went home that night as the doctors advised me to. They said James was in the best possible care. It was hard to leave him. He was all swollen and blown up with drugs to keep him comfortable.

I went home to look after Frankie, Ollie and George. I phoned Chris. He was concerned and understanding but he still hadn't grasped the enormity of the situation. He thought I was over-reacting as he'd listened to what Roddy had said on the information he'd received from the midwife. The following morning I phoned Chris to tell him I was on my way back to the hospital. I had just come off the phone to the doctors and they gave me no guarantees James would make it. At this point, they weren't exactly sure what was wrong with him. I told Chris he really should come home. This was the Thursday morning, the day of the game against Valencia.

We had a huge row over the phone, as Chris didn't believe me. He said I was over-reacting and that James would be fine. I was raging and told him I didn't want to be with him, didn't like the way he didn't believe me. I was really upset. In the car on my way to the hospital, I knew Chris wasn't himself during that conversation, he's usually very supportive and always believes me. I wondered if this was his way of dealing with it, that he realised how bad James really was but just couldn't bring himself to face up to it.

So, I phoned Doc Roddy again and tried to explain the seriousness of the situation. By this time, I was at the hospital and Dr Coutts was walking by. I handed my phone to him and told him to tell Roddy exactly what had happened. I then went back on to Roddy and he apologised. He had no idea the full extent of what James had been through and was still going through. Roddy had based everything on the information he had received from that midwife the previous day. Roddy now knew everything. Roddy then asked for my permission to tell Martin O'Neill. They then went and told Chris. Chris collapsed. He didn't play that night and stayed in his hotel room. It was unfortunate he couldn't get a flight immediately. Celtic were flying back right after the game and he had to wait until then.

I also had the other children to think of. They knew something wasn't right because James wasn't in the house with them. I told them he was in hospital but didn't want to worry them too much. Frankie and Ollie just started to cry.

I was totally taken aback when Sam told me the doctors had to resuscitate James. My head was all over the place and I wanted to go home to be with my family. I spoke to Martin O'Neill and told him I wasn't in the right frame of mind to play. I felt numb with it all. I don't even know if numb is the appropriate word. Martin was very supportive and understood my position. The club tried to get me flights out on the morning of the game and they all bent over backwards for me. I'm eternally grateful for that. I stayed in the hotel as the players went to the game at the Mestalla Stadium.

Alan Thompson was out of that game and he stayed back with me and was very supportive. It was good to have company at that moment. We sat in the hotel room and watched the game. It was then I started to think about decisions. The decisions we make in life. The referee could flip the coin for the captains to decide who'd kick off, but at that moment it was all so insignificant. In the grand scheme of things, what great difference does it make which side you kick into for the first half?

And it took me back to Sam's decision to call the hospital the previous morning. It was the right thing to do, yet as she sped through red lights, she could have been wiped out by a lorry.

I then wondered if a premature baby such as James would have it in him to fight back to health. I had no idea if he'd have the strength and resolve to live. But he did. He showed he was a fighter. Thankfully. The overwhelming thing about it all was that I didn't really understand, in the early part, the consequences – just how bad James was and how lucky he was to survive. It was all down to Sam's motherly instinct to call the hospital and rush him in immediately. Had she stopped at the traffic lights, there's a good chance James would have died. Had Sam not been pro-active and taken him to hospital, James would have died. That is 100-per-cent fact.

Had I been at home that morning, James wouldn't be alive today. If Sam had asked me what I thought about James, I would have said, as I normally did, that he would have been fine and that I'd give the club doctor a call. I'd called Roddy many times in the past about the kids or taken them to see him. But I was never in a rush to do it. I wouldn't have had the urgency Sam had. I could never relate to coughs and colds being split-second decisions. In terms of having that split second to make up your mind, I have not, and never will, make a decision as important as the one Sam made that day.

When we landed back in Glasgow after the game, I went straight to the hospital. I can still remember all the attachments to his body as he lay on a life-support machine and he looked totally helpless. I felt terrible. As a dad, I just wanted to pick him up, cuddle him and make everything go away. But I was helpless as well. It was a horrible situation to be in. The life-support machine was keeping him alive, tubes and leads going into his nose, arms and stomach.

It wasn't until I arrived back in Glasgow that they diagnosed what exactly was wrong with James. He had a condition called RSV (Respiratory Syncytial Virus). It's basically a cold to us but hits young babies hard because they are so small. They usually get it between the months of November and February. When he came out of hospital after being born prematurely, he was getting stronger, improving all the time, he was putting on weight and was getting there. But then he contracted RSV. The pipes to his lungs were so small they blocked up with secretions. His lungs had stopped working but his heart had carried on, trying to compensate for that. Eventually his heart couldn't cope with the extra strain and it packed in. It's quite a common virus for babies over the winter months and it can be very dangerous.

I sat there talking to James, hoping he'd come through it all. I was thinking about what life would be like without him and what life would be like if he survived. What he would look like when he got older. How his life might pan out. But you just have to get on with things, visit the hospital every day, do what you need to do. We were there all the time but we also had our other children to consider and it became mentally tiring and draining. We couldn't neglect them, of course, so there was a balance to be struck between James and our other three boys. Looking back, it was horrendous but you get through it. You have no choice other than to get through it. We just got on with things, as any parents in our position would have done.

He was in intensive care for six days and was then allowed into the ward on oxygen. He was there for another three days. When we got him home, we kept him indoors for four or five months. We didn't take him anywhere, we were so scared something would happen to him with all the winter germs. We were very protective. No one touched him unless they washed their hands first.

We were also given a heart-monitor to take home with us when James got out of hospital. It clicked all the time and if James stopped breathing, it triggered an alarm. Thankfully, it never happened.

Had James been sleeping in bed, rather than in the car with Sam, that morning back in November, he would have died. We were lucky he had his lapse in the morning. Someone was definitely looking over us.

We all got through it and the most important thing is that James is alive and well and healthy. He has to wear hearing aids now but that is a small price to pay.

Sam: The reason why James is partially deaf is not from when he was born, it resulted from that period afterwards when he was so poorly. It could have been down to the drugs he was administered or the lack of oxygen that got to his brain. The doctors got to him just in time, as the next stage for him would have been for his brain to be affected and that would have left him brain-damaged.

We didn't realise until he was four that he was partially deaf. We used to shout at him and he would just ignore us. Or so we thought. But he couldn't hear us. He'd be watching the television and the volume would be up ever so loud. We just didn't realise.

When we moved to Birmingham, a teacher at his nursery school detected something was wrong. She asked us if we'd had his hearing checked. We did get his hearing checked in Glasgow but they didn't spot anything unusual, as James didn't want to communicate.

We knew his speech wasn't at the stage it should have been but were told it was maybe because he had a dummy. We never suspected anything was wrong with his hearing. We felt so stupid for not noticing it.

The headmistress, an ex-nurse, organised a test for us with an audiologist who told us he had a hearing problem. We moved to Norfolk. I quite liked the idea of moving back to Norfolk where Chris was from. We had lived in Norwich briefly together before Chris was transferred to Blackburn. We saw doctors at Norfolk and Norwich Maternity Hospital. Within two weeks, he had his hearing aid. James has a massive hearing loss for high-pitched sounds. Also, some words he had never heard before, words such as cat and rat. Simple words. The day we walked out of the hospital with his hearing aid, he asked me what that strange noise was. It was the sound of him walking, his feet striding along, hitting off the floor. He'd never heard that before. I just smiled but with tears in my eyes. It's amazing the things we take for granted.

We used to let him away with all sorts, because we felt so guilty and felt so lucky he was here. But we've knuckled down with him now.

When he was about seven, he asked me, 'Mummy, why can't I hear?' and I explained everything to him. I was crying and then he nearly cried. He can lip-read, which is another help for him. But the most important thing is that he's still with us and he's a healthy, headstrong little boy who's also very kind and sensitive.

To be totally honest, the hearing aids aren't overly nice to look at but the over-riding thing for me is that we're still extremely lucky to have him. Some children in the hospital at the same time as James unfortunately didn't make it. James was one of the lucky ones. So, a hearing aid is a small price to pay. He has also grown up to be a determined little boy and I think that must stem from when he was in the hospital as a baby. He answered the questions I had in my head back then in November 2001. He is most definitely a boy who will not be beaten easily. He is a lovely singer and loves his music. And when he's had enough of any of us, he'll turn his hearing aid down a little bit! He's a happy, well-adjusted boy with a great sense of humour and is always laughing.

The hospital were brilliant and as far as we were concerned, they kept James alive. We are eternally grateful for that. They keep many, many children alive day after day and the work they do at Yorkhill is second to none. I know it's their job to do that, but I can't stress highly enough how important their jobs are and it makes football seem insignificant. Saving the life of a child or scoring a goal? There's no comparison. Shouldn't even be mentioned in the same breath.

Doctors and surgeons have to make quick decisions on how to keep children alive. I think we take that for granted. I can't understand what must go through their minds when they are faced with such a decision. A life-changing decision in seconds is real pressure. And they must get the decision right. If they make a wrong judgement call, then it could be fatal. You do hear sad stories about when doctors do make mistakes and it gets highlighted. But the good work they do every day doesn't get highlighted enough. It must be so stressful. My brother Ian is a consultant neurologist in Australia and I know from his job the incredible pressure that he is under. He often has to break shattering news to patients, such as telling them if they have MS. He feels stress and pressure, allied with sorrow, but ultimately he knows it's a very worthwhile job.

We have many doctors and nurses to thank for the way they've treated our sons, all of them delivered by emergency Caesarean section, all born ahead of schedule. Frankie was born in Norwich, premature at thirty-five weeks, on 1 June 1995. I was playing with Blackburn Rovers at that time. We went back to Norwich for a holiday, visiting friends and family, and he was born there. Oliver was born 8 May 1996 in Blackburn at thirty-seven weeks. George was born in Blackburn on 3 September 1998 at thirty-four weeks.

James was next and then we had Harry. He was born in Glasgow on 15 April 2003. He arrived seven weeks early and weighed 4lbs 7oz.

Sam: I was scared when I fell pregnant with Harry because of what happened with James. It wasn't a planned pregnancy. We only told a few people I was pregnant. I used to go to school to drop the boys off wearing a big coat to hide my tummy. Harry was born at thirty-three weeks. He was in intensive care for a few days on c/pap to help with his breathing. But he was fine. He was just four weeks old when the UEFA Cup Final was in Seville. I didn't want to go to the final, purely because I didn't want to leave James and Harry behind. But Chris talked me into it, told me I couldn't not go with Frankie, Ollie and George. This was probably going to be the only time they'd see their dad in a European final and he didn't want them to miss out on the whole experience.

It broke my heart to leave James and Harry behind. I didn't have five kids to go away and leave them all the time. But I'm so glad I did go to Seville. It was a wonderful experience and really great for the older boys.

Sam is a huge part of my life and a fantastic mother to our boys. I met Sam after an England under-21 game in Portsmouth. It was 1993. I stayed down and went out on the town after the game and bumped into Sam in a nightclub. We exchanged numbers and kept in touch over the phone for six or seven months. During that period, she had proved herself to be a less than great timekeeper. She failed to turn up for one game when I got her a ticket to see me play for Norwich against Queens Park Rangers at Loftus Road. It was her loss – I was outstanding that day. Well, at least that's what I told her! It was a cracking game but actually I wasn't that good. But I forgave her for not coming.

She came up to Norwich to see me soon after and we've been together ever since. We got married on 31 January 1995 at Hirst Green, near Blackburn. We have no girls yet and it's all my fault, as any man in my position would tell you!

We are delighted with the family we have and we are proud of our sons. And just like James, our other boys Frankie, Ollie, George and Harry are all very special. Football has helped provide our family with a nice life but the most important thing is, and always will be, that we all have our health.

2

THE GOOD LIFE

I was born a healthy baby on 10 March 1973 in Peel Street Hospital, Nottingham, the fourth child of mum Josephine and dad Mike. I had three elder siblings, brother Ian and sisters Rachel and Lucy. When my mum knew she was going into labour, she was at home with Dad and they phoned for an ambulance. She had never been in an ambulance before and was quite excited. She left my dad with my three siblings and they all complained to Mum about him later. He gave them Marmite sandwiches on wet plates and couldn't put a nappy on my sister, Lucy.

Dad might not have been much of a cook but he was a fine footballer. He played for Norwich, Chester and Carlisle. Unfortunately, a medial cruciate ligament injury on his right knee ended his career. He could have tried to continue playing but wasn't prepared to risk playing professionally after that. He was just twenty-seven.

He pursued another career and studied to be a PE teacher at Loughborough University. We lived in a place called East Leake at that time and Dad then got a teaching job and we moved to just outside Norwich, to a place called Horsford. That was our family home and my parents still live there.

I had a happy childhood. We weren't a wealthy family but we were comfortable. We had a nice house, with a bit of land. We had goats, chickens and geese. It wasn't a farm, just a smallholding, but we were like the people in the classic seventies sitcom, *The Good Life*. I was brought up on goat's milk. It tasted sour and horrible. The butter from the goats was horrible, too. My mum used to tell me to drink my milk up because it would make me strong. She would spend lots of time reading books to me and always made sure my brothers, sisters and I were brought up well, knew right from wrong and were respectful and well mannered. A solid, no-nonsense upbringing.

I liked having animals but one thing I didn't like was when I was sent out at night in the dark to shut the chickens in. I was petrified. I used to think there would be someone there with a knife, waiting for me. I've always had a vivid imagination. I was terrified of our geese, as was my dad. He would never go into the pen without a broom. I was also scared of mice and spiders, which isn't too good living in the countryside!

I always seemed to be frightened and my imagination used to run riot. I used to think someone was going to break into the house. We had a three-bedroom house and I shared a room with my brother Ian. Ian's bed was closest to the window and then, when he moved away to university in 1986, my younger brother Johnny moved into the room. He was three at the time and I made sure Johnny then got the bed closest the window. I used to make out that it was to get him some fresh air but it was really to protect myself in case someone came through the window, so that they'd get him first. Never happened, of course, but it didn't stop me worrying about it all the time.

Johnny was a late addition to the family. He was born in 1983 but had myself, Ian, Rachel and Lucy doting on him. I would often look after him. I'd bath him, change him, get him ready. My mum banned me from looking after him because she felt I was going to make him stupid because I liked a bit of mischief. It was difficult for him in some ways. He may have felt like an only child because of the age gap between him and the rest of us. But he's a sensible boy. So, Mum was right to relieve me of my duties!

My parents always said I was mischievous as a child but never nasty. I'd have tantrums and fall-outs with my parents and siblings, which would usually result in me threatening to run away and I'd set off on my bike. But when I got to the end of the driveway, I'd say that my chain had fallen off or I had a flat tyre.

I was always encouraged to study and work hard on my school-work. I once wrote a story about a footballer and Mrs Robinson, my teacher, asked me to write about something else. So I wrote about a cricketer. I just loved my sport. That was my life, what motivated me. When I was with friends we'd organise sports days in our garden. It was great fun. I'd be dribbling with the ball in the garden, doing a commentary and pretending to be John Robertson. I'd practise kicking the ball through the centre of the tyres and hitting the ball with my left foot off the garage door to improve my game.

I was good at high jump and a decent cross-country runner. I loved playing snooker and darts, too. I just wanted as much sport as I could get, really. At Christmas and on birthdays, I wanted sporty presents – football strips and football boots. The *Shoot* and *Match* annuals were always a must. I enjoyed reading about the big stars of football at that time.

I went to the local village schools in Horsford. At Horsford Middle School, I was heavily influenced by the then headmaster Steven Slack. We used to play lots of sport at school and I was lucky back then that Steven was in charge. His love of sport was brilliant for a sports-daft pupil like me.

I attended Hellesdon High School, where my dad was a PE teacher. It wasn't the natural high school for me to go to but it made sense to go there, travel in with my dad, that kind of thing and maybe so he could keep a closer eye on me.

We were a very sporty family and all pushed by our parents

to do well academically. My elder sisters and brother adhered to that, put the hours in studying. I didn't. Ian was a good sportsman, good at gymnastics and football, but didn't want to head the ball as he felt it would damage his brain cells. He knew what he wanted to do, aimed to get into medicine and is now a successful consultant neurologist in Australia. As I always tell him, Ian is the second brightest in the family after me. I've got a lot of admiration for him, going to university for seven or eight years and working exceptionally hard. I think it's a good thing to know what you want to do when you're fifteen or sixteen and you can aim for it, push yourself and hopefully achieve it.

I played lots of football, of course, throughout my school years and played cricket during the summer when I was a bit older. It was a great way to make friends. I played for Horsford Boys at under-12 level but at that point we were younger lads, playing at nine and ten against boys a couple of years older than us. We used to get thrashed 15–0 and more on a regular basis. I remember we once drew 0–0 and it felt like we'd won the World Cup. We got better as we got older and started to win more games, which was just as well. I'm so competitive that I used to take it personally when we lost games and I even cried a few times when we lost at training. I took it very seriously.

I liked the fact that we were a village team and we had a bond, local boys together. Football has changed now for kids of seven, eight, nine and ten. They travel from all over to play for one club and sometimes are attached to a professional club from the age of six. I'm not sure that is good for boys. I think it's best not to be signed up at such a young age, but to enjoy youth football without any major pressure.

Dad encouraged me to enjoy sport. He just wished I would give as much attention to my schoolwork, but football was my main passion. I knew, however, from my early teens, I needed to get fitter. Dad helped me with that. I'd come back from school games on a Saturday and we'd go to my dad's school for some gym work. It helped me build up my strength. We'd also go there during holidays. My dad would also put circuit training on at the school at 7.30 most mornings for pupils who wanted to get fitter. There was always a good turnout and the kids benefited from it. I wasn't a natural athlete but the fitness regime definitely helped me.

Being born in Nottingham, I supported Forest. They were my team. Years later, of course, I met my idols in Martin O'Neill and John Robertson. I had these amazing preconceptions about what great people they were and as much as I would like to say it was a massive disappointment, having got to know them now, I just can't find anything bad to say about them! They were good to me at Celtic and they both worked well together, along with first-team coach Steve Walford.

John and Steve would sometimes join in with the players on a Friday for a game of five-a-sides. They couldn't move but had some lovely touches. Martin didn't join in and some players, not myself I may add, reckoned it was because he didn't have the technical ability of John and Steve. But Jackie McNamara and Neil Lennon never could judge a player!

I got a Nottingham Forest top for Christmas one year and I never took it off. Trevor Francis was also a player I admired from that team under Brian Clough. To win the European Cup two years in succession – 1979 and 1980 – was a truly incredible achievement. They were a great team and Clough was an exceptional manager.

I was glad to be able to follow in their footsteps and realise the dreams I had when I was a kid, and I have my parents to thank for that. Not forgetting my Nanny Sutton, too, who was always very kind and supportive. I'd often go to her house, and she always had food ready for me. She couldn't do enough for me. She came to visit me as often as she could when we lived in Scotland. Sadly, she died in May 2010. I was very fond of her and miss her. She put a lot of work into keeping scrapbooks of my career, from when I started at Norwich, all the way through, and she did the same for Johnny. I now have those scrapbooks in my possession and treasure them because my Nanny put them together.

Before I made the back pages as a professional footballer, Nanny would come and watch me play as a kid. But as she probably well knew, my journey to becoming a professional wasn't going to be straightforward.

3

THE LONG WAY
TO CARROW ROAD

I started playing organised football at the age of eight or nine for my local village team, Horsford, in the Norfolk Sunday league. As I've said, in the early days, we weren't overly successful. I can remember only drawing one game in my first season and losing heavily most weeks. Many of the boys, like myself, found it tough playing against the older, tougher and stronger boys in this age group. But the experience was invaluable and as we grew older together, we developed into a decent team and won cups and leagues a couple of times. It was an exciting and enjoyable time as most, if not all, of the boys attended the local village school. I spent all my spare time outside of school and during the holidays playing football at the village recreation ground. We loved to play games of 'Headers and Volleys' and 'Wembley' and other small-sided, made-up games.

There was a good little group of us – Jason Wright, Mark Rix, Julian Makin and his younger brother Wayne, and Neal Pyle. We were friends and I suppose we were inseparable when it came to football. Like most boys of our age, we ate, drank and slept football. We loved to pretend to be the stars of that era – Kenny Dalglish, Trevor Francis, Bryan Robson. And John Roberston, ominously. As the team improved, so did I. I'd play five-a-side tournaments during the week after school. I'd also play football for the school and on a Sunday. It would have been difficult not to get better. As a consequence of me getting better, I was asked to attend a trial at the Norwich City FC Centre of Excellence. I was also selected to represent Norwich Schools and we played games against other area School Select teams such as Yarmouth and East Dorset.

I was still attending Horsford Middle School at this point. Every Monday I'd leave school and get a lift to my grandmother's house in nearby Hellesdon. She would feed me and then walk me to the house of another boy around the corner, Neal Carey. He was also on trial at the Norwich Centre of Excellence and his dad, Peter, would drive us to the training ground at Trowse, on the other side of Norwich. We both attended for a few months and football-wise I felt reasonably comfortable. I wasn't the best but I was by no means the worst, either.

I was growing all over the place, all arms and legs, and I probably looked uncoordinated and clumsy at times – ok, nothing has changed there, then! When it came to the decision being made as to who the club would sign on a schoolboy form so that they could continue at the Centre of Excellence, I was rejected, deemed not good enough. I took it really badly. I didn't like the feeling of rejection and I was devastated. And embarrassed.

I liked the fact my school friends knew I attended Norwich City on Monday nights and when it stopped I felt I had lost face. I was very self-conscious and at that age I was either twelve or thirteen and thought I would never be a professional footballer. Even though my parents tried to encourage me and keep my head up by saying that time was on my side and that I could still achieve my dreams, I thought that was it. Game over for me.

Dad was once told an interesting statistic by a coach at youth football level, that only one in 5000 kids who play football at the age of twelve, thirteen and fourteen will make it as a professional. It's a frightening statistic.

I hated Norwich City for rejecting me. I was too young and just not mature enough to understand their decision. My dad told me I was going to be a late developer and that I should keep practising, become fitter and stronger. Inside, however, I was fragile. I was very young and at that time I didn't believe my dad. It was clear-cut in my mind, simple and straightforward – I'd been kicked out and my big chance had gone.

Looking back, I should have believed in myself more and in my dad, Mike. He had a good professional career as a footballer. He started on the groundstaff at Norwich City at fifteen, making his debut for the first team at eighteen. At the age of twenty-two, he moved on to Chester City and then Carlisle United until his knee injury forced him to retire from the professional game at the age of twenty-seven. He still played local football when I was really young. I can remember him playing for Great Yarmouth. He was a great reader of the game and a lovely passer. He had to learn to jump off his other knee after retiring from the professional game and that couldn't have been easy. He was a big influence on me and didn't give me false hope. He always told me the truth, even if at times I didn't like it.

He was and still is an extremely fit man. At times, I thought he was extreme in pushing his fitness on me and my older siblings. My grandparents on my mother's side lived in Lowestoft, a pretty seaside town on the east coast with a lovely beach. It was very picturesque, especially on lovely summer days when most families would enjoy a leisurely stroll along the sand; some of the kids would have their buckets and spades and others would be paddling in the sea. All of them, at some point during the day, would enjoy an ice-cream. The Sutton family? Well, my dad used to have us running up the sand dunes and slopes. It was all in good fun, but his drive and knowledge on fitness and how to build strength and stamina were very beneficial to me.

I was never a natural athlete, I was very skinny but genetically it's fair to say I had more slow-twitch fibres than fast ones. But through cross-country and beach running and circuits before school days when I moved up to the senior school at Hellesdon, I developed a base in general fitness. But my body wasn't developing as quickly as I would have liked. Physically, I could have been described as gangly.

After the rejection from Norwich City, my attitude changed towards football. Looking back, I pretended I wasn't interested in becoming a professional footballer and that I wasn't bothered. I could take football or leave it. It was a kind of defence mechanism I suppose and I started to really take a strong interest in cricket – and quickly harboured hopes of becoming a first-class cricketer. I had always liked cricket from a young age but football had been my first interest.

I began to go to coaching courses from the age of twelve at Notre Dame School in Norwich and as well as playing at school, I joined the local cricket club, Horsford. I wasn't outstanding or prolific and, up until the age of fifteen, I had never scored a lot of runs on a consistent basis. But I really enjoyed the game and I turned myself into a reasonably capable batsman. I was selected for the Norfolk under-15 team. Norfolk is a minor county in cricketing terms but at the youth age group, we played first-class counties. In my first game, against Nottinghamshire, I scored 85, and that was a big surprise and a real confidence boost. I scored a couple of 35s against Lancashire and Yorkshire, 70 against Cambridgeshire and 105 not out against Northamptonshire. With this form, I was selected for a Midlands trial and I was very proud and considered it a good achievement.

There were four regions in England – the North, the South, the West and the Midlands – that took part in a cricket competition called the Bunbury Festival, which was started up by the former Bee Gees manager David English. David has worked tirelessly on this and has managed to raise hundreds of thousands of pounds for charities with his work.

The tournament was a round robin and I was selected to play for the Midlands at the Beckenham and Sydenham Bank grounds in Kent. Prior to this, I had scored a 70 not out in a warm-up game at Collingham Cricket Club in Nottinghamshire for the Midlands against the North, so I was full of confidence. But in my first game I struggled badly. I faced a bowler who was far too good and fast for me and I was out quickly. It wasn't the fact I was out that was the problem – it was just that I was out of my depth. Other boys in my team were so much better and I could see that clearly. It was another sporting blow.

I was dropped for the remaining two games and left the tournament after it finished knowing I didn't have a prayer. These boys were miles ahead of me, so much better. I found myself coming up well short. I then lost hope of becoming a professional sportsman. I wasn't being defeatist; it was just that I was very sub-standard at cricket at the level that was required.

I was still playing football regularly for my school and on a Sunday. I also played for the county and Norwich Schools. I was performing decently but still didn't harbour any hopes of becoming a pro. When I was fifteen, I went for England schoolboy trials at Trent Polytechnic in Nottingham for a week, as a representative of Norwich Schools. It was a good experience but I wasn't selected. A young Jamie Redknapp was at the trials. I don't know whether he succeeded getting into the side or not back then.

I represented Norwich Schools in a game at Great Yarmouth and Dave Stringer, the Norwich manager, attended the game. At full-time, he told my dad I hadn't shown any real sign of improvement. Well, I suppose at least I was consistent. I now had to start thinking about what path I was going to take. At school, I was reasonably sound academically, but I was lazy and didn't try anywhere near hard enough. I loved sport, nothing else. I wanted to be a sportsman, not confined to an office for the rest of my life. But I was realistic enough to know that it looked very doubtful that my dreams would be fulfilled. My GCSEs came around and I was under pressure. My brother Ian and sisters Rachel and Lucy had passed all of their exams before me. I comfortably broke the record and ruined the family tradition as I only passed six out of nine.

One exam in particular summed up my laziness. My maths paper number was 1305. Unfortunately for me, I thought that was the time it started. At 9.20 the phone rang in the house and my mum answered a call from Dad at the school. He was very angry and asked her why I wasn't in the school for the exam that had started at nine. I cycled the three miles to school in a panic and my dad passed me in the car going the other way, gesticulating, not in a friendly way. I'd failed again. It seemed a recurring theme. I did actually pass my re-sit at Maths. That time I was on time, in fact I was early.

My elder siblings had gone into sixth form. Ian then studied medicine and Rachel and Lucy both got their A-levels and are now businesswomen.

Given my track record, my parents advised me not to go into the sixth form and to look for a job instead. I agreed and sat a multiple-choice exam to try and get a job as a clerk with Norfolk County Council. To my astonishment, I got a letter through the post offering me the job. I was excited. I was going to earn money during the week and leave my weekends free to play sport – cricket in the summer with Horsford and football for the rest of the year. Through my teens, I used to go to the cricket club on Tuesday and Friday nights, and play or watch at the weekend. I was often kindly picked up and dropped off by the now president Marcus Wilkinson. Marcus took me under his wing and found jobs for me. He was and still is a real character. He used to get the heavy roller started, and I'd jump on and drive up and down on the wicket. Marcus would give me a wave from the bar. I enjoyed the cricket on and off the pitch, so a job during the week with the council and being allowed to play sport at the weekends didn't seem a hardship. Far from it.

But within the space of a few weeks my life had changed forever. My dad phoned Graham Turner and asked if he would give me a trial at Wolverhampton Wanderers. My dad had played with Graham at Chester. I was set to go and it was very kind of Graham to agree. Then Norwich intercepted and my dad phoned Graham to give him the news. My dad was a good judge of a player and he thought that I had potential but was by no means outstanding. A Norwich City scout agreed with him and it was time to go back to Norwich to try again.

The opportunity to try out for Norwich came about because my school team were still in the County Cup competition and we progressed to the semi-final. We played Caister High School at a neutral venue in Norwich, the Hewitt School. It was a nice pitch, surrounded by a running track, and Graeme Wren, a teacher at the school, was also a Norwich scout. He attended the game and I scored a hat-trick in a 4–0 win. My dad took our team and knew Graeme. Graeme told my dad that he was impressed with my performance and came to watch the final at the same venue against Yarmouth High School. Again I played well and scored another hat-trick in a 4–0 win. Off the back of these two games, I was offered another trial at Norwich City Football Club. It was near the end of the season and I had a week or so training with them, and then a game against a team at the club's training ground.

The team we played against were hopeless and I scored ten goals. My luck was changing. I was offered a few more games until the end of the season. I think I played two more and then I was offered a YTS contract for the following two years. I loved Norwich City again. I was sixteen and on top of the world.

The contrast in my feelings then compared with three or four years earlier was incredible. I hadn't seen this coming. Norwich City must still have had their doubts but they'd taken a chance on me. I was positive now and my confidence grew overnight. In my mind, I had been given two years to prove myself worthy of a professional contract. Two years was a long time and it wasn't going to be down to luck as short-term trials can be. I felt I had a genuine chance and this was going to be down to myself.

Looking back, there couldn't have been many, if any, better clubs to start at. Norwich were in the top division but they had a small squad and a history of developing youth – the likes of Dale Gordon, Jeremy Goss and Ruel Fox had progressed from the youth ranks into the first team. It was an exciting time.

The first thing I noticed and liked very quickly was that we were always in and around the first-team players. The training ground at Trowse had two big changing rooms – one for the first team and one for the youth team and younger professionals. Each youth team player was given three professionals to look after and other jobs to do during the day. Typically, we would arrive before nine in the morning, put out the training for our professionals, clean the boots and make sure the changing rooms were spotless. After training, we would collect the kit, take it to the laundry and then sweep up the dressing rooms. We would then scrub floors, clean the toilets and showers, and brush down the players' boots.

The youth team coach, Keith Webb, made sure we kept the place in an immaculate condition and made sure we took our duties seriously. The professionals would sometimes send us down to the local bakery for a sausage roll or a pasty and a drink before training. How times have changed diet-wise!

My first pre-season was at the University of East Anglia and we used their facilities and grounds to run around. The training was physically gruelling, as pre-seasons normally are and that never changed no matter what club I was playing at throughout my career.

Keith Webb instilled in us that it was important to train as hard as possible and to try and beat the first-team players at running. It was a natural for some first-team players to run within themselves at pre-season but the youths were told they had earned the right to train in this manner. We had not by any means and we were pushed hard by Keith. On the pitch and in the training I felt ok. I knew my position in the pecking order as a first-year YTS boy. I had only played boys' football previously, so in my mind I felt I was a long way off playing first-team football. But being in the environment so close to the first team every day I could see clearly how the progression would work.

I started playing under-18 football in the youth team. We played in the South-East Counties league against the likes of Spurs, Arsenal and Chelsea. Some of the second-year YTS boys had played in the reserves the previous season and would again this season. This I used as a motivational tool. If I could forge my way into the reserves quickly, I'd be one step away from the first team. The first team had some really good players at that time, like Ian Crook and Robert Fleck and others who had come from Tottenham after being released. We learned a lot from the first team, including the importance of a good first touch. That was drummed into us week in, week out.

My dad recommended I go to weight training, in my own time, so I started going to sessions with a man called Chris Roberts who owned a gym in Norwich. He was a body-builder and Dad had known him for years. Chris designed a programme for me to try to develop my strength and power. Quite a bit of weightlifting was involved and I found it very beneficial. Craig Bellamy used him in later years and so did my brother, Johnny. It made a difference to my physique and was another crucial part of my development.

Norwich only carried a small first-team squad, so they looked to the reserves when they had injuries. Whoever was playing the best in the reserves was next in line. It seems to be much more difficult for a player nowadays to find a way in to the first team, with so many more obstacles in terms of bigger squads and more foreign players. At the time I started in 1989–90, there were not many foreign players around, although a Scandinavian influx had started.

For myself, I could see a logical progression, a route to the top. I just needed to perform well but that was by no means a certainty. Fortunately, I started to progress quickly and grew in confidence on the pitch. I started playing centre-half in the youth team as well as centre-forward. It was a bit daunting at first and I was nervous but I grew into that defensive position, which helped with my confidence and my development. I learned from the centre-forwards and the centre-halves I played against, and I thought it was a massive positive to have two strings to my bow.

The coaching was intense and the training very competitive. We had a lot of drills and it was very well organised. We were taught how to play specific positions and the strikers were taught about basic runs and movement. I was learning all the time. The senior staff – Dave Stringer, Dave Williams and Mike Walker – were always very pleasant to the younger players and full of encouragement. But I wasn't so sure about Keith Webb. He was a relatively young coach but I felt he was overly nasty at times in those days. Looking back now, I think he was the way he was to try and toughen us up. But I felt at times he was overly aggressive and he and I certainly didn't see eye to eye. He would often play in the training games and on one occasion he caught me with a bad tackle on the shin. I had a bad injury and I was out for a long period with a haematoma. I had to have a special shin pad made up out of plaster to protect the injury. I was furious and resented Keith for this, thinking he had kicked me on purpose. Of course, now, I look back and see things differently. But I did use Keith as a motivation and I wanted to get on at Norwich in spite of him rather than because of him. I think it was natural for boys not to like their youth team coach but, again, looking back, he was a big part of how I progressed in the game. He didn't single anyone out specifically but he seemed to give the younger boys a hard time. At first I didn't understand this but I now realise he was trying to get the maximum out of everybody; he was teaching us the pecking order and that we had to work harder and harder to climb the ladder. We had to earn the right.

However, I didn't cover myself in glory off the pitch at this time and I did leave myself open for criticism from Keith and the Youth Development Officer, Gordon Bennett. When I arrived for my first day at Trowse, I was joined by six other boys and most of them knew each other from the schoolboy teams at Norwich City. The second-year YTS boys obviously knew each other from the previous season. I was extremely nervous at first, I was very quiet and in the dressing room I felt very uncomfortable. On the pitch I was fine but off the pitch I had never experienced the football dressing room environment. It was a brutal place.

I was brought up in a sleepy Norfolk village and now I was mixing with street-wise boys from tough backgrounds. It was an unforgiving environment and I was scared. Some of the older boys would try to intimidate the younger ones, me included. Back then football clubs didn't have Human Resource Departments you could go to with any grievances, not that any of us would have used it had it been available. I didn't know how to react at first; I couldn't always work out what was said as a joke and when people were being serious. The dressing room is an unforgiving place. Gradually I started to stand up for myself as all the first-year boys did. It was a good learning curve. We were all competing with each other for a place in the team and the ultimate aim of a professional contract. It was tough at first, especially as a lot of boys had moved away from home for the first time, me included. I had moved into digs in Norwich, as the bus service into Norwich didn't run regularly enough from Horsford to make commuting a possibility. It was a massive change.

I gradually grew into the environment and then began to thrive in it. I found the banter exciting and the dressing room was now a place I wanted to be. You had to be sharp to survive in the company of guys like Lee Power and Stephen Rocastle. They were incredibly sharp and street-wise.

I was improving on the pitch and started to play reserve football in my first year. As a consequence, I think I became more confident, more vocal and definitely cheekier. It's fair to say Keith Webb probably found me unbearable. My mum and dad knew exactly the frustration Keith was feeling, as they were having it with me too at this stage. They knew I could be a real nuisance.

As a YTS player, I earned £29.50 in the first year and £35 in the second year. We were given a bus pass and had our digs paid for. We were there to play football, but we were getting to an age when young men like to have a drink and go out for a look at the local talent. So, at Christmas time, it was always handy to get a tip from the professional players we looked after. I looked after Paul Blades, Tim Sherwood and Ian Butterworth. Unfortunately, the tip didn't come free. The youth team players had to stand on a bench in the first-team dressing room naked and sing a Christmas carol. If the singing wasn't good, bars of soap, football boots, anything that came to hand was hurled at you. Funnily enough, none of the first team rated our singing. It was a good adrenalin buzz, though. Butterworth, the club captain, only tipped me £10. Blades and Sherwood were much more generous and tipped me £20.

The first-team lads liked to lull us into a false sense of security. The first Christmas I was there it snowed and the youth team were offered a snowball fight against the first team. We would just throw snowballs at them, but some of the younger players were chased and caught and then stripped naked. It was a good learning experience all the same. As time ticked by, my confidence grew and some of my behaviour, coincidentally off the pitch, became more stupid and I made some bad errors of judgement. I didn't drink alcohol before I joined Norwich City, but some of the boys did and I decided to try it. I began to enjoy some good nights out in the city centre pubs and clubs but after one such night, we were called into the office by Keith Webb and Gordon Bennett and they read us the riot act. We had no idea how they knew we had been out the night before and had another night out planned for that evening, but they had not sanctioned either night out. We were shocked. How could they know about this?

We were then told that any player stupid enough to go out that night would be in serious trouble. Myself and another lad, Colin Loss, discussed this and thought it was a fairly safe bet to go out, as Keith and Gordon wouldn't think any of us would be so stupid as to even contemplate it. To make matters worse, Gordon drove past us that evening about eight o'clock, close to the train station in the city. We waved at him and he waved back. We contemplated going back to our digs immediately but we discussed it and were now even more confident than before that Gordon would surely go home, thinking we couldn't be that dumb. We had a great night out, or so we thought, but the end of the night must have come as a shock for Colin. When he returned to his digs, Gordon was waiting for him and he was furious. I had returned to my digs in a different part of the city, unaware of what had happened to Colin.

The next day, I soon found out. We were both in massive trouble and I thought I was for the sack. My parents were called in to the club and Colin and I were told to scrub all of the training ground floors with a toothbrush. It took ages. The following day, I went in for a meeting with Gordon and he placed me on a final warning. There was a protocol, apparently, but I'd gone straight to the final warning. I apologised profusely. I was stupid and too clever for my own good. My parents told me I had been hanging by a thread and was lucky to still be at Norwich City. They also told me I was stupid and irresponsible. They told me the right things to say to Gordon when I was called in and I'm sure that without their help and guidance at that time, I would not have been at Norwich City any longer.

Colin left the club soon after the incident. To this day, I don't know what went on between him and the club. All I did know was that I was very fortunate to still be given a chance by Norwich City. My dad felt it was unfair Colin was shown the door and I wasn't, and I can see his point. Gordon Bennett spoke to my dad about the situation and my dad told him if he felt it was appropriate to sack me then he should do so. My dad was doing a little bit of coaching with Norwich kids but didn't want any favours for me just because of his position at the club. I was extremely sorry to see Colin go and I knew I was lucky to stay in my job.

It was real wake-up call. Afterwards, I really knuckled down, as I was so scared of getting the sack. I made sure I went out only when we were given permission. I still liked a night out, most boys of that age do, but I had wanted the best of both worlds and had been properly put in my place.

The move away from home and into digs was going well, though. I enjoyed it and it was good fun with some of the lads. The first house I stayed in didn't last too long, however, as I had to move out due to an ant infestation. I then moved to another house with a few of the lads. One weekend, the woman in charge went away and left us with her Siamese cats. One of the cats was pregnant so she asked us to keep an eye on it. The next morning we woke up and the cat had given birth but had eaten her new-born kittens. There were legs and afterbirth everywhere – it was horrific. We ended up getting into trouble and we had to leave the digs, which was a bit unfair – it wasn't our fault. But that was all part of the learning process, the adventure of being a young footballer away from home.

At the beginning of my second YTS year, I was playing regular football for the reserve team. It was a great experience to play against players such as Paul Walsh, Vinnie Samways and Mickey Hazard. I was making my way through the ranks at the club and I found reserve football to be really good for me. Back then, reserve football was really competitive and I used to play against some really tough central defenders, top-team players that were on their way back to fitness for the first team, or guys that might have been banished and were waiting for a transfer. I quickly learned I had to be aggressive to survive at that level and, more importantly, show I had enough in me to make the step up to the first team if required.

I knew that central defenders were told to 'leave one on the striker' from as early in the game as possible. That was the way the game was. I was a victim of some of those tackles quite a few times, especially when I was younger and naive. Terry Hurlock caught me with one when I was playing against Southampton. He just ran into me and absolutely floored me. Totally leathered me. It was a lesson for me. The physio ran on to give me treatment and asked me where it hurt. I told him 'everywhere'. But it was exciting and I knew I had to be more aggressive. It was something I had to learn and was a big tool to have in the locker.

I played many games at centre-half. I think the coaching staff fancied playing me there more often. I felt when I played at the back I could read the game quite well. I could assess situations and give myself time.

Mike Walker was the reserve manager and he was very good with me. He helped me tremendously but was also very tough with me and the other younger lads. But he was very fair and a tremendous motivator. He simply wouldn't accept players not pulling their weight. He also knew what buttons to push back then. He liked his players to be very aggressive and the work ethic was extremely important. He demanded a high standard but was also understanding as long as honest mistakes were being made. Mike drilled it home that he wanted us to learn from our mistakes and not repeat the same errors over and over again. By Christmas in my second YTS year I felt confident I'd be offered some kind of contract, as I was doing well in the reserves and was playing regularly. David Williams, the first-team coach, often played with us and said nice things to me. I appreciated the compliments.

By now, I was occasionally joining in with the first team in training when they were short of numbers. Nearing the end of the season, a number of injuries occurred in the first-team squad and I was given a place on the bench for a game against Queens Park Rangers. We were 2–1 down and I was given the last ten or fifteen minutes at centre-forward. We got back to 2–2 and with a few minutes to go, I scored the winner from close range and my name was up in lights for the first time. And to do it at Carrow Road felt great.

Before the season finished, I came on as a substitute against Liverpool at Anfield and played against Ian Rush. We lost 2–1 but I didn't feel out of my depth. It was a great experience. I was very nervous going on in both games, but once I had been on for a couple of minutes the nerves finished and I absolutely loved it. I was getting hungrier and hungrier for more. I wanted it so much.

The contract I wanted so badly eventually arrived and I was given a two-year deal on £175 per week just before the end of the season. Ironically, myself and another boy, Tim Wooding, were the only two lads offered contracts from our age group, as not one of the schoolboy forms lads, signed from the time I was rejected, were taken on. Just two years previously, I was all set to work for Norfolk County Council as a clerk and now I was playing football in the top flight of English football as a professional footballer. It was incredible and I should have believed more in my dad.

Looking back, you can never pick and choose the way your life works out normally but I was happy with the way my early football career worked out. I think it was the right way to do it. I think it was better not to be on a 'schoolboy form' and instead just go about my business as a normal footballer enjoying the game with my pals. Then, getting in the back door at sixteen and into the YTS system was perfect for me. Getting that second chance was great, the way I'd choose to do it all over again. Unless you are exceptional at twelve or thirteen, then, in my opinion, it's best not to be attached, because I feel players can end up pigeonholed. People then have pre-conceived ideas about you and about what you can do. It suited me to not have it happen that way, although the rejection was hard to take.

Now, I don't know the exact statistics, but very few kids who sign schoolboy forms with clubs actually make the top team at that club. They are either released and move down a level, or they go out of the game because they're not good enough. It's a massive let-down when you are told you're not good enough. Some kids start at a club at five or six years old and then get released at sixteen. It must play havoc with your head. Effectively, it can feel as if your dreams are ruined. I defy anybody not to feel really depressed when they are released. I was depressed and distraught when I was released at twelve. I tried to paper over the cracks at the time but it stayed with me over the following years. I just kept at it and enjoyed playing in different positions in a much less pressured and structured environment.

As a young player looking to start out on a professional career,

Norwich suited me down to the ground. There was a natural progression through the ranks if you were good enough, which gave me the feeling that it was possible to succeed. And although you can't stereotype clubs, historically, there are plenty with strong youth set-ups that win most games but don't actually get a lot of players through from the youth team to the top team. At those clubs, many players get released because there's simply nowhere for them to go, there are too many players in front of them cluttering up the reserve team. I have a lot of admiration for players who persevere after that sort of disappointment.

My brother, John, was with Tottenham Hotspur as a kid but was released by them. I have so much admiration for John because of the way he handled that situation, the way he stuck at it and now look at him. Firstly, he went on trial at Leicester for no money. Not a penny for six months. He's been up the road on trial, down the road on trial, across the road on trial, absolutely everywhere to prove he was good enough to be in the game at a good level. I don't how John managed to keep going. The amount of times managers said, 'Sorry, you're not what we're looking for.' It is a brutal business, really.

John had very good spells at Millwall and St Mirren. He has a fantastic mentality. He had a good spell at Motherwell and really excelled there in his final season (2010–11) and scored seventeen goals for them. Motherwell were keen to keep him but he signed for Heart of Midlothian, which I believe is another step up. I know Neil Lennon considered taking John to Celtic but I think the move to Hearts is the right one for John, as he should play there most weeks.

He is a talented striker and I believe he has the ability to move up another level. John has a few years left in his career, whereas my time has long gone. But my early experiences at Norwich were mostly beneficial and stood me in good stead for the challenges that were ahead of me in the game.

4

LEARNING AND EARNING

Dave Stringer was the manager who gave me my debut and for that I'll always be eternally grateful. Dave played hundreds of games for Norwich. He was a good club man, had Norwich at heart. He wasn't flamboyant; he was a quiet, studious man, not a ranter or a raver. He didn't say silly things. My impressions of managers as a young player was that they would rule by an iron fist and by fear. But Dave was never like that. He was very straightforward and fair. The young professionals had a good upbringing at the club.

Dave resigned from his job in May 1992 after we finished the season in eighteenth place. Results weren't good enough and he was replaced by Mike Walker. Mike was more vociferous than Dave, more aggressive, but very fair. If you performed well, he'd lavish praise on you. If you didn't do well then you'd certainly know all about it. He was a very smart man. He'd never let you rest on your laurels and that was a good thing for all the players, but especially the younger ones. He made sure we kept striving to be better and better. There were no grey areas with Mike. I understood Mike and you were left in no doubt what your role in the team was and you were expected to run around and to be aggressive. It was clear under Mike that you had to give your all – that was the least he expected.

I didn't think it would be easy for Mike to go from reserve manager to first-team boss. He would have had decent relationships with some of the first-team players but would then have had to change his role a bit, be more aloof. But in my mind, Mike did it brilliantly. He coped really well with the transition; he distanced himself from the players and had the respect of the dressing room.

Mike liked his suits, liked to be well dressed and look good. He was nicknamed the 'Silver Fox' by the players. But his appearance didn't hide the fact that he was very hard working. He turned out to be the most successful manager the club had had in a short period of time and he got us into Europe. He was very good for my developing career, too, and he was a real football man. He was very efficient at handling the delicate blend between youth and experience and that was one of the keys to our success. Mike might have been lucky to inherit some really good senior players who were at his disposal, but he also knew how to treat them and make them tick.

Training was a bit more intense under Mike. There was no standing off during training games and you had to close opposition players down, and show Mike you had the sort of committed work ethic he expected. I had been used to this in the reserves anyway so it was no problem for me.

Mike's management style was also different. He could be quite brutal at times and sometimes lose his cool. He was very aggressive in the dressing room if he felt people weren't pulling their weight. He was very tough on me at times and I was unsure how to take him on occasions. He never allowed you to shirk things and demanded 100 per cent at all times, but the constant demand for effort seemed to work as I can't honestly remember any player not giving their all under Mike.

Mike had been an integral part of me getting into the first team, so naturally I was pleased when he took over. I had started to carve out a career under Dave Stringer but suddenly under Mike I felt I was starting to make great strides.

Being a young player and going into the first team, naturally I was nervous. But team-mates such as Ruel Fox, Ian Crook and Mark Bowen were big influences on me and really helped develop my game. Another player whose help was invaluable was the ex-Rangers striker Robert Fleck. He was the top striker at Norwich at that time and a cult hero. He always offered the young players plenty of encouragement and he always had time for you. It meant a lot to me that he gave me that time.

Being in the first team, I started to earn more money due to the bonuses. I also signed a new deal, moving my wages up to £500 per week. I'd never experienced money like it. But having the extra money in my pocket also signalled the start of a few problems for me off the park. I never spent my money wisely. I suppose, like most young guys, I enjoyed having a bit of money but not as much as I enjoyed spending it. I bought myself a car, I was enjoying nights out in the bars or spending money at the casino and gambling on the horses. I was really poor at managing my money and I quickly got myself into debt.

I became very lax because I thought I had cracked it. Maybe things started to go to my head. My wallet was getting bigger but so was my head. More money meant more gambling – the horses, the dogs, the fixed odds, the casino. You name it, I was losing money on it all.

On the park, I was still doing really well and was now a regular first-team player, and soon after I signed another new contract. It was only six or seven months after signing my previous contract. This time I moved up to £1000 per week plus a signing-on fee. I also had good bonus money and decent incentives. Happy days. But in all honesty, it made the situation off the park even worse. The more money I had, the more reckless I became.

The first-team players came in every morning with a newspaper and we'd all look at the horseracing cards for the day. One or two of the lads would get a tip on a horse and would pass it to the other boys. Over the piece, I lost hundreds of pounds on so-called nailed-on 'certainties'.

The Yarmouth greyhound track was just twenty miles away from Norwich and we'd often go there after training to spend an evening. There were usually eight races and I'd have a bet on every one of them. From there, we'd often end up in the local casino in Great Yarmouth. I wasn't living a proper lifestyle and I wasn't exactly a model pro. My off-the-field shenanigans were quickly getting out of control but I was enjoying life.

And at least my performances on the pitch for the first team belied my attitude off it. Team-mates like Ruel Fox, Ian Crook and Mark Bowen were teaching me how to play the game at the top level, my game knowledge was developing all the time.

Myself, Ruel Fox and Lee Power became very close and spent a lot of time together. We had a lot of fun getting up to plenty of antics. We used to play a game called 'Spoof' which was a guessing game involving coins and whoever lost had to do a forfeit. One night, we were playing it while driving past a field of pigs. We got chatting, had a 'Spoof' and the loser had to go into the field, catch a pig and give it a kiss. Suffice to say I lost. I spent twenty minutes chasing pigs around this field. However, I wasn't quick enough to catch one.

Another time, I was with Lee and a local car dealer called Wayne we used to knock around with. The car dealer was driving and we bet him that he couldn't do 100 miles per hour down this little country lane. He got to about forty miles per hour going around the bend and he hit a tree. I was in the front passenger seat, wearing my seat belt, thank goodness, and was fine. Lee was in the back seat, hit his head off the passenger seat and had a bloody nose. Wayne, the driver, was really shaken, which was understandable. We were lucky to get away with it and, of course, Wayne didn't win any money from us because he didn't win the bet.

I started to receive a fair bit of attention from the press. The newspapers gave me some rave reviews about my performances on the pitch, which made me feel great. I had bought a nice house in Thorpe St Andrew on the outskirts of Norwich, so I now had a mortgage payment to meet every month. Buying the house was a sensible thing to do. It was one of the few things that I spent my money wisely on but I was still frittering away money on the roulette tables and the horses.

Within a short space of time, I racked up gambling debts and credit card debts of more than £5000. I knew I had to get a grip on the problem because it was getting out of control. Had I kept gambling at the rate I was going and if I continued to bankroll everything on my credit card, then I would probably have ended up in tens of thousands of pounds worth of debt. But before it went too far, I decided to face up to my problems and do something to sort out my financial situation when I realised that my debts were leaving me struggling to pay the bills. It just seemed like a ridiculous situation. There I was, earning more money than I'd ever seen before in my life, yet I was left with less money than when I was a first-year YTS trainee.

It wasn't hard to work out why I'd got into this mess. I was very young when I moved away from home and I was drinking too much, although not to the extent that it made me miss training. My parents could see I wasn't living life the way I should be and they suspected I had one or two problems. They were also worried about the company I was keeping. My mum was especially worried. She used to cycle almost eight miles, three or four times a week, to my house in the morning to make me my breakfast and also, no doubt, to keep a check on me. But it wasn't enough to prevent me from gambling too much and spending heavily on the credit cards.

I knew I had to do something and confided in my parents. When I needed some home-truths then the place for me to go was back to my parents' house in Horsford. I told them the situation I was in and they said they would help me. They gave me sound advice. To get things back on track, they told me I had to do two things – give up gambling and concentrate on paying back the debts. Following their advice meant I kept my house and didn't have the worry of all that debt hanging over me.

My mum took control of my income for a time and her solution was pretty drastic. She gave me £10 a day to live on and that was it, with no more access to cash. There I was, at the age of nineteen, a first-team player at a Premier League club in England, one of the up-and-coming talents, and I was living on £10 a day. If only people knew!

I felt it was a drastic measure at the time but there's no doubt that it was very effective. It was the only way to get me out of the mess I was in. I was simply gambling too much and losing too much money – I knew that. But I never felt I had a gambling addiction. I did like the buzz, it was exciting and it helped to kill the long days after training when there was nothing much to do. Some players get really sucked in and can't get out of the addiction. Paul Merson has been very open about his gambling addictions. What I lost financially was only a fraction of what he's been through, but it's all relative; what I lost was a lot to me at the time, especially as it could have meant me losing my house if I'd carried on like that for much longer. I still enjoy an occasional bet but I'm not mad on it.

Over my career, I was never really one for card schools, especially the serious ones, and there were some heavy ones on the team buses on the way home from games or in the hotels the night before we played. Mostly the lads would play Brag or Shoot Pontoon and some schools had a fair bit of money riding on it. I didn't like that; it left my stomach in knots. I didn't want to lose big money and never really got involved. I suppose I didn't have the balls for it.

When I moved to Blackburn and was on considerably more money than I was ever used to at Norwich, with all due respect, winning £50 on a horse wasn't going to give me a buzz or make a difference to my day. I don't mean that to sound arrogant, but to win big you had to bet big and I never had the balls to place huge sums on a bet, whether it be a horse, a dog or a game of football. That's the problem with gambling – to get a real buzz you need to be taking a real risk and for some people it becomes incredibly addictive and a way to make them feel alive.

Having said that, I did enjoy a bit of luck now and again. We played Carlisle in a Rumbelows Cup competition and I had been playing at centre-half for a while. I was put up front that night and a few of the lads backed me at 12–1 to get the first goal as I was on penalties. I scored both goals in a 2–0 win, both headers. I also missed a penalty for my hat-trick, a horrendous effort from me from twelve yards. I bet £20 on myself to score and a few of the rest of the lads also won money on me. I don't see anything wrong with players backing someone to score a goal or backing their team to win. It's different if they put money on their team to lose. That's unacceptable and that should never go on in the game of football. It's unfortunate that it does, although I think the rules are so strict and stringent now and bookies are so on the ball that it rarely happens. It's pretty much forbidden for professional footballers to bet on any game of football nowadays and I think that's the right thing, especially when you look at how much is at stake for the clubs, the players and the fans.

My financial concerns didn't stop me from doing well on the park. The Norwich dressing room was a lively place with some really good characters and talented footballers. Strong friendships were formed and it was all great fun. Some mornings we'd go for breakfast before training to a little cafe and have a sausage sandwich or a fry-up and a cup of tea. Lee Power would meet up with myself and Ruel Fox for that early morning bite to eat. Ruel would travel from Ipswich and stay with me. We were friendly and knocked around together. At that particular age, the times were enjoyable, we had few responsibilities and I found both of them incredibly funny to be around. We spent a lot of time laughing.

In the 1992–93 season, when we finished third in the league, I played at centre-half and I think we had a negative goal difference. I was quite raw and very aggressive. I was a young player and sometimes let my enthusiasm get the better of me and made some rash decisions. I remember being on the end of a few hidings. I played in a 7–1 defeat at Blackburn. After that game, I was fairly hacked off with Ian Butterworth, my central defensive partner, because he gave an interview where he said he had told me to keep my head up and not let the defeat affect me. I was angry. In fact, if memory serves me correctly, Alan Shearer had put him on his backside on the track at the side of the pitch and scored a goal. I felt Ian was passing the buck. I was bad that day but, in fairness, he was worse. Bearing in my mind, also, that I was a youngster and he was the senior pro. But Ian used all of his experience in the post-match interview to deflect any negativity away from him and put the spotlight on the rookie, myself. I learned another lesson that day, this time about how players look after themselves even after the game.

Up until Easter, we had a genuine chance of winning the Premiership. Then we had two games that ultimately defined our season – Aston Villa and Manchester United at home. Unfortunately, we just came up short, but it was a really exciting period and I don't know whether I fully appreciated it all at the time. I was young and thought this was just normal, the way it was in football. I wish I'd relished it all a little bit more.

We lost 3–1 to Manchester United in the first of these games.

Defensively, we were poor and United thoroughly deserved their victory. We were 3–0 down at half-time. We then lost narrowly to Villa, 1–0. It was a very evenly contested game but the upshot was that we just weren't good enough that year. At this time, the supporters wanted the chairman, Robert Chase, to throw money at the club and take us to the next level. We'd finished the season in third place, a very creditable result for a team outside the usual big names. It could have been better, of course, but we felt we had done well and done the club proud.

My progress continued as I remained playing at centre-half throughout the 1992–93 season. Then, towards the end of the campaign, there was a shortage up front and I was given a chance to play centre-forward. It turned out to be the definitive period of my career. I scored a hat-trick at home to Leeds and the club decided to keep me up front from there on. I relied on good service and I was lucky to play with such good attacking players. I was given a chance and I took it. I played the last dozen or so games as a striker and went on a run of goals. I scored ten goals in that period until the end of the season.

We got to the FA Cup semi-final in 1992–93. We beat Southampton in the quarter-finals and I scored the winner, a looping header over Tim Flowers in extra-time to win 2–1. Neil Ruddock was centre-half for Saints that day and he was a tough guy to play against, a real powerful presence on the pitch. We played Sunderland in the semi-final and lost 1–0. John Byrne scored the winner for them. He'd scored in every round of the tournament that season for them. During the game, I had a decent chance to score from fifteen yards but I didn't quite get over the ball. It was all a bit of an anti-climax after getting that far in the competition but it just wasn't our day. We were also missing a fully fit Robert Fleck, our talisman. He'd broken a rib and hadn't recovered fully, but had he been 100 per cent then it might have been a different story. FA Cup finals are the games you dream about as a kid and you work towards as a professional, and when you get so tantalisingly close to Wembley, it's really tough missing out. Especially when you have the opportunity to affect the result.

At the start of the 1993–94 season, we went to Sweden on tour and I played up front in the pre-season games in which I took part. There was no doubt now, in my mind, that I was a striker. It turned out to be a phenomenal season and I scored twenty-five goals in the Premier League. My tally for the whole campaign was actually twenty-eight, as I scored three more in other competitions.

Yet we didn't start that season particularly well. Manchester United beat us 2–0 at home on the opening day of the season. We then had two tough away games – at Blackburn and Leeds. I scored a couple in a 3–2 win at Ewood Park. That was on the Wednesday night. Then on the Saturday, we turned in an incredible performance to defeat a strong Leeds team 4–0 at Elland Road. Foxy got two at Elland Road and I scored as well. Jeremy Goss got the other goal – a sensational volley that was later voted Goal of the Season. There was no disgrace in losing to Manchester United at home but it did put a bit of pressure on us going away to two difficult venues after that. In all honesty, we'd have settled for a point in both games but we ended up with six. The team got real confidence from that.

Myself and Efan Ekoku were forming a good partnership and Mike was happy with us. But he was concerned with other areas of the team, worried about the fragility at the back. He tinkered with the system a little bit to make us more difficult to score against and shored it up at the back, going with a three-man central defence and effectively playing a back five. It was a switch from 4-4-2 but he felt it necessary. I think he wanted it mainly for our games in Europe that season but he used it very often in our league games, too. When you try a new system, it can take a while to adjust and you often get teething problems.

However, the defenders were given that little bit of comfort in the knowledge that, at the top end of the pitch, Ekoku and I were flying. We were a great out-ball for the defenders, with Ekoku's pace the main reason for that. I would do my bit by holding the ball in and then giving it to Foxy out wide or to a runner from the centre of the pitch. We also had Ian Crook pulling the strings in the centre of midfield. We were really well set up as a counter-attacking side. Crook would get his head up and spray the ball, and Foxy would take on full-backs.

We then had a 5–1 win at Everton. Ekoku scored four and I scored one. We knew they were a tough team to play against especially at Goodison Park and my partnership with Ekoku continued to blossom. Because of his phenomenal pace, I could play percentages with him. I could win flick-ons and hook balls on without having to worry about being totally accurate as his pace was so good. His pace could make a pretty average ball into a really good one. He could stretch our markers and leave space for me, which made my job that bit easier. Had he not been as quick, I would have had to be more exact and that would have made my job so much more difficult. I was really lucky to play with him in that side. We had so many different attributes in that team, especially when we attacked, and although I was still learning the game, I was growing in confidence all the time.

We played Vitesse Arnhem in the first round of the UEFA Cup that season. It was Norwich's first-ever European game. Technically, they had qualified twice for Europe in the 1980s, but were denied the chance as English teams were banned at the time because of the Heysel tragedy. We were at home in the first leg and I enjoyed that night – packed house, under the flood-lights. Very special. It was 0–0 at half-time and then John Polsten scored from close range. Ekoku scored a superb volley from an acute angle and then Crook got the vital third. That was extremely comfortable to take over to Holland. I played a more withdrawn role in Arnhem, defending from the left-hand side. We left Ekoku up front, used his pace as an out-ball and he had a number of goal-scoring chances. The game finished 0–0 and that scoreline flattered Vitesse, as Ekoku had a few chances but couldn't convert on the night. Our system was extremely effective and working well.

We then played the mighty Bayern Munich and amazingly we knocked them out, in what was arguably the biggest night in Norwich City's history. Did we expect to beat them? No, we didn't, although I think we felt capable of causing an upset on our day. I think at the time we were the only British side to have beaten them on their own pitch, the Olympic Stadium. Lothar Matthäus led that team. Jan Wouters, Mehmet Scholl, Thomas Helmer and Christian Ziege also played. They had a team full of superstars.

We scored fairly quickly through Jeremy Goss. It was the most famous goal in Norwich's history. It was a superb volley. Then Mark Bowen scored with a deft header at the back post and we won 2–1. In the second half, we had come under extreme pressure and Bryan Gunn had to make a succession of saves to help us win.

Bayern were severely aggravated at losing to us in the first leg but we were a capable side. We actually thought we had a chance after winning the first game, but knew it was going to be difficult as we didn't have great experience in European competition. We also thought Bayern would have played better. Despite the fact that we had beaten them, there was still apprehension in our dressing room for the second leg, and rightly so. Bayern took the lead after just five minutes at Carrow Road and we knew we were up against it. We quickly realised we had to shut up shop for a period to stop them from gaining momentum but, eventually, we grew into the game and found our rhythm. Then Jeremy Goss scored again, this time from close range in the fifty-first minute. At the other end, Bryan Gunn made some important saves once again. The atmosphere created by the Norwich fans that night was like nothing I'd experienced ever before. It was such as memorable occasion. They nearly lifted the roof off when Goss scored.

We got tremendous publicity from this game, and it seemed that most of the country warmed to us and wanted us to do well. We were the underdogs taking on mighty European teams and beating them. However, it shouldn't have been that much of a shock to us because on our day, we were very capable of beating the best teams in England at that time. Sure, against Bayern we rode our luck a couple of times but that was always going to happen. But it wasn't a fluke we beat them over two legs because, on balance, we deserved to win.

Next up for us was Inter Milan, the Italian giants, a team packed with household names such as Dennis Bergkamp and Rubén Sosa. We played well in the home leg but, with ten minutes remaining, we conceded a penalty. We narrowly lost 1–0. It was my first experience against Italian opposition and it's fair to say their defending was extremely physical and uncompromising. It was a good lesson for me to play against Bergomi, one of the best defenders in Italy at that time. He was very clever physically in the way he used his body and blocked me.

We faced the daunting task of trying to overturn the one-goal deficit in the return leg. We had to go to the San Siro and win. Simple as that. We went there without some key players, as Ian Butterworth, Ian Crook and Rob Newman were all suspended for previous bookings. We started the game relatively well but Ekoku and I missed two good chances. I snatched at mine and put it wide from the right-hand side of the box. We missed Crook in that game as we lacked the incisiveness of his passing. We were punished late on and Bergkamp finished off the tie to leave us all shattered. It was very disappointing as we wanted to replicate what had happened against Bayern, but we came up a little bit short this time against a very street-wise Italian outfit. They were well drilled and well organised. They were difficult to score against and effective going forward. It was nice to play in the San Siro even though we didn't perform that well.

My career was progressing well, though. I was now playing for the England under-21 side, travelling away from home around Europe to play in various games. We played over in Turkey and in other countries, and it was all part of my education, part of growing up. We lost 1–0 to the Turkish team. They had Hakan Sükür in their team and he was a cult figure in his country at that time. We had the likes of Steve McManaman, Jamie Redknapp, Darren Anderton and Lee Clark; it was a good team.

The first time I joined the squad I had felt a bit nervous. Most of the lads were playing for the so-called big clubs, such as Liverpool and Newcastle. I was from Norwich, an unfashionable club, albeit the club was doing well. But I never felt inferior in any way, football-wise. In fact, I was glad I was a Norwich player because I often reminded myself that had I not been at Norwich, I didn't think I would ever be in the England under-21 squad. Had I been with a Manchester United or an Arsenal, I would have been lucky to play in the first team because of their bigger squads and more intense competition and that would have denied me the chance of representing England at international level. I was very lucky, in that respect, to be playing first-team football in the Premiership in a very successful side under Mike Walker.

I enjoyed playing for the England under-21 side. I played both centre-half and centre-forward for my country at that age level. I scored my only goal against San Marino. I'd also played in the wonderful Toulon tournament in the summer of 1992 when we knocked Brazil out in the group stages and also defeated Scotland. We beat the host nation France in the final.

There was a bit of an issue with the FA that summer, as I had booked a summer holiday and then they called me into the squad. I didn't even know what the Toulon tournament was. I had paid a lot of money for my holiday and the FA did not want to compensate me. At first I told the FA I didn't want to play in the tournament, as I had booked this holiday. Eventually I had to cancel the holiday and I lost a lot of money. England demanded I play for them in the tournament and I suppose, thinking about it now, I was happy they didn't take no for an answer, as I enjoyed the tournament and representing England in it. But it was a sore hit for me financially.

I signed a new deal at Carrow Road in December 1993 and my new contract included a goal bonus. On Boxing Day 1993, we played Tottenham at White Hart Lane. I scored twice – one from half a yard and the other a volley from about six yards from a Foxy cross. I was on £500 per goal if we won or drew. I was delighted. I had just earned myself an extra £1000 for scoring from a combined distance of seven yards. Nice earner. I know people question the wisdom of giving players a goal bonus and I fully understand that. But I was never going to refuse that sort of deal when the chairman, Robert Chase, offered it to me. Personally, I don't actually agree with a goal bonus. It can maybe make players selfish. I have played with players in the past that would try to score from the corner flag – and they weren't even on a goal bonus. There's no doubt it was at the back of my mind and I was obviously keen to score in every game. I remember we lost 5–4 at home to Southampton one day. I scored twice but I wasn't entitled to my £1000 because we lost the game. I think that was the only time in my career I shouted at the Norwich defenders and told them to liven up a bit!

I was having a really good period during that season, scoring lots of goals. I was really enjoying myself at this stage of my career on and off the park. But at that time, looking back, I was acting like a complete arsehole off the park. I could go overboard with certain things. But I was a bit of a Jack the Lad in my younger days at Norwich. Myself and other team-mates must have been hard to control.

I really believed in all the publicity and hype that surrounded me. I didn't want that stage of my life to end. I'd pick up a newspaper and on the back page I'd be linked with a move to Bayern Munich, that kind of thing. It was all very exciting and I got sucked right into it. I was scoring goals and I had money in my pocket. Amazingly, my looks must have changed overnight when I got into the first team because I never got a second glance when I was on a night out as a youth-team player.

We used to work our social calendar out around the games. When I was at Norwich, we played on a Saturday afternoon at three o'clock. We had a game on a Tuesday or a Wednesday night every now and again. But most weeks we knew our schedule. Train Monday and Tuesday. Off Wednesday. Train Thursday and Friday. Play on a Saturday. Off on a Sunday.

As a single man, I had a social routine, too. We knew the nightclubs to go to. We'd go to Ritzy's in Norwich on a Wednesday night. On a Saturday after a game, if we were away from home, we'd get through a lot of alcohol on the team bus travelling back to Norwich. We were so far away from most other places, we'd have at least a three-hour journey every second weekend. And we'd have a right few beers on the bus.

Mike Walker would come up the back of the bus and never minded the players having a few drinks. We'd stop halfway home and have fish and chips to soak up the beer in preparation for going out when we arrived back in Norwich. Suffice to say times have changed now, professionally for the better, enjoyment-wise for the worse. It wasn't frowned upon to have fish and chips and a few beers after the game, it was part of the routine, all part of the fun really. It was yet another part of my life as a footballer I really enjoyed. Even things like staying in hotels the night before games were exciting. Getting nice meals, that kind of thing. In general, being treated like a superstar. I liked that. And then to top it all off, you'd go and play at a top venue such as White Hart Lane, Stamford Bridge or Old Trafford.

It was the same when I first started out playing for the reserve team. I liked going for a pre-match meal on the way to playing somewhere such as Swindon or Arsenal. The good thing about the reserve side back then was that you got to play at the real stadiums, whether that be Highbury, The Dell, Upton Park, places like that, rather than at the training ground, as is the case now for a lot of reserve teams. The reserve team would play against the London clubs and it was brilliant and exciting to play at such grounds. When I played for Norwich youth team, we played at training grounds and the like, but we knew the reserve team played at the real stadiums and it was another incentive to climb the ladder.

Playing at the glamorous venues becomes par for the course after a while and it is a bit of a shame to lose that excitement, but it's just part of being a footballer. One thing I never took for granted was scoring a goal. There's no better feeling than scoring in front of your own fans, especially a vital goal in a game that had plenty riding on it.

The more I scored, the more confident I became and being totally honest, my success at that time as a footballer was down to the players I was playing with. They were all perfect for me in different ways. Foxy's creativity was priceless, Crook's ability to execute the eye-of-a-needle pass and Ekoku's pace helped me so much – all reasons why I progressed so well at Carrow Road. As a footballer, at that stage of my life, I was on a roll, lapping up all the positive press and headlines. Even when I played badly in games, the press wouldn't give me a hard time. I was rarely criticised by the press at that time. It was rather nice, actually.

Off the pitch I was still full of it and on the pitch I was full of confidence. I finished the season as record goal-scorer for Norwich during the course of the 1993–94 season with twenty-five Premier League goals to my name. But, I'll repeat, I was fortunate to have so many good players around me and a good manager in Mike.

Mike didn't really mind, within reason, what you were up to off the pitch, but when you came in to training he expected you to give 100 per cent, be totally committed. At Norwich, the running wasn't scientific – they just used to run us till we dropped. That's the way it was. You'd do horseshoe runs, box-to-box runs, sixty-second laps and lots of doggies. Back then, the idea was to make you as tired as you could be, really. Pre-season training was similar, some players were physically sick. Sports science has progressed from the early days. You'd do some gym work, sit-ups and weights, that kind of thing. I had some structure to my gym work through my personal sessions with Chris Roberts a couple of times a week.

It was usually on a Tuesday that we'd run really hard. The consolation was you knew you were off on a Wednesday. The irony was that we'd do all this running and then clear off to the local cafe for egg and chips. As well as chips, we got our other carbohydrates into our system through pints of lager! Really, when you think about it, it was pretty silly. But it was bloody enjoyable. Of course, when you're younger, you don't suffer from hangovers and you can survive for a couple of days with a few hours sleep here and there.

In my years at Celtic, we'd be sitting on the coach coming home from away games wearing these skins to help get your body to recover quicker. We were told to drink shakes and energy drinks, it was all about recovering as quickly as we could and preparing properly for the next game. Occasionally, I would question the wisdom of it all. Sometimes I'd have a couple of bottles of beer the day before a game and then go out and score on a Saturday. As my career progressed, sports science improved, so our habits got better. Sports science dictates how we look after ourselves and standards have improved dramatically. However, my preference would have been to go through my entire career in football living my life as it was during my early days with little pressure, no worries and lots of fun. I'd have been a happy man. But I understood that managers and clubs have wanted to find ways of improving the performance of their players and having an edge.

Back then, there wasn't the huge backroom staff that clubs carry nowadays. There are more than a dozen at big clubs now from dieticians, a video analysis team and even goalkeeping coaches. Football was more basic back when I started out. Mike Walker often left you to your own devices and that was why I also felt he was a good manager. But when you do well, it means other people covet you and it led to Mike leaving Norwich to take over as manager of Everton. At that time, I felt really upset and truly disappointed he was gone.

When I first joined Norwich, I had no idea, obviously, how my own career was going to go. I felt I had got into the club through the back door and probably didn't think I'd ever play in the first team. Things changed quickly. I did work hard to improve my game. I also listened to what I was being told. Gradually, I worked my way up the pecking order inside the dressing room and Mike definitely raised the level of my own self-expectation as to what I could achieve in the game. I wanted him to stay but understood his reasons for leaving.

John Deehan took over from Mike and results started to slip. We went on a run of ten games without a win. We finished twelfth in the league. Foxy was sold to Newcastle. I was devastated to see Foxy go. He was a brilliant footballer and a really good person. We were very good mates. Deehan replaced Foxy with Neil Adams from Oldham. Neil performed well at Norwich but he just wasn't Foxy. That said, I didn't want him to be Foxy. Neil had a good career at Norwich but Foxy was on a different level. It just wasn't the same after Mike left, it all started to crumble, at least it felt that way. It was at that point questions were asked of Robert Chase and why he hadn't opened the purse strings. It was accepted Norwich were a selling club, but what people wanted to know was, where was the money going? Players were being sold but few were being bought for anything like the same money.

I started to get linked with other clubs. I began to receive strong interest from some really top clubs and I was excited. Of course, money then starts to come into the equation. What I was earning at Norwich was nowhere near what my potential earnings were going to be elsewhere. This was in the March of that 1993–94 season and I had just turned twenty-one. What guy of my age wouldn't have been excited at the prospect of being loaded and ready to sign for one of the top clubs in England?

Mike Walker on Chris Sutton

We rejected Chris when he was twelve or thirteen because we felt he wasn't good enough. We then took another look at him a few years later and he was still very raw. But he was tall and we felt it was worth taking a chance on him because of his height. When he joined the club on the YTS scheme he was very enthusiastic, keen to work hard and learn. I was reserve-team manager at that time and had discussions with the other coaches about him. We debated several times whether he'd be a centre-half or a centre-forward. He was tall and aggressive, both good assets for either position. We spoke to Chris about it and he made it clear he wanted to be a striker; he clearly fancied the glory of being a goal-scorer in preference to being an unsung hero.

But he also had things he needed to work on to make the step up. He was a gangly lad and his first touch wasn't nearly good enough. We told him, nagged him day in, day out if truth be told. He had to work on it and to be fair to him, he put in the hours to improve his first touch and game awareness. Chris's father was also a footballer for Norwich and he must have benefited from his father's advice, too.

Chris was a bit of country boy when he first arrived at Norwich and definitely wasn't as street-wise as some of the other lads on the YTS. He had to grow up very quickly. He also received one or two funny looks because in his first year or so at the club, he didn't behave and act like a typical footballer. On the way to games on the team bus, the lads would play cards or watch a video. Chris always had his nose in a book, and I mean proper reading. It was English literature. He came from an educated background and that doesn't always go down well in a dressing room.

But when he got a few reserve games under his belt and then broke into the first team, I could see a change in him. In terms of the way he behaved off the park, he became what you would describe as a typical footballer. He was friendly with Ruel Fox and they got up to a few naughties off the pitch. We had to pull them in and keep them in check. When he was in the youth team, Chris had to be hauled in a couple of times and threatened with being turfed out for the way he behaved off the pitch. He'd break curfews and go for nights he shouldn't have. So, by the time he played for me in the reserve team and then when I became first-team manager, I knew all about him. Norwich isn't exactly big and there was no hiding place. He also thought he was being cute with some of his antics but we caught him out. He was a bit of a handful for a while, a silly lad. But we were usually one step ahead.

When he played for the first team, his first touch was better and he had a nice turn of pace. He wasn't blessed with blistering pace, but he was quite deceptive and had a little burst in him over a few yards. He was also very opinionated in the dressing room, arrogant at times. He'd come and see me if he wasn't playing, and I'd tell him to go away and improve on his first touch, that was key to him becoming a top player. As was the case when he was younger, he took it on board. I didn't mind him having an opinion, actually, it didn't bother me. Some players moan behind your back but at least Chris was man enough to moan to my face.

He quickly became a real asset to the team and I couldn't do without him. He scored twenty-five goals one season and was quite incredible for us. He scored goals and linked the play, holding the ball up. I couldn't have asked for more, to be truthful. His form attracted attention and Blackburn Rovers offered £1 million for him and Ruel Fox in 1993.

Robert Chase was chairman at the time and informed of the offer. I laughed at it, told him it was peanuts. Chris was worth at least three times that on his own, never mind a joint bid for Fox. But the chairman wanted to accept, wanted to bite Blackburn's hand off for it. I managed to convince him it was wrong to accept. I would have quit the job had he taken that money. I knew he wouldn't spend enough money to strengthen the squad and I sort of accepted that, but I wasn't going to stand for him selling the best players for a ridiculously low amount of money.

Around a year or so later, we sold Ruel to Newcastle for more than £2 million and Chris to Blackburn for £5 million. That was fair enough. It was just a pity Norwich sold its best players. We could have built on some of our achievements if we'd spent the money on decent new players but the chairman didn't make enough funds available for that and I think the club suffered badly as a result.

I left for Everton in January 1994 and I was accused of being greedy by people at Norwich. It wasn't about money. I had a few months left on my contract and the chairman said he would sort it out. He never did, it was never forthcoming. So he had backed me into a corner and I had no choice but to accept the security Everton offered me. John Deehan was my assistant there and took over from me. The chairman just stamped all over John. I felt sorry for him. The club was relegated. John never really stood a chance.

I had great times at Norwich. Chris was good for me and I hope I was good for him. I just wish he had scored the couple of chances we had the night we played Inter Milan in the San Siro in the UEFA Cup. We were 1–0 down through a Dennis Bergkamp penalty and then Chris had two good chances inside fifteen minutes. He missed both. Maybe the occasion got to him, I'm not sure. At least the dressing room was a calm place that night. The same couldn't be said of our game against Bayern Munich in the previous round. We had a Scottish kitman called Jock Robertson. He was well into his sixties and was about 5ft 3in tall. He was a lovely man and enjoyed a laugh and a joke with the players. But Chris used to take it too far sometimes. Prior to the Munich game, he wound Jock up about the state of the kit and that it wasn't clean enough. He then threatened to throw Jock into a skip. Jock lost his cool and was trying to get at Chris. He was jumping up, throwing punches at him and it had all broken loose. I couldn't believe it. Here we were, minutes away from one of the biggest games in the history of the club and there was a riot in the dressing room. Chris just didn't know when to keep his mouth shut.

But he matured into an excellent footballer and he could have played for England at centre-half. That's how good I thought he became in that position. I remember we played him there when he was a kid as an emergency against Liverpool and he was outstanding, up against Ian Rush. He could tackle and could come out of defence with the ball. But he hated playing there. I thought he could have gone on and developed into a Tony Adams type. But his ego got in the way and he insisted on grabbing the limelight as a striker.

He worked hard to improve his first touch and with our help he polished off his rough edges. It led to his move to Blackburn and the chance to play for the full England team. But his stubbornness ruined that. He should have agreed to play for the B team under Glenn Hoddle. He must regret that decision. I know I was disappointed at the time when he refused to play. It was silly of him. But he still had a good career and we enjoyed some wonderful times together at Norwich.

5

FROM A CANARY TO A JAIL BIRD

The interest in signing me intensified towards the end of the 1993–94 season. The chairman, Robert Chase, in an attempt to end the speculation and put the fans' minds at rest, stated that I wouldn't be sold at the end of the season and if the club did sell me, then he wouldn't be at the club at the start of the new season. I can understand why he said that, but he maybe would have been better saying nothing because we all knew I was going to go.

In the end, I spoke to Manchester United, Liverpool, Arsenal, Tottenham, Leeds, Chelsea, Newcastle, Sheffield Wednesday and Blackburn. It was a helluva lot of clubs and it was hard for me to get to grips with it all. It was flattering. I was in a very fortunate position.

Tottenham chairman Sir Alan Sugar phoned my dad and asked us to go to his house to visit him, with a view of getting me to sign for his club. My dad politely declined on my behalf.

But only two clubs agreed a fee with Norwich – Blackburn and Arsenal. They were willing to pay £5 million for me. So, at just twenty-one, I was on the verge of moving for a British record transfer fee at the time.

Manchester United, I understood, would pay £4 million, no more than that. Sir Alex Ferguson had been impressed with my form on the pitch for a couple of years but told my dad he thought I should spend another season at Norwich. He was also doing his homework about me off the pitch. In fact, so much so that, allegedly, a couple of former SAS men followed me around for two weeks to check on my behaviour. They returned to Sir Alex with a good enough reference. During the summer of 1994, Sir Alex phoned my dad at his school. He said to my dad that he thought it would be best for me to stay at Norwich for another season and then he could assess me more during that period. But Dad broke the news to him that I was on my way to Blackburn.

I had played some good games for Norwich against United. I had scored forty-three goals in 127 appearances for Norwich, which was a good return considering I played my first forty or so games at centre-half. My favourite goal for the club was in a game against United at Old Trafford. The ball broke out to me at the edge of the box and I took it on the half-volley with the outside of my left foot and it flew straight into the corner. It was a great goal. There was a little bit of fade on the ball and it looked like I meant it. The reality was that I just got my head down and struck it.

I also remember one when I played a one-two with Jeremy Goss and then bent it into the top corner on the half-volley against Liverpool. I thought that was a fantastic goal, one of my best ever. A few years later, when Bruce Grobbelaar was under investigation for match-fixing, he said, allegedly, in a national newspaper, that my goal that day was one of the ones he let in deliberately. There's no way he let that one in on purpose!

My move came down to a choice between Highbury and Ewood Park and it didn't take long for me to up my mind. Arsenal were a massive club and I discussed things on the telephone with George Graham. It was very tempting. Blackburn had made me a great offer and, having spoken to Kenny Dalglish on the telephone, the prospect of playing with Alan Shearer and in a Blackburn team that had run Manchester United close the previous season was enticing, especially as success didn't seem too far off. I quickly made my mind up to sign for Blackburn and travelled up to the North West. I met the chairman, Robert Coar, at his house and signed terms on a five-year contract there and then. Norwich had agreed a fee with Blackburn and they gave me permission to talk to the club. But I wasn't allowed to tell anyone; I was sworn to secrecy by Robert Chase.

I travelled back to Norwich and had a meeting with Robert Chase. He told me he was going to call a press conference to stop all the speculation about me leaving the club because he had previously stated that if I wasn't at the club for the start of the new season, then he wouldn't be there either. He also said he would make it known at the press conference that he would test the water with other clubs and if a club came up with a £5 million transfer fee for me he would let me go. It was surreal because I had already signed for Blackburn. I wasn't totally comfortable with Robert Chase's press conference but I had no choice, I had to go along with it. But it was misleading to the Norwich fans.

It wasn't good practice from Robert Chase but, in general, he had the club's best interests at heart. At the time, I was with all the fans and the players when they pleaded with Robert Chase to loosen the purse strings and build on the success we had under Mike Walker. But, as we all know, it's easier said than done. I always thought Robert Chase had his own interests but he did a lot of good for Norwich City Football Club. He had a big part in the building of the new training ground and the redevelopment of Carrow Road. As is natural, football chairmen always seem to be pilloried. And in my time at Norwich, Robert Chase came in for a lot of criticism. But I think it's fair to say he was a shrewd operator.

On a personal level, as much as I was excited at moving to a bigger club and earning more money, I was quite reluctant to move away from Norfolk. But I knew it had to happen and that I would have to pack my bags and live elsewhere. I had been with Sam for a while by that stage, too. With the way things were for me at that particular time, I decided to settle down, which was a good thing. Blackburn seemed the ideal place for Sam and me to set up a new home.

Joining Blackburn was really exciting. I was joining a club with a very ambitious owner in Jack Walker, who at the time was prepared to spend money and back Kenny Dalglish. I joined players such as Alan Shearer, Paul Warhurst, Tim Flowers and David Batty – all top-class players who had joined the likes of Jason Wilcox, Colin Hendry and Stuart Ripley at the club. Blackburn were on the up. They were paying big money for players and paying them lucrative wages. Blackburn had beaten off Manchester United to sign Alan Shearer, and Tim Flowers chose Ewood Park in preference to Liverpool.

I had scored four goals against Blackburn the previous season. We beat them 3–2 and drew 2–2. I scored a double at Ewood Park and a double at Carrow Road. Now, I was set to score goals for the club and was excited at the prospect of playing along-side Shearer. When I played centre-half at Norwich, I played against Shearer when he was playing with Southampton. I always thought of Alan being exceptionally strong and good at holding the ball up. He wasn't the tallest of strikers but he was very powerful in the air. And his goals really took off at Blackburn.

Naturally, the thought of playing with Shearer was a big factor in my decision to choose Blackburn ahead of every other club. Kenny Dalglish was also a huge factor. I wasn't a Liverpool supporter, but in my youth I'd have had to be very stupid not to know exactly who he was. He was one of the greatest players in the game and was very famous. When I met him, he impressed me and I was very comfortable in his company. His enthusiasm was infectious.

I'd be lying if I said the money wasn't a factor. I was on a reasonable wage at Norwich but nothing like what I was going to earn at Blackburn. This was a fresh start for me and one I was nervously looking forward to.

I had a going-away party the night before I was due to go to Blackburn for the official press conference. I was to be paraded at the club as a record transfer fee in Britain. A few friends and team-mates attended the bash in Norwich. It's fair to say a lot of alcohol was consumed and things got a bit out of hand. I was at the forefront and enjoying my evening. I was twenty-one at the time, had a high opinion of myself, and enjoyed the attention and adulation I was getting.

My leaving night was going well. Then all hell broke loose. Going from one pub to another, I jumped right inside a convertible car headfirst. I caused a little bit of damage to the indicator by bending the lever. Suffice to say it was a pretty stupid thing to do. It was alcohol-fuelled and although in jest, it was a decision that backfired spectacularly. The owner of the car, who wasn't in it at the time, must have reported me to the police. I was oblivious to this as I stood at the bar in Tombland, an area in the centre of Norwich, enjoying myself. Then I got a tip-off that the police were coming, so I nipped out the fire exit and into a taxi to make a quick getaway. The next thing I knew, the taxi was being followed by three police cars and they pulled us over. We were surrounded. You'd have thought I'd killed someone.

I was taken out of the taxi and into the back of one of the police cars. They took me to the police station and put me in a cell. I thought it was an over-reaction from the police. I wasn't formally arrested, but they were going to have their moment with me and I was cautioned. It was reckless behaviour on my part, though.

Eric Serruys, my friend, went back to my house where I lived with Sam and told her what had happened. She then phoned my dad and the club to notify them. My dad wasn't best pleased. I was more scared of him than the police, for sure. I didn't know how I would explain to him what had happened.

It wasn't a brilliant night, really. It makes me cringe just thinking about it now. It was brainless behaviour. I was really upset with myself because I had let a lot of people down. I went to Robert Chase's house straight from the police station. He was very kind and looked after me. We then flew up to Blackburn from Norwich Airport in a small aircraft. Thankfully, Sam had gone out and bought me clothes, so I didn't travel in the same gear from the night before.

The whole journey was a nightmare and I was very worried about how the incident would be reported in the press. My mind was all over the place and at the forefront of my thoughts was that I might have jeopardised everything all for the sake of a stupid night out. I was concerned Blackburn might pull out of the deal, not wanting to bring someone who was drunk and disorderly to their club. I should have been tucked up in my bed that night instead of being out on the town.

The following day should have been one of the best of my life but I was hungover, anxious and tired. The only thing I kept reassuring myself with was the fact that I had already signed. Pen had been put to paper. Today was just about me being paraded in front of the media. I suppose Robert Chase would have been just as pleased as me that the deal had already been signed. Otherwise he might have seen £5 million disappear.

As I'd feared, news of the incident hadn't taken long to become public knowledge. It was all over the television, radio and newspapers. I was terrified about what Kenny's reaction was going to be. Thankfully, he just laughed it off. He was very good about it. That was such a relief, as he would have been perfectly entitled to give me a rollicking and possibly not want that type of character in his dressing room. In that respect, I couldn't have had a better man to look after me and manage me at that time of my life.

Thankfully, I didn't end up in court over that incident. I was given a stern warning, though. That was probably the kick up the backside I needed at that stage. In many ways, I had behaved like a prat and had some things coming to me. I got too big for my boots. I suppose I was just twenty-one but my behaviour should still have been better.

Headlines had followed me throughout that final season at Norwich. The national press were interested in me and I attracted headlines whether I played well or played badly. I liked the adulation; I enjoyed the attention but definitely preferred it when they were talking about events on the pitch rather than off it.

When I started with Blackburn in the summer of 1994, I was very nervous and excited. Whenever my performance dipped, there were questions about whether or not I was worth £5 million. I didn't handle the criticism well but Kenny was always there for me, always backing me.

I went on pre-season tour to Norway with Blackburn and my first game was on a Saturday afternoon, a friendly against a side called Steinkjer. We lost 2–1 and the press felt I didn't play to an acceptable standard. The following day the *News of the World* ran with a back-page headline of 'Sutton has a Steinkjer'. I actually thought my performance wasn't too bad. However, this was my introduction to being a high-profile footballer who was now up there to be shot at. It was the first negative press I had received on that scale for my game on the park. I didn't like it. I failed to understand it.

Of course, I'd had negative press after my off-pitch antics, but I couldn't understand why they had gone from being so positive about my abilities on the pitch to then having a right go at me. I thought this shouldn't happen. I understood the game, in terms of how the media works. I didn't like the negativity. I thought everybody would be reading it and sharing the negative opinions that were being expressed about me. But, of course,

I had to get used to it and learn to live with it. I suppose, in many ways, I made a rod for my own back.

However, I was always my own worst critic and I should have disregarded some of the nonsense that was written about me. Some people had some real cheap shots at me. Sure, there was some constructive criticism and that was absolutely fine. The rest wasn't. I just couldn't understand why, all of a sudden, I went from being a very good striker at Norwich to having people question the £5 million transfer fee that was paid for me. I had only been with Blackburn for a short space of time, even before a competitive ball was kicked, and already some were forecasting that I'd be a waste of money.

On the opening day of the season, we drew 1–1 with Southampton and I missed a few chances. I got flak for that. It was on my mind a little, I suppose, but I was fine in the next game when I scored on my home debut in a 3–0 win against Leicester. Things continued to improve and I grabbed a hat-trick in a 4–0 win against Coventry. That really settled me down. I didn't have a feeling early in the season that we were going to win the league but we won ten games on the spin. We weren't a brilliant footballing side, but we worked hard and were very effective. We relied heavily on our wingers, Jason Wilcox and Stuart Ripley. They were super fit and got up and down that line. We made sure we were efficient and got the ball forward into dangerous areas.

The team was the same fairly often – Tim Flowers as keeper, Henning Berg and Graeme Le Saux at full-back. Tony Gale and Colin Hendry were the central defenders, with Ian Pearce playing alongside Colin in the second half of the season. Mark Atkins and Tim Sherwood were the central midfielders. Tim was an intelligent footballer and a good captain. Mark was a very under-rated footballer but Kenny appreciated him and so did the players.

Mind you, I think Mark was the only player Kenny ever lost

the rag with in training. We were playing a game of five-a-sides, which Kenny loved to play and he was brilliant, although he could be stroppy. One day, Mark went right through him and Kenny ended up on the ground. Well, he gave Mark some amount of abuse. It was very unusual for Kenny. I don't think Mark tackled him ever again.

That said, we had a good camaraderie at the club. We were like a well-oiled machine, very efficient and we continued to churn out results, with the SAS partnership going from strength to strength on the pitch. The goals flowed for both of us before Christmas. I scored the winning goal away at Chelsea and two goals at home against Liverpool in a 3–2 victory. After Christmas I dried up a little bit in terms of my goalscoring, but Alan seemed to go from strength from strength. I, like most people in the country, marvelled at his goalscoring prowess. He was a machine. When he got half a chance he buried it. He had a low back-lift and such power in his shooting and was incredibly strong in the air, especially for a guy of his size.

He was ruthless, very single-minded and had a self-belief I'd never encountered before. I can't honestly remember him missing a chance that season, such was his efficiency. The Rovers machine ploughed on to get result after result, grinding it out. We had big personalities with the work ethic to match anybody and with Kenny cleverly knowing which buttons to press at the right time. Kenny was instrumental in keeping us focused and as relaxed as we could be.

My partnership with Shearer had played an important part in Blackburn securing their first title in decades. Throughout the season there were constant murmurings about my relationship with Alan. The murmurings continued after Alan left for Newcastle at the start of the 1996–97 season. I suppose as a renowned striking partnership people expected we'd be great mates on and off the pitch. I would like to think we both had a healthy mutual respect for each other on the pitch. Off the pitch it's difficult for me to put into words how I felt. It's hard to explain but there was always an underlying feeling from me that there wasn't any warmth towards me from Alan. Alan was one of ten other team-mates in a big squad of players. We didn't have to be best mates off the pitch even though we got on okay. I felt Alan's relationship with Mike Newell may have been the reason for the way I felt. They were a strike partnership the previous season and were best mates.

I was brought in by Kenny and broke up the Shearer/Newell partnership. I felt at the time there may have been a bit of resentment towards me. I may have been feeling a little insecure, I don't know. I had moved for a British record transfer fee and maybe stole the limelight away from Alan for a short period. I really wanted his approval. I was still very young at twenty-one and it was my first move away from Norwich, where I was brought up. Maybe I felt slightly vulnerable at that time. I was very high profile but hardly experienced in life at dealing with situations. I was a big fish at Norwich but was now in a pond with the biggest fish in the country at Blackburn.

At certain times, like when I scored my third goal in a 4–0 victory against Coventry City, Alan didn't come over to celebrate with me and this left me very unsure about what he thought about me. The following season I felt Alan had a strong influence on Ray Harford when it came to team selection. It was the way I saw things at the time. At football clubs key players often do have a big influence at times. Whether I was right or wrong, it was the way I felt then. Alan has had an incredible career and it was a privilege to play alongside one of England's greatest ever strikers. I'd like to think the SAS partnership will be one the Blackburn Rovers fans remember for a long time. It was certainly a season I'll never forget.

At the start of April, we had a very significant week when we won two difficult away games. The first was at Everton and I scored the opening goal after twelve seconds. It was great to get on the score sheet. Alan scored the other one. We were two up and then they came back to 2–1. They piled the pressure on and there was an almighty scramble inside our box, which seemed to last for about three minutes. Talk about hanging on for dear life. We got away with the points. It was an ugly performance from us, but it was a huge three points and a massive win. It was also my first goal since I found the net for us in an FA Cup replay at Newcastle at the end of January. We lost that tie and also lost early in the League Cup to Liverpool. Going out of the competitions allowed us to focus fully on the League.

From Merseyside we headed to London to play Queens Park Rangers. We won 1–0 and I scored the winner. It rounded off a great week for the club and I also felt pretty pleased with myself. We got on the bus that night and for the first time I think we thought the title was in the bag.

But it wasn't going to be as straightforward as that. We began to slip up in many games and lost at home to Manchester City, who were struggling to avoid relegation and managed to beat us. Despite that defeat, we were still five points clear with four games to go. It was a healthy lead and we thought we couldn't lose it from that position, but we still kept frittering points away.

By the time we played at home to Newcastle, the title was back in the balance. Had we not won that night, the title may well have stayed at Old Trafford. But we beat Newcastle 1–0. Alan scored the goal. Tim was outstanding that night in goal; he pretty much won the game on his own for us. I remember in his post-match interview he kept talking about having the bottle to win the title and he was absolutely right. I think in an interview a few days' earlier, Sir Alex Ferguson had questioned our bottle to win the title and this was Tim responding to him in the best possible way. As a team, we knew we had the ability to go all the way, but would we have the nerve? Would we be able to keep our composure? Kenny had won titles as a player and manager with Liverpool but none of the Blackburn lads had won a title. It was a real test for us.

Eventually, the title race came down to the last day of the season. We were at Anfield to play Liverpool, and Manchester United were away to West Ham. It was all to play for but we should never have let the situation get to that point. We needed to win the game to guarantee the title and I think many people thought Liverpool would lie down to us because of their affection for Kenny and their dislike of Manchester United. Let me assure you, they didn't give us an easy ride that day. And no Blackburn player expected them to. They beat us. Thankfully, West Ham managed to draw against United and Hammers keeper Ludo Miklosko had an outstanding game, pulling off save after save.

We played in a tired manner against Liverpool. I felt I had no energy left after the first ten minutes. I didn't sleep well the night before and I just wasn't in a relaxed frame of mind. I was maybe over-anxious, felt nervous and drained. We played all of our games at high intensity and it took its toll on us. We lost the game 2–1. Shearer typically gave us the lead in the first half but John Barnes levelled in the sixty-fourth minute. We were hanging on and then Jamie Redknapp scored an injury-time winner for Liverpool. Thankfully, Manchester United couldn't beat West Ham and only managed a 1–1 draw at Upton Park.

Despite the defeat against Liverpool, we had performed well throughout the season and in the end, we deserved what we got winning the title. We had eighty-nine points and United had eighty-eight. It gave us a crack at the Champions League. It was only one team that got into that brilliant tournament in 1995 and we were delighted to get it and the money that came with it. Manchester United had to settle for the UEFA Cup. They may well have felt their championship challenge took an almighty blow when they lost Eric Cantona halfway through the season. Cantona was banned for the season when he assaulted a Crystal Palace fan with a kung-fu style kick after he took exception to the fan verbally abusing him. But having said that, they signed Andy Cole from Newcastle in the January for £7 million – to break the British transfer record that I had held for my move to Blackburn – and Cole was terrific for them.

Some crucial things didn't go our way during the season, such as the unexpected loss to Trelleborgs in the UEFA Cup first round. There were also league disappointments, particularly when we lost both games to Manchester United. Decisions went against us in both games. I'm not saying we were robbed of the points, but it didn't help us in the first game when referee Gerald Ashby sent off Henning Berg. It was a poor refereeing decision. In the second game, we scored to make it 1–1 but the reaction of their players and the way they pressurised the referee got the goal disallowed. That made us feel even more bitter towards the Manchester United players and management. After that game, Kenny Dalglish said sarcastically in an interview that these things even themselves out. Now, had we drawn one of those two games, then we wouldn't have needed to go to the final day of the season. Had we drawn both games, we'd have won it comfortably.

When I played at Blackburn I used to hate Manchester United. Subsequently, over the years, as time went by, I've grown to quite like Manchester United and have real admiration for what they've achieved as a club. But we wanted to beat them badly when I was at Rovers because they had dominated for so long. They probably felt that they would keep on winning leagues and that we wouldn't be a major threat to them, but we managed to overcome them and win that title in 1995.

When we won the title, some small-minded people wanted to go down the road of saying the club 'bought' the title instead of giving us credit for what we had achieved. We had a fairly young squad; it wasn't like we had a team full of experienced thirty-year-olds. At the end of the day, you can spend millions and millions of pounds on players but it doesn't guarantee success. We had to be well managed and credit goes to Kenny for that side of it. I liked the way he always backed the players. If you performed poorly, he would never have a go at you in public. He gave us his backing even if he knew we hadn't played up to the standard he demanded. I just wanted to go out and do well for him. He knew his football, knew the strengths and weaknesses of the players. He had achieved so much in the game and is one of the greatest players ever to play on these shores and beyond. He was also very humble and modest. I played under him for a year and it was a very enjoyable experience. He spoke very well and was an inspirational talker. He kept things very simple and enjoyable. He liked a laugh and a joke but you knew where the line was with him. And one thing that was crystal clear about him at all times was that he hated losing.

Others also played their part and Ray Harford was also important to our success. Ray was Kenny's No. 2 and took most of the training sessions. His ability on the training ground complemented Kenny's brilliant man management.

And then there was Jack Walker, the man who had invested so heavily in the club and who took great delight from winning the league. All the players were delighted for him. He was a really nice man. He had bought the club five years earlier and taken them from the old Second Division to the Premiership title. Yet for all the money he spent on big-name players, he retained a feeling of community and made sure Blackburn was a family club. Jack Walker epitomised what the club stood for and that was hard work. Blackburn is a real working-class area and it was nice to see the Rovers fans have something to celebrate. Jack wasn't flash in any way. He started his business with nothing and built it up. He wanted to put his money into Blackburn Rovers Football Club and he was rewarded. He just wanted his hometown club to do well. It was never about him, he wanted all the attention to be on the players and the fans.

I felt relief as much as anything when the referee blew the final whistle at Anfield. I kept thinking more about how I would have felt and what people would have said if we had lost it, thrown it away. I think a lot of the lads were thinking the same thing but we never spoke about it. It would have been a helluva collapse but such things have happened. But we got there; we made it. It took me a few days to realise what we'd achieved and then I started to appreciate it. I walked around with my chest puffed out. Winning the Premiership title with Blackburn can never be taken away from me.

I don't know how Kenny was feeling in the pit of his stomach before the game, but he spoke well and tried to keep us on the level. He would have been disappointed and upset had we not won it. But we got there and I was delighted for him. It was Blackburn's first title win since 1914. Unfortunately, my old club Norwich were relegated that season along with Ipswich, Leicester and Crystal Palace. I felt for the Norwich fans and my former team-mates.

After the game at Anfield, we went back to a hotel in Preston to celebrate. I had a few drinks and I felt so relieved. The over-whelming feeling was one of satisfaction. It's the only Premiership title I've won. I signed the previous summer with that intention and we accomplished it. I scored fifteen goals in forty league appearances and that was satisfying, too. Alan was the top scorer in the Premiership and won the Golden Boot for his thirty-four league goals.

I just wish we had kicked on from there – became a top, top club and established ourselves as a major force. Kenny was voted Manager of the Year by his peers, but he decided to stand down as manager and moved upstairs to a role as Director of Football. I don't know why he chose to do that but it was just never the same without him as manager. It was a great club with some good, honest people in charge and the 1994–95 season is one that Blackburn fans, the players and I will never forget.

Kenny Dalglish on Chris Sutton

We watched Chris closely for a wee while. He was attracting attention from a lot of other English clubs. He was instrumental in getting Norwich to the top of the league. They came to Blackburn as league leaders in the October of the 1992–93 season and they lost 7–1. Chris played that day, maybe as a defender.

But he knew how to score a goal and we needed another goal-scorer. I wanted to team Chris up with Alan Shearer. I knew Chris would be ideal to play alongside Alan. Alan was never going to be left out of the team so we needed someone to play with him who would also score goals. I spoke to him to try and sell what we had and he had to buy into it.

His dad was involved in the discussions. His dad was influential on him. I made it clear to the Blackburn board that I wanted Chris and I was delighted they shared that determination to bring him to Ewood Park. I was away on holiday when the fee was agreed between Blackburn and Norwich. It was a record transfer between British clubs. When the Blackburn chief executive phoned to tell me we had secured Chris I was thrilled.

The fee was a lot of money but I had no problem with that. For me, a fee is never important if you are getting the right type of player and the right type of person. Chris fitted the bill, although he did have that problem the night before he was paraded at the press conference in Blackburn. Well, he had already signed so there was no way we could pull out of the deal!

Seriously, that was never a problem for me. I told Chris to put that incident behind him and look forward.

He played very well for us that season. He scored a hat-trick early in the season against Coventry City in a 4–0 win. The best game he played for us in the title-winning campaign was when we went to Highbury to face Arsenal in August 1994. Jason Wilcox got red carded and we moved Chris back to centre-half. He was up against Ian Wright and didn't give him a sight of goal. Chris was outstanding that day and we got a 0–0 draw. It was a vital point. He was a brilliant centre-back and I wouldn't have minded him playing there for us. However, he'd already had the taste of blood as a goal-scorer and once you have that, it is hard to move away from it, especially to a less glamorous role.

He scored plenty of goals for us up until Christmas and then it became a bit more difficult for him. Very few defenders could handle him and Alan together. Even if one of them wasn't quite on top of their game, the other would be on form. One of them would always be inside the box, looking for a chance. In fact, most of the time you'd find the two of them inside the box. He was honest on the pitch and gave the team everything he had. He put in a great shift. It might have gone unrecognised but it wasn't unappreciated.

He wasn't an easy striker for defenders to play against. He was a great outlet for us. He also had a better first touch than people gave him credit for. He was mobile, had a decent turn of pace and was a good finisher. But, despite things going well for him on the pitch in his first few months, I know he wasn't always at ease with himself. Most of the problems Chris felt he had were self-inflicted. It was all in his imagination. That must have been his problem at Chelsea, too. How a player of his ability went to Chelsea and wasn't a success, I'll never know. He must have had self-doubts there, too.

Maybe if you're not the most confident person in the world, and it might sound strange because someone has just bought you for £5 million, anything anybody says that might be a bit tongue in cheek or a bit of a joke, if you don't feel it's truly welcoming, then you're going to enlarge it in your mind and it will affect you. Chris, to be honest, was his own worst enemy when it came to that.

Now, he might have had a wee sort of an issue with Shearer but that was all in his mind. Maybe Chris came to the club thinking 'Goodness, that's Alan Shearer, England's centre-forward, what am I going to do here?' He didn't look too unhappy when they scored though and they each seemed to enjoy it when the other put the ball in the back of the net. So, it was all in his own mind as far as I'm concerned.

He used to come in in the morning and I would pass him in the corridor and sing to him: 'We're not so manic now.' I'd smile and he'd tell me where to go! He was just a big shy guy. He found it difficult to look people in the eye. Sometimes you could barely get a 'hello' out of him. But he was a really nice lad, really nice.

The whole group of players we had that season were terrific, fantastic with each other and that was reflected in the way they played. They were a good lot to be around.

Alan and Chris were lucky to have Stuart Ripley and Jason Wilcox down either flank. The pair of them worked like Trojans and set up chance after chance. Yet, probably the best finisher we had at the club was Mark Atkins.

All of the lads had to do their bit and then some. Believe it or not, we didn't have a huge squad. When I think back to it now, we were knocked out of the UEFA Cup by Trelleborgs in the first round. Had we progressed in that tournament then it might have cost us the league.

The players made it all possible and, of course, it would be remiss not to mention Jack Walker. Jack took the club up a few levels with his financial input. The players were well paid but they weren't on fortunes. Sure, they were on good money but they weren't on wages that other clubs couldn't have matched. Clubs need to buy players to win the league. Tell me a club that has won a title without buying a player? People claimed we bought our way to the title but that was a misconception. Negative things were written and said in the media and it was rather unfair. Other clubs and supporters became jealous of Blackburn Rovers and the Rovers fans loved that fact. They thought it was great and lapped it all up.

Jack funded the players but the club got some return on the players. Henning Berg was bought for £300,000 and sold to Manchester United for £5 million. The club doubled its money on Chris and quadrupled its money on Alan. Colin Hendry moved for more than a £3 million profit to Rangers. Tim Sherwood went for more than a £3 million profit when he joined Tottenham. Graeme Le Saux was a £4 million profit. Those guys all served the club well and then made the club a tidy sum of money. In the end, it worked out well for everyone and I was proud to be a part of that team and that Championship-winning season.

6

THRONE OFF COURSE –
LIFE AFTER KING KENNY

Ray Harford took over from Kenny Dalglish in the summer of 1995. Kenny decided to move upstairs to a Director of Football role after we had won the title. Kenny was always going to be a near impossible act to follow. He won the title with an unfashionable Blackburn for the first time in eighty-odd years. It was always going to be tough for Ray to make the transition from coach to manager. Being second-in-command, as Ray was, is totally different from managing. Relationships and friendships would have been formed with a lot of the players in the previous few years Ray had been at Blackburn. This is nothing new, it happens at all clubs.

In my opinion, it is then difficult to keep your distance when taking over the reins and Ray struggled to make this transition. He was close to certain players. Alan Shearer was one of them. I felt Ray was definitely influenced by certain players when it came to team selection. I suffered because of this. I had no proof but it's what I felt.

Prior to the season starting, Ray had used the phrase, 'If it ain't broken, then don't try to fix it.' We had won the Premiership title and sticking with the same side seemed reasonable. However, from the outside, it may have looked like we should have made a major impact signing or two so we would be able to carry on the momentum.

Ray's 'if it ain't broken' phrase didn't apply to me. Within a few games, I was left out of the starting line-up and I wasn't happy. He reverted back to playing Mike Newell as Alan Shearer's strike partner.

I hadn't done a great deal wrong but it was certainly a rapid change in fortune from the previous season under Kenny. I wasn't that arrogant to think I couldn't be dropped, but my form wasn't that bad and, in my opinion, it was ridiculous for Ray to replace me so early. I found the situation farcical and it led to a number of run-ins with my new manager.

I challenged Ray and asked why I had been left out and who was picking the team. He told me he was the manager, he picked the team and my performances hadn't been as good as they had been the previous season. I told him we'd only played three competitive games and I hadn't been that bad. I told him it was unjust and that I wasn't happy, and that if things didn't change I'd have to consider my position. I let it go for a month or so and nothing changed.

My dad came up for a meeting with Ray and myself, and it was very similar to the previous meeting. I wanted my dad there. This time I told Ray I wanted to leave. I knew I could have secured another good move comfortably at that stage, but he told me I couldn't go and I'd have to get on with it.

He was punishing me twice. I was raging.

The team on the pitch hadn't started the season well and eventually I started to get some games – but as a centre-half, only occasionally up front. I wasn't enjoying life under Ray. I'd lost faith in him and I did not trust him one bit. He was a good coach and, looking back, a far better coach than I gave him credit for at the time, but that was because I didn't like him as a person. I think it's fair to say the feeling was mutual. I got through a disappointing season for the club and myself but I was far from happy under the new manager.

Normally when a player is unhappy, he will speak to the assistant manager or first-team coach. At most clubs, one, if not both of them, also have a role between the manager and the dressing room. If you have a grievance, you would speak to them first and see if it could be resolved without having to go directly to the manager.

John Robertson and Steve Walford were particularly good at that role when they were at Celtic under Martin O'Neill, but I didn't feel there was any kind of 'buffer' between manager and players at Blackburn. Derek Fazackerley and Tony Parkes were Ray's assistants. In a team meeting at the training ground, Ray had been quite critical of me in terms of my attitude at training and Derek Fazackerley just nodded and agreed. Rather than offer a different perspective and maybe try to help resolve the situation, all he managed to do was virtually repeat word for word what Ray had said. I told Derek to shut up, that his opinion didn't mean anything to me and that he was a budgerigar. He wasn't overly happy with my comments. But I felt isolated. I didn't feel I had any support whatsoever from the manager or his backroom staff. That's why I decided to get on the front foot. However, I didn't always react in the greatest possible manner. That's fair to say, for sure. And, in some ways, I regretted what I said to Derek. In hindsight, it was something I probably shouldn't have said. He's a decent guy and a capable coach.

We had started the 1995–96 season in the Champions League with a buzz around Ewood Park but it had quickly gone flat. We eventually finished the league in seventh position but we were in the bottom half for most of the season. We were knocked out of the Champions League when we finished bottom of the table in the group stages.

Over the summer, I seriously contemplated my future and I

felt I could have got a good move. But then Alan Shearer was sold to Newcastle just before the start of the 1996–97 season for £15 million. He had been an incredible player for Blackburn and was virtually impossible to replace. I had started the pre-season not sure at all about my future but after Alan's departure, things took a dramatic twist in my favour again. Ray got me into his office and told me that I was going to be the main man that season. I was going to play centre-forward all season and he told me how much he rated me. I nearly fell off my chair. I was stunned at this U-turn. In fairness, he said that we had to put last season behind us and he was right.

The team had a disappointing start to the season and I missed the first four games due to injury. When I was fit again, I was selected to play the first game at home to Derby County and it was live on Sky. I wasn't particularly fit, as I'd just come back from injury and was pushed in without any reserve games. We lost the game 2–1. I played ok, nothing special. But I did score the goal.

The next day, we had a debrief in the changing rooms at the training complex at Brockhall Village. Ray said, in front of the players, that he was so pleased to have me back in the side and went on about how well I had played against Derby. He then told the players to give me a round of applause. I nearly collapsed out of shock and embarrassment. The players were loving it, taking the mickey. I don't think I've ever gone so red. The likes of Jason Wilcox had a field day with it for weeks afterwards.

The previous season I was so out of favour and now I was flavour of the month. As much as I was happy back playing in the team and up front again, I couldn't believe the change in Ray's attitude. He was so positive about me – it was incredible. Being cynical, I trusted him even less after this, if that was at all possible. But I was playing again so I just kept my head down.

The next twist was Ray resigning due to poor results just six games later, on 25 October 1996. Looking back, the start of our campaign was nothing short of disastrous. We had four points from eleven games but somehow survived. I don't think any side had ever recovered from that kind of start and stayed in the Premier League. Our league form was bad enough but the low point was a defeat to Second Division side Stockport County in the League Cup.

In all honesty, I wasn't sorry to see Ray go at that time. We had never forged any sort of relationship when he was the coach and we certainly didn't click when he became manager. However, you can't change history and there is no doubt that Ray played an integral part in Blackburn Rovers winning the Premier League in 1995. Blackburn supporters will always be eternally grateful for Ray and Kenny's success and rightly so, but he and I just never got on.

Tony Parkes took over from Ray as a caretaker manager, initially. He had been at the club a long time as a player and then a coach. He worked under Kenny and Ray in the same capacity. He knew the players and was a good club man. In terms of being a manager, though, Tony struggled to stamp any authority on the players. He was not a strong character but he was a nice man. I think it was difficult for Tony to step up and take over as manager after previously being the players' confidant. The players virtually managed themselves for the rest of the season. In a way, you have to give Tony credit for that as he wasn't forceful or a dictator.

There was also a bit of spirit back in the dressing room again. Tim Sherwood, the club captain, was inspirational. Tim was a really clever footballer, very street-wise on and off the pitch. All the players looked to him for leadership and he didn't let us down. He was the captain when the team had won the Premiership title but this was an altogether different challenge.

Tim had the ear of the dressing room and, in my mind, was

practically the manager during that period. After Ray's departure, we changed the system to a 4-5-1, in an effort to toughen up and become much harder to beat. We had a really aggressive central midfield of Tim, Garry Flitcroft and Billy McKinlay, and this midfield trio were the catalyst for the side. They set the standard with their work ethic and commitment. They were like a pack of hounds. We finally won for the first time that season by beating Liverpool 3–0. I scored two goals and Jason Wilcox scored the other one. It was our eleventh game of the season.

That win gave us belief and we went from strength to strength. It was the first time I had played up front on my own as a central striker. The game plan was to use me as the focal point of the team, and to get runners from the midfield area to run off me and beyond me. I had to have my share of flick-ons and touches for this to work and it really suited my game with the likes of Kevin Gallacher, Sherwood and Wilcox bombing on. We were very resolute and difficult to beat with a goal threat at the other end. We had good players and I was enjoying my game again. We eventually dug our way out of trouble to avoid relegation and finished in fourteenth position. After having just four points from eleven games, it was a decent achievement. It was European form we showed.

I think Tony was very fortunate to inherit such good players from Ray. We had top players and we shouldn't have been languishing anywhere near the bottom of the table. We were under-achieving. Jeff Kenna and Graeme Le Saux were the fullbacks. Colin Hendry and Henning Berg were the central defenders. And we had Jason Wilcox and Kevin Gallacher down either flank of the five-man midfield. It was a really good team.

There was a great deal of speculation as to who the next manager was going to be. Being Blackburn manager was still an attractive position. Sven Göran Eriksson was actually announced as the new manager, just before the end of the season. Everything was agreed. He had decided to leave Lazio and join us in the summer. But then he changed his mind. It was a farce. Tord Grip, his assistant, had started to come and watch our games towards the end of the season and give reports to Sven, to prepare him for his arrival. Needless to say, it was a great shock when he then turned down the job to stay at Lazio.

Roy Hodgson was appointed during the summer. Roy arrived with a fantastic pedigree and a great track record as a boss. He had won countless championships in Sweden and was successful as manager of Switzerland and Inter Milan. He took Inter to a UEFA Final. Roy brought a whole new element of professionalism to the training. It was the first time I had encountered double training sessions on a regular basis. The training was very interesting – different from anything I had seen under previous regimes. It involved a lot of game-related functional sessions. It was very structured, detailed and methodical. Roy broke the game down in great detail, down to the individual's roles in the team environment. It was new to me and I learned so much from him. Roy's knowledge was incredible and everything he said made sense. He was very hands-on in training; he took most, if not all, of the football sessions. And he didn't delegate any of the functional sessions to his assistants, Tony Parkes and Derek Fazackerley. At times, Tony and Derek would put on a passing drill or a bit of circle work for the warm-up before the main training took place. Roy would then step in. Roy also brought an Italian fitness coach, Arnoldo Longoretti, to the club. He put us through our paces physically. Again, this was very new to me and a lot of the lads.

We also had a gym programme – upper body stuff – and we were monitored. Previous to this, most of the other players and I would go into the gym anyway but now it was compulsory. We started to get our weight and body-fat checked regularly. It was a very professional set-up. I didn't always enjoy two sessions a day. I actually felt for the first time I had a proper job. Footballers working hard and having double sessions? It was unheard of.

Before the start of the 1997–98 season, Roy brought in the Swedish striker Martin Dahlin from Roma. He had a great track record and was a good guy. He had scored goals at the top level. But he had problems with his back and struggled for a lot of the season because of this. For me, the season ended up well in terms of my level of performance. I had learned so much from Roy and my understanding of the game was getting better all the time. Roy gave me confidence in abundance through his training and man-management.

The team responded to Roy's methods almost immediately. We started the season strongly and played some great football and I built up a good partnership with Kevin Gallacher. Kevin was a very intelligent player; he suited my game. He was slight in stature but very sharp. He had good link-up play and was an excellent finisher.

In the first couple of months, we were on a roll, memorably beating Sheffield Wednesday 7–2. I scored a couple in that one. We also beat Aston Villa 4–0 away and I scored a hat-trick. Unfortunately for me, Dennis Bergkamp stole the show and grabbed the headlines in the papers. My hat-trick was good – a half-volley with my right foot from the edge of the box, a swivelling left-foot volley from about twelve yards and a close-range volley from a Jason Wilcox cross – but Bergkamp scored a sensational hat-trick on the same day for Arsenal at Leicester City. His third goal was one of the best I've ever seen. A diagonal ball came over his head from the left-hand side of the box and he had instant control. He then had a keepy-uppy to sail past Matty Elliott before placing a half-volley finish to the far top corner of the net past Kasey Keller. It was just brilliant.

The highlight of the season for me, in terms of a team

performance and enjoyment, was beating Arsenal 3–1 at Highbury just before Christmas. We remained top of the Premiership after that game and that was special, especially off the back of the previous season's events in which I caused a furore. Arsenal were at the peak of their game and it was arguably their strongest-ever team. The spine of that side was David Seaman, Tony Adams, Martin Keown, Emmanuel Petit, Patrick Vieira, Ian Wright and Dennis Bergkamp. We played them off the park and Gallacher scored a sensational volley past Seaman. It was a very sweet victory.

Highbury was a venue where the opposition fans really detested me. In fact, anyone connected with the club tended to despise me. It was because of an incident in the game on 19 April 1997. Arsenal were fighting for a place in the Champions League and we were trying to avoid relegation. They were 1–0 up through a David Platt goal and were trying to kill the flow of the game at every opportunity, which is their right and what teams do under such circumstances. However, I felt they were maybe overdoing it a bit. I certainly wasn't the only player in our team to think that way. We were all fairly agitated with their antics. We wanted back into the game and needed a goal but they were taking their time when they had a free-kick or a throw-in. Their physiotherapist took his time when he had to come onto the pitch to give treatment to Stephen Hughes after Sherwood tackled him. Vieira played the ball out to let the stretcher on. Then Ray Parlour came on to replace him. There was about one minute of normal time remaining at this point.

They took an eternity with the treatment and there was a feeling from us that enough was enough. During the time it took for the treatment, a few of us had discussed what we were going to do at the throw-in. We decided to throw the ball back to them but I was to chase it down. I chased down Nigel Winterburn and, technically, didn't let him clear it. He was trying to shield the ball out for a goal kick and ended up kicking the ball out for a corner for us. The Arsenal players were extremely angry, and there was a skirmish or two inside the box as they made their feelings known to me. Vieira pushed me and I pushed him back. We were both booked. From the corner we scored a brilliant goal through Flitcroft, a half-volley from the edge of the box. We were ecstatic and Arsenal were going nuts, mainly at me. They missed out on a Champions League place to Newcastle that season on goal difference so you can see why they were so angry.

I think I played the final three minutes of stoppage time on the touchline, as close to the tunnel as possible. It's the only time in my career I played left wing. When the referee blew for time-up I nipped into the tunnel and into the safety of our dressing room. The Arsenal players were livid and Martin Keown led the charge to get at me. My team-mates made sure none of the Arsenal players got into our dressing room. That said, I would have sorted Martin out if it came to a head-to-head!

I was severely criticised for the incident by Arsenal and sections of the English media and, in many respects, I can understand their grievances. I suppose I didn't cover myself in glory but I only did what I felt was right at the time. Technically, was it the right thing to do? Well, in terms of sportsmanship, no, it wasn't. But then, if you want to talk about sportsmanship, then by the letter of the law Arsenal should have played at a normal pace. But all players will try to waste time when they are in front; it's part of the game. All teams try to slow the game down when they are ahead and the team that is behind tries to speed it up. We've all been on both sides of the fence when it comes to that. That's the way football is and that's the mentality players have. Quite simply, there is hypocrisy in football.

It's all about trying to win and we were fighting for our lives that day. It's an emotional game. I got fed up with the way Arsenal went about their business in the closing stages, really it was as simple as that. As a team, in the main, we made the decision to charge that ball down when we threw it back to Winterburn. I was blamed for it and I've been able to live with that. Had it not been me that charged it down, it would have been one of my team-mates.

In the post-match press conference, Tony Parkes criticised me, said that I was young, naive and shouldn't have chased the ball down. However, in the dressing room, he was completely different. He was delighted we scored that goal and praised me for my role in it.

And for Arsenal, to blame us for them not getting into the Champions League was absurd, quite frankly. They played three league games after we faced them. In their next game, they drew 1–1 at Coventry. Then, on 2 May, they lost at home 1–0 to Newcastle. In my opinion, that's the game that killed their Champions League chances. Had they not lost that day, they would have been fine. In their final game, they defeated Derby 3–1 but they'd simply left it too late.

I was never well received at Highbury, anyway. I was always on the receiving end of a fair bit of verbal abuse at that ground, especially when I went back there the next time in December 1997 and we beat them 3–1. I got pelters that afternoon. It was nice to silence the home fans with that victory though.

That wasn't the end of it between Arsenal and me. In October 1998, we played them at Ewood Park on a wet night. Vieira broke my nose. We had a corner kick and as I went up to head the ball there was serious contact between his elbow and my nose. It was full on and incredibly painful. My nose was squelching all over the place and my eyes were watering. It was the first time I'd had my nose broken. I was on the deck and I looked up at him. I couldn't see very well, but I'm fairly sure he was grinning at me.

Needless to say, I wasn't happy. I received treatment and

managed to carry on playing. But my focus wasn't totally on the game. I wanted to get Vieira. I waited for the opportunity. I thought my chance had arrived later on and I flew at him with a two-footed tackle, in and around his hips. Well, at least that's what I aimed for. But I missed him completely and ended up on my backside. When I got back on my feet, Petit immediately pushed me back to the floor again. The referee, Dermot Gallagher, red-carded me. It definitely wasn't my night. Thinking back on it now, it's comical but the red mist came down for me that night. I've never watched that incident again and I never will. It was a bad night all round. I wasn't long back in the side after an ankle injury and Hodgson certainly wasn't happy that I was now going to be suspended.

But that's the game. Players can sometimes lose their heads and I was no different at times. Things go through your mind and I wanted to get back at Vieira. Some players will let their elbows fly about and catch opponents in the eye or the cheek-bone. I've caught players with my elbow, but I've never tried deliberately to seriously injure an opponent. I've been an aggressive player and tried to protect myself when it was needed. I didn't want to put Vieira out of the game for a few weeks but I did want to let him know that I wasn't having him breaking my nose. I was angry, that's human nature, or my human nature.

Vieira and Petit were an outstanding partnership in the middle of the park for Arsenal. They were like a well-oiled machine. They could look after themselves physically and thrived on any form of battle on the pitch. In terms of all-round ability, I'd put Vieira ahead of Petit.

It can become very heated on the pitch and any striker will tell you about what it can be like when you're on the receiving end of a bad one. Sometimes I was not thinking straight. But when the centre-half is battering through the back of you time after time, then it can become frantic. You lose a high ball to the centre-half and then you lose another one. You become frustrated and you want to do something about it because you don't want the centre-half to dominate you. So, you become more aggressive.

When I first started playing, you could get away with a lot more and defenders would use their arms for a bit of leverage and to protect themselves. You can't do that now because of the new laws. If you dare step out of line, the likelihood is that television cameras will catch you out. You now can't tackle from behind or use your arms. The game was much more physical a few years ago. I think there have been some perfectly good tackles in games in the past couple of years but players have been given a straight red card because of the uncertainty over what is a suitable challenge or not.

I remember I used to try and count to three when the ball was played up to me and I had to hold it in, waiting for support. Then the defender would just smash through the back of me. Really whack me. I knew it was coming. It wasn't nice. I rarely ever made it to the count of three. Many a night I'd go home bruised and battered. When I first started out and during my career at Blackburn, there used to be some top defenders such as Gary Pallister and Steve Bruce. Arsenal also had a terrific back four, with their success under George Graham built from the defensive foundations of Tony Adams, Martin Keown, Lee Dixon and Nigel Winterburn. Those Arsenal lads were brutal to play against. Really brutal. But they were also very good players. The flip side was that when I played at centre-half, I would do the same to strikers.

But Roy always played me as a striker. I scored goals under him and was very happy. In his first season, we felt good about ourselves. That 3–1 win at Highbury just before Christmas gave us more confidence and we felt really great.

However, after Christmas, for no real reason, our form dipped.

It was a major disappointment. At the turn of the year, it looked like we would be challenging for the Premier League title. By the end of February, we were out of the race. A 5–3 win over Leicester, managed by Martin O'Neill, was one of the few high-lights of the second half of the season. I scored a hat-trick in that game. There was a doubt I was going to play in this game as I felt unwell, but after scoring early on with a deft flick from a Damien Duff cross, I brightened up. The third goal was a chip into the far corner, over Kasey Keller, who was standing on his line. And I actually meant it.

We were still in the shake-up for a UEFA Cup spot going into the last game of the season. We were to play Newcastle at home and we had to win. On a personal level, I had a chance of winning the Golden Boot for being the Premier League's top scorer. We were drawing 0–0 with two minutes to go and I scored with a direct free-kick from the edge of the box. I drove my shot past Shay Given and the goal meant we finished sixth to get the European slot. It was the only free-kick I ever scored in my career. I also ended up joint top-scorer in the league along with Michael Owen and Dion Dublin on eighteen goals.

I thought I'd scored with a direct free-kick five or six years later in a game away to Livingston. But it was disallowed. It was an indirect free-kick. I didn't notice the referee raising his hand to indicate that! No wonder the Livingston keeper never dived! I felt a real clown as I turned towards the Celtic fans to celebrate.

After a good break, there was a lot of optimism as we started the 1998–99 campaign. Roy brought in Kevin Davies for £7 million. He'd scored some brilliant goals for Southampton the previous season. I started the new campaign up front with Kevin but our partnership never really clicked. Kevin found it hard and was very quickly judged on his goals tally. His all-round game was decent, but he was very young at the time and didn't seem the most confident person. Things didn't work out for him at Ewood and he returned to Southampton the following summer. His career really took off soon after and he became an established Premier League player at Bolton.

We didn't start the season very well and as confidence started to diminish, results suffered. One of the biggest blows was losing in Europe. Blackburn played in the UEFA Cup under Hodgson in September 1998. We played French side Lyon and drew 2–2 in the Strade Gerland, which was a good result. The return leg was at our place and we fancied ourselves to go through but we blew it and lost 1–0. It was a desperately disappointing result and once again we failed to make any impact on the European stage.

To a man, I felt we all let Roy down. We became sheep, following one another. His training was more important than ever and we had to believe in him, but we made excuses. We crossed the white line and nothing had changed from the previous season in terms of Roy. Roy was totally professional and couldn't do any more, really. He gave his all. In my mind, us players were totally responsible in the end for Roy getting the sack.

I'm loath to criticise the Blackburn board because they were good, decent and honest people, and had the club's best interests at heart. But I felt the decision to sack Roy was wrong. I'm 100-per-cent certain that if Roy had stayed on as manager, we would have stayed up. History tells us that with Roy's record since.

Roy has proven time and time again what a great manager he is. He stabilised Fulham and took them to the UEFA Cup Final. I thought he was very unlucky to lose his job at Liverpool under strange circumstances but he once again showed his qualities when he kept West Brom in the Premiership in 2011 when they looked to be well on their way down. He took over those clubs when they were in far worse positions than Blackburn were at that time. We were a good team but Colin Hendry being sold to Rangers was a blow. Near the end, Roy paid the price and was removed from his job in November 1998.

Brian Kidd came in to replace him the following month and was given around £25 million to spend on new players in January, when he brought in Keith Gillespie, Ashley Ward and Jason McAteer. What I found strange was why Roy wasn't given funds like that. If Roy was given the same amount of money to spend, then I'm in no doubt we would have stayed up. He made some terrific signings – Stéphane Henchoz immediately springs to mind. But Roy had his hands tied, in many respects.

Brian became the fifth Blackburn manager I had played under in five years. He arrived with a big reputation and was previously assistant to Sir Alex Ferguson at Manchester United at Old Trafford, where he had enjoyed much success.

Where Roy was extremely analytical, Brian was completely different. The football training changed dramatically again. The functional stuff was gone and the fitness coach had left. The new manager had his own methods. Under the previous fitness regime, we had done a lot of structured gym work and we'd do 600-metre runs once a week. We had a sprint hall built at Brockhall Village. Under Brian, we'd do a lot of shorter runs, with shorter recovery time. The training was high-intensity without any real structure. It was more like stuff I had been used to earlier in my career. Everything was off the cuff. I suppose after Roy, everything else would seem rather simple.

Brian Kidd brought in Brian McClair as his assistant. I'd played against him many times and he was a top footballer. He was a very studious and quiet guy. The manager was the motivator, the enthusiast and was very vocal. It was hard to make sense of his Mancunian rants at times.

I was struggling with an adductor problem and didn't play in much of the second half of that season. The manager must have got a bit of a shock after being used to sitting at the top of the table with Manchester United. It was always going to be very difficult taking on a side as low on confidence as we were at that point. As hard as he tried, he couldn't get any momentum going and couldn't stop the slide in form. And bearing in mind that Brian spent £25 million, none of the signings made much of an impact, if any. The club went down. I was disappointed. I only managed to play seventeen league games that season and scored three goals.

It was all a bit of a mess. Blackburn was a proper football club and had real supporters who knew the game. They didn't deserve relegation. I had always felt Blackburn Rovers was a friendly and family-orientated club from the top down. The board, with Jack Walker at the helm, were always very kind and approachable. They put the football club's best interests at heart and they certainly didn't deserve this.

Blackburn is a small town but is a real football hotbed. And despite having many other clubs close by, such as Bury, Preston, Burnley, Accrington and being near Manchester, the support was great and the fans turned out in numbers all the time.

My five years at the club were certainly eventful and very memorable. It was a very happy period in my life on and off the pitch. I loved living in the North West. I'd only ever really known Norfolk and it was a change for me in so many ways, but it turned out well. I was told it rained all the time up north but that wasn't strictly true! When we first moved there, we bought a house in the Forest of Bowland, in a village called Chaigley. It was very picturesque. Sam and I became good friends with the farmer next door, Stan, and his wife Joan. We have stayed in touch over the years but, sadly, Stan died last year from cancer. We enjoyed their company and they were real Lancashire people, very down to earth.

Sam and I felt so much at home in that area that we got married there on 31 January 1995. We married in Hirst Green Church, a few miles away. We had a reception at Northcoate Manor, which is a small hotel and restaurant. It's a cracking place. Jack Walker used to stay there when he came over from Jersey for games. All the players came to the wedding and the reception, my brother Ian was my best man and his speech was great, very articulate and well delivered. He didn't leave too much on me!

But I was playing the next day in a re-arranged league game at home to Leeds United. It had been postponed from earlier in the season due to a waterlogged pitch. So, we didn't exactly enjoy an extended honeymoon. Tim Flowers was sent off in the game in the first half and I had to move back into midfield. That's about all I remember of the game.

Away from football, our home life felt good; we had three sons by that point – Frankie, Ollie and George. We also had two dogs, Fernandez and Antonio. I used to enjoy walking them on Longridge Fell on my own and didn't see anybody for miles. It was lovely when it snowed, absolutely picturesque.

But as soon as the 1999 season finished I had a decision to make. I wasn't against staying at Blackburn and trying to help us win promotion back to the Premiership at the first time of asking, back to where the club belonged. I was very comfortable living in the area. We'd moved house again, deeper into the Forest of Bowland to Chipping. Life was good off the pitch. I was paid well and not under too much pressure. But I was getting itchy feet. I had never played outside of the top league and maybe my ego was telling me that I didn't want to start now.

My name was circulated to test the water and I was unsure what would happen. The feedback, however, was positive and I was sure I could secure a good move, but just how good was dependent on a lot of things. I went to see Brian Kidd and he understood I wanted to move on. He assured me the club wouldn't stand in my way if they received an acceptable offer.

I suppose my stock was still high. I had been the top scorer in the Premiership the previous season and had been a consistent performer before that for a few years – although, admittedly, there was the occasional stinker. The two clubs who showed the most interest in me were Manchester United and Chelsea. It was very, very flattering to get clubs of that size showing any interest. But it soon became clear that Chelsea were really keen. As is the case with most transfers, there was a bit of sparring but then it all moved on very quickly. As soon as I spoke to Gianluca Vialli, I was really excited at the prospect of playing for him and I just wanted the deal to be concluded as quickly as possible. I was going to play under another great striker. I was buzzing at thought of playing in West London for a club on the up with some of the best footballers in the world.

Everything was good again. How could I go wrong?

Roy Hodgson on Chris Sutton

When I got the job at Blackburn in 1997, one of the things I looked forward to was working with Chris. He had an excellent reputation in the game and I knew he would be influential in the plans I had for the team. I teamed him up with Kevin Gallacher and they formed a fantastic partnership. They played a huge part in the success we had that season, qualifying for Europe. We finished sixth and, considering our budget, that was about as high as we could have hoped to finish.

Chris has said he felt fragile when I arrived but I can't say I noticed that. Sure, when you're a striker and you've maybe not scored goals then that does dent your confidence, and nearly being relegated has a negative impact. So, for him to say I lifted him and took his game on is rather nice of him. Maybe I didn't detect any fragility as I may have been somewhat fragile mentally myself when I arrived at Blackburn. I had previously been at Inter Milan and we had just lost the UEFA Cup Final to Schalke 0–4 on penalty-kicks. I was very keen to win that and wanted to leave Inter on a high. It maybe took me a while to recover from that.

I could sense from the first meeting that Chris was totally on board with what I was trying to do, in terms of the tactics and the training. You can look into the eyes of a player and know one way or another. He wanted to improve and didn't want a repeat of the previous season when the team came very close to being relegated. He was an intelligent person and had very good game knowledge. I'm indebted to Chris for buying into my plans that first season and his willingness to do so definitely had an effect on other players. We played some nice football and Chris scored many important and fabulous goals.

Doing so well in the first season, however, was always going to make my second season in charge extremely difficult. It was always going to be a struggle to better the first season. We lost Kevin to a broken arm when he was on international duty with Scotland and Chris had ankle problems. Their absence was a major reason why we struggled. We also lost Colin Hendry to Glasgow Rangers and Tim Sherwood was being courted by Spurs. He wanted to leave but a transfer fee couldn't be agreed. So, he stayed with us but mentally he wasn't there. All of those things contributed to us struggling in the league. You need players to be onside and if you don't have enough of them standing shoulder to shoulder with you, then it makes life as a manager extremely tough. Then, when results weren't going our way in the second season, players looked for excuses. That's just the way it is.

I liked Chris as a person and rated him highly as a player. When you are a manager, you have to fall in love with your players and they help you become the coach you want to be. Chris tried management at Lincoln and he would pop in to see me at Fulham a couple of years ago, more to see his good friend Billy McKinlay. I could feel a growing sense of frustration in a couple of our meetings. He could come to terms with the lack of ability at that level but found it hard to relate to players not having the desire to succeed and give their all. I don't know if he will try management again but he will have gained invaluable knowledge from his time at Lincoln. If he doesn't go back to it, then he will have other things to occupy him. He has a very supportive wife in Sam, a lovely lady, and has a large family to keep him occupied and focused. Chris is a very balanced human being and a very nice lad.

He often made me laugh when we were at Blackburn. I used to love the camaraderie he had with Billy McKinlay. They'd often wind each other up and it would result in a game of wrestling before training. Billy was at least six inches shorter than Chris but he'd give it his all as they rolled around the grass. I loved their antics. They were bubbly and I feel that rubbed off on the players.

Chris moved to Chelsea from Blackburn and it didn't work out for him. But I was pleased to see him recapture his form at a massive European club such as Celtic and help them achieve success in Scotland and in Europe. He deserved that good fortune and success, that is for sure.

I feel for him that he didn't play more times for his country. It was a difficult one for all of us when Chris decided he didn't want to be involved in the England B squad. It was difficult for me to give advice when Chris came to speak to me about it. The trick, I would say, is for national team coaches not to have B games. That, perhaps, would avoid conflict and situations arising such as the one Chris had with Glenn Hoddle. I suppose I hoped Chris would see his inclusion in the B squad as a route into the main squad. But he decided not to look upon it that way. I thought he could have been an asset for Glenn and if he had played in the B games, it may well have turned out that way. But we'll never know.

He says now he regrets the way he handled that whole episode. Well, hindsight would be a wonderful gift to be given. We live life for what we believe is right and most beneficial at the time, not what we might think we'll feel ten years down the line. But I suspect it will be a minor regret Chris has. He has enjoyed a wonderful career and nobody can take that away from him and no decision he made years ago should spoil his other achievements in any way.

7

PLAYING FOR ENGLAND –
THE B ALL AND END ALL

When I was at Norwich, I received international recognition. That gave me extra confidence. I was learning how to play the position of centre-forward, getting better and better, improving my all-round game awareness. In terms of goal-scoring, I had one exceptional season at Norwich, it was 1993–94 and I scored twenty-eight goals, twenty-five of which came in the League, still a club record for the top division.

That 1993–94 season proved to be the catalyst that really launched my career. Everything seemed to happen so fast for me that season and my form led to my name being mentioned for the international team. Terry Venables was manager of England and I never really expected to be involved. I was still rough around the edges. Andy Cole was also in the frame as he'd had a fantastic season at Newcastle. At that time, I never claimed to be worthy of a starting place as I still had plenty to learn.

Terry was a clever guy and had a great managerial career. He must have had a look at me and felt it was best to go with the tried and tested. I had no problem with that. I think it was fair. In terms of goals, I was up there but maybe not as an all-round striker yet. I was nowhere near as polished as strikers such as Ian Wright and Alan Shearer at that point. Terry named me in his squad for a get-together in April 1994. I was invited to Bisham Abbey for training. Ian Crook, my Norwich team-mate, was also asked.

I was quite nervous at going to spend a few days with the stars of our game. Other new faces included at that time were Jamie Redknapp, Andy Cole and Jason Wilcox. I felt I trained well and settled in fine after being very nervous.

The following month there was friendly at Wembley against Greece and some parts of the media and ex-players expressed surprise I wasn't included in the squad. Instead, I played in a B international and we defeated Northern Ireland 4–2. I was subbed in the second half. I was pretty average that night and didn't perform anywhere near to the level I could have done. It was frustrating, but I was still young and felt international recognition of any sort was to be welcomed. Terry never selected me to play for the full England side.

I did get capped by England but sadly only on one occasion. I feel I should have had more caps. But to say I shot myself in the foot is probably an understatement. There was much more attention on my game after I moved to Blackburn in July 1994 for £5 million. It was a British record fee for a player at that time and I was under pressure. But my stock had gone up because of that move. I was at big-spending Blackburn who fancied pushing Manchester United all the way for the Premiership that season.

The first England squad of the season was named the following month for a friendly at Wembley against the USA. Venables didn't include me. At that time, maybe it was a good thing. It allowed me to focus completely on Blackburn. I didn't have quite the same attitude in the November of that season, when there was another friendly game, this time against Nigeria. By this point, I had scored fourteen goals for Blackburn and felt ready for the step up to the international squad. Venables chose to snub me.

I was very disappointed. My form was very good, my partnership with Alan Shearer was prolific and developing all the time.

The theme of being overlooked for my country continued. In early 1995, games were played against Republic of Ireland and Uruguay. I was at home twiddling my thumbs, yet I was desperate to be involved. Even when Alan Shearer pulled out with injury, I still didn't get a sniff. The likes of Andy Cole and Les Ferdinand were ahead of me in the pecking order. They were good players but at that time I felt very confident, as good as anybody.

Venables was then replaced by Glenn Hoddle and I was glad of the change of manager. Clearly, Venables didn't fancy me. I thought the introduction of Hoddle would signal the start of something good for me at international level but, instead, it only signalled the end of my very brief career playing for my country.

The 1995–96 season I had at Blackburn under Ray Harford set me back in terms of my international career. That was the season leading up to Euro 96. But I didn't play enough games for my club and played very few games at centre-forward. I was never a front runner for a place in the Euro 96 squad so it wasn't a great surprise when I wasn't selected.

I got back on track the following year. I started the 1997–98 season very well. Roy Hodgson was by then the Blackburn manager. I scored a hat-trick in a game against Aston Villa, amongst other goals. I started the season very strongly. It was going to be an important campaign as England would be off to the World Cup finals at the end of it and I wanted to be on the plane to France.

I scored nine goals in the first few weeks but wasn't given a look-in for a game against Moldova. A crucial match away to Italy in Rome was next on the fixture list and I was left out. Stan Collymore was included instead of me and, in terms of goals, Stan hadn't had as good a start as me. He was at Aston Villa and initially struggled to score. My non-inclusion created a bit of debate in the media. Some felt I should have been in. Quite a lot felt Hoddle was perfectly correct not to choose me for the A squad since there were so many other quality strikers around. Blackburn manager Roy Hodgson spoke publicly in my favour as did my strike-partner at Rovers, Martin Dahlin.

Whether he felt a bit of pressure to include me or whether it was totally on merit, Hoddle chose me for a friendly at Wembley against Cameroon. It was November 1997 and by this stage I had scored eleven goals for Blackburn that season. I came on as a sub. I got the last eleven minutes of the game when I came on for Paul Scholes. Scholes and Robbie Fowler scored in a 2–0 win but I didn't get enough time to make an impression. That said, I was proud to make my debut for my country, it was one of the highlights of my career.

Sure, I wanted – and felt I should have had – longer on the pitch. But after being snubbed for game after game, it was just a relief to finally get on the pitch in front of the England fans.

Hoddle then announced a plan to play three B international games – Chile in February, Switzerland in March and the month after that, Portugal were the opponents. He felt it would be beneficial to assess as many 'fringe' players as possible in the build-up to the World Cup. Hoddle clearly saw me as one of those players and chose me in his B squad to play against Chile.

By that stage, I felt my form was a good as it had been at any time during my career. When you look at my statistics then, you can see what I mean, it's there in black and white. I had scored fifteen goals in the league and was the joint top-scorer in the Premiership at that time.

There was just no way my form had dropped in the build-up to the Chile game. If anything, my game was stronger, improving all the time under Roy Hodgson. I'd go so far as to say my all-round game was as good as it was at any time during the Premiership-winning season. A couple of players were injured and a couple of players came from nowhere to jump in ahead of me, among them Michael Owen and Dion Dublin, and that miffed me. But Glenn felt it was right for me to play in the B game against Chile and I wasn't having that. His reasoning was that it was best for someone like me to get a full ninety minutes in a B game than ten or fifteen minutes off the bench in a full international.

I was hacked off about the situation, really upset. I spoke to Roy Hodgson and told him my feelings about Glenn Hoddle and the England situation. Roy was a good listener and a real players' man. It was good to have someone like that to talk to, to open up to. Roy is a proper football man and I respected his opinions on football and life.

He understood my predicament. He could see how upset I was and he didn't like to see that. I told him I wanted to phone Hoddle to tell him I didn't want to participate in the game against Chile, which was to take place at The Hawthorns, home of West Bromwich Albion. Roy played devil's advocate and said I should be careful about this, as I'd be making a rod for my own back. But it was my decision and I had to make the call.

Roy also asked me to speak to Paul Ince before making the call. Paul was a senior England player and Roy had managed him at Inter Milan. I spoke to Paul. Paul made it clear to me what I should do, really. He advised me not to walk out on England. He explained the consequences of such action. I should have listened to Paul. But the situation was eating away at me and I couldn't let it drop.

I would have preferred to see Hoddle face to face but had to settle for a telephone conversation. I got through to Hoddle at the FA offices in London and told him my feelings. The conversation started off by me explaining my thoughts on the England situation and my disappointment at being left out of the A squad, when in my mind my form was getting better and other strikers had dropped out through injury.

I wasn't aggressive in my tone; I kept my composure and remained factual. I just went through things. I made it clear I was not going to turn up for the B game. I told him I felt my form was good and it didn't feel right for me to be dropped from the main squad.

Hoddle's response was: 'You don't want to wear the England shirt, that's your choice.' He repeated that over and over and over. He never offered me any form of explanation.

I thought the manager of England could have been more articulate and more open with his answers. I didn't expect him to change his mind. But he kept repeating the same thing. I found it quite pathetic, to be truthful. I felt I deserved an explanation.

But he was the manager of England and it was his right to do and say as he pleased. Looking back, he didn't have to explain anything to me. He was England manager. I was just a peripheral player in his mind. It was just disappointing the way it all panned out, really. It hurt that he didn't rate me highly enough to warrant a place in his full squad. My ego took a knock.

In my time, I've made some pretty quick and hot-headed decisions and that was definitely the biggest one, in terms of football.

When Hoddle was a player I marvelled at him. He was so skilful and an exquisite passer of the ball. Always accurate, whether it was a simple five-yard pass or a forty-yard diagonal. He was a brilliant player to watch. Yet, his inability to communicate in the way I expected totally staggered me. I was bitterly disappointed with him.

I knew what the consequences for me would be for making the telephone call to him. I was prepared to go for it and I didn't want it to continue to eat away at me. I defy anyone who was in my shoes at that time to say they wouldn't have felt the same way as I did. But other people may have handled it differently and possibly most would have handled it in a much better way.

Hoddle was quick to let the media know the situation and I

took plenty of flak for it all. My God, I took flak. From the tabloid columnists who inferred I had a flaw in my character, to Alan Shearer who had his say at a press conference. I didn't feel surprised that Alan chose to criticise me in the way that he did. I have admitted in this book I did the wrong thing in turning down the chance to play for my country. It just reaffirmed to me that when I had had my doubts about Alan's frostiness towards me at times at Blackburn, I had read the vibes correctly. As a former team-mate I would have expected him to toe the party line and adhere to an unwritten rule amongst so-called team-mates and say something along the lines of 'it wasn't a decision I would have made by any means but Chris is his own man and Chris makes his own decisions', rather than what he did say which was, 'it's Chris's loss, not England's'. Alan was probably correct. But he never phoned me or tried to cajole me into changing my mind. But then again, why would he?

Gary Lineker also criticised me but urged me to reconsider. I certainly asked for criticism, it just came in different forms at times.

Again, thinking about it now, I should have got my head down and accepted the situation with the B squad. I should have played and not attracted attention to myself.

Hoddle had plenty of options – from Robbie Fowler to Teddy Sheringham to Shearer to teenage sensation Michael Owen. Owen was starting to establish himself as an international player. But I'd had a good season. I won the Golden Boot for the English Premiership – I scored the same amount of goals as Owen and Dublin. My form was as good as it had ever been. I'd have loved to have gone to the World Cup in France in 1998.

I knew making the phone call to Hoddle would end my England career under him. I felt at the time it was the right thing to do. I had to be true to myself. Looking back, I should have kept my counsel. But biting my tongue is not something I've always found an easy thing to do, particularly when I feel strongly about something. With the benefit of hindsight, I realise it wasn't the smartest thing to do. That telephone call, which lasted less than five minutes, had a major negative effect on my international career. It was a massive error of judgement and I'd handle it more wisely if it happened today. But that's life.

I reckon I would have got a few more caps as the years progressed. International games went through a stage of friendly games against lowly opposition. The managers would make six or seven substitutions at half-time and the friendly games didn't feel as though they had a lot of meaning to them. It was different, of course, when it came to major tournaments and qualifiers. I realised there was a pecking order and I was well down the list. There was Shearer, Owen, Sheringham, Cole, Fowler, Wright and Ferdinand.

That said, the one cap I do have can't be taken away from me. I was really pleased to play for England. I was only on the field for a short time and I only touched the ball on a few occasions, but it was still a great experience.

Hoddle was replaced by Kevin Keegan after the World Cup finals. The slate was wiped clean. Keegan promised me he'd judge me on my performances, not what I had said under previous regimes, and I was in a few squads when he was England manager. I was at Chelsea at that time and my form wasn't great, so I wasn't expecting much. I would turn up for squads and the established and experienced players would be there. I'd just keep myself to myself, keep my head down and train hard. Didn't make any difference, though. Keegan never played me. In fairness to him, the way my form was at Chelsea at that time, I'd have been lucky to get a game for Andorra.

Sven Göran Eriksson came in to take over from Keegan. He came to Scotland to watch a couple of Champions League games. I know people in England don't rate the SPL very highly and I agree that it isn't as strong as the English Premiership. But when you play for the Old Firm, every team is desperate to beat you and there is intense pressure to win every game. Lose a game and you'd think the club was in a state of collapse, such is the reaction from fans and media.

Sven came to our games and there is no better place to judge a player than in the Champions League because there is no doubt it is a cut above the English Premier League. Some might say the standard is on a par with international football. But I've no idea if he watched me closely with a view to selecting me in his squad. Yet, I thought I played relatively well. From what I remember in the home games I played for Celtic, we were very good. I was playing with confidence and my partnership with Henrik Larsson was flourishing. We caused a lot of problems to some of the top European defenders.

We had a good record and picked up some fantastic results. I felt I made a decent contribution in those games. And then, at the end of the day, you are who you are, where you are in the pecking order, really.

Was I a better option for England than Shearer? No, of course I wasn't. Shearer scored thirty goals in sixty-three appearances for England, a strike rate any player would be proud of. But I did have my strengths. Some players just had better attributes than me. The standard of English strikers was frightening at that time. I mean, when you think that a phenomenal striker such as Ian Wright only got thirteen starts, it tells you all you need to know. Les Ferdinand only got seventeen caps and he was an incredible striker. Other gifted strikers also found it hard during that era. Andy Cole only got fifteen caps and Matt le Tissier made just eight appearances.

I would have liked my club partnership with Shearer to be have been given a chance at international level. In our first season at Blackburn, it worked particularly well and we won the title.

I enjoyed playing with him. He was an unbelievable striker. But that's the way it goes. And, like I said, my problem was with the protocol and selection process.

At least I had some great times for my country at under-21 level and made thirteen appearances, scoring one goal. We played in the prestigious tournament in Toulon in the summer of 1993 and we beat France 1–0 in the final. Lawrie McMenemy was in charge of us at that time. Graham Taylor was the England gaffer. I made my debut for the under-21 side nine months earlier when we defeated Spain 1–0 in Burgos. Darren Anderton scored the winning goal.

My earliest memory from when I was a kid is of watching the 1982 World Cup in Spain. I recall Bryan Robson scoring a goal after twenty-seven seconds against France. I used to like watching Robson. Trevor Brooking was also a hero of mine from that era.

Moments have stayed with me from other World Cups and Gary Lineker was a stick-out from 1986 in Mexico. He was a great striker and had a fantastic career. In the 1990 World Cup finals in Italy, it was all about Gascoigne. Gazza was a big player in England. He was up and coming and very exciting. He was incredible to watch. I think just before he joined Lazio he was the best in the business. He was superb at the 1990 finals. He was the most amazing player I've seen on a football pitch, a total cut above any other player I've been on the field with. He was doing back-garden flicks and displaying his silky skills on a matchday, brilliant to watch. He made it look easy. He played as though he wasn't feeling an ounce of pressure. Of course, one criticism that was always levelled at him was his temperament. But, in most environments, he was like a twenty-one-year-old playing against a twelve-year-old, he just looked so far in front of every other player.

Gazza had talent that most guys could only dream about. He stood out in that World Cup. Everyone had sympathy for him when he burst into tears as he realised that he wouldn't have been able to play in the final after a second yellow card in the semi-final against Germany ruled him out. Of course, England were knocked out on penalties, so they didn't make the final anyway.

That was a massive World Cup. The whole of England was desperate for the country to do well. I was a youth team player at Norwich at that time. For me, it was more memorable than Euro 96.

Bobby Robson was manager of that team and he was a great manager, and a respected and talented football man. He got the best out of players and had a record that would have stood against any other manager after his achievements with Barcelona, Ipswich and Sporting Lisbon, to name but a few clubs. He deserved to take England all the way to the final of the 1990 World Cup. Who knows what could have happened after that.

On reflection, I regret the way I handled the situation with Hoddle. On a personal level, I would have loved to play in a World Cup with England but blew my chances of getting to France 98. In the end, playing for my country will always be a highlight of my career.

8

A STAMFORD BRIDGE TOO FAR

Gianluca Vialli had a presence about him. He was a world-class striker in his day when he played in Serie A, in England and at international level for Italy. He made it clear he wanted to sign me for Chelsea in the summer of 1999. Pierluigi Casiraghi had picked up a serious injury and Vialli needed to bring in a proven striker to fill that void. He had many great foreign players at the club, quality ones such as Gianfranco Zola, Frank Leboeuf, Gus Poyet and Marcel Desailly. Vialli wanted the presence of another Englishman in his side. Dennis Wise was at the club and youngsters such as John Terry and Jody Morris. I agreed to go there and it was very exciting. I was looking forward to it. The fee was £10 million, a staggering amount of money. But I couldn't wait to get started. My wages had increased a little bit but not substantially.

When I went to Chelsea, I was at a good age and I felt ready for another big move. There was a lot of different nationalities and in many ways that made it quite exciting. Some of the players were extremely high profile such as Desailly and Zola. Leboeuf too. I'd had a few run-ins with Frank when I was at Blackburn. The main one came when I played against him at Stamford Bridge in April 1998 and we won 1–0 thanks to a Kevin Gallacher goal. I think Frank criticised our team's style of play in the lead up to the game and said we were overly physical. After the game I had a go at him in the press conference. But I should have kept my counsel. He was a really good footballer and read the game well. But I always felt I could rough him up a bit, that he didn't really enjoy the physical side of the game. I tried to use that to my advantage when we played against each other. We got on fine after that falling-out, although we were never great mates. We were both professionals and in football there are many cases in which you play alongside people but you don't necessarily have to get on. We all know how that works. I didn't dislike Frank, he was a decent enough guy.

Gianluca was assisted by Ray Wilkins and Graham Rix. We also had an Italian fitness coach, Antonio Pintus, who was very good. But when I arrived at Chelsea for pre-season, I hadn't played a lot of football since the previous Christmas as I'd had problems with my adductors. I arrived there not as fit as I could have been. I had a decent enough pre-season in terms of the work I was doing, but I didn't play in all of the games because I'd had a niggle or two. I wasn't as physically fit as I would have liked.

Training had changed so much from when I was a young pro at Norwich to what I experienced under Roy at Blackburn with the double sessions. The game had moved on. Pre-season used to be about long runs and trackwork. The balls would come out after a few days. At Chelsea, it was about taking your body fat, stuff like that. There wasn't so much long distance stuff but there was a little bit of trackwork. At Chelsea, the most we'd run was 1000 metres in one go. There was also a lot of gym work and prevention work before the training session on the pitch got underway. We used to do that as a group; it was part of your day. Previously, I'd only done that off my own back when I wanted to.

I always enjoyed training. I was never the quickest player and I was never a great sprinter, but I was a decent endurance runner. In a lot of ways, I enjoyed pre-season and always realised the importance of it. That was down to the importance my dad placed on fitness when I was younger, taking me to the sand dunes. Being fit made me feel strong mentally. The pre-season games were just about getting minutes under your belt. The results were secondary, really. When I initially arrived at Chelsea I wanted to impress.

Physicality was a big part of my game and I used that during matches. In training at Chelsea, I eased off on the physical side; players do that with age. In my younger days at Norwich, I was full-on; I'd fly into tackles. I was doing it to impress. But I was always in control of what I was doing, unless I got hacked off with a player coming through the back of me. Some players couldn't switch off and used to train the way they played. John Terry was like that at Chelsea. When I was there, John was coming through the ranks and had everything to prove. He was a good player. He used to be ultra-aggressive and that has obviously helped him become the player he is today.

Johan Mjällby was the same at Celtic. It was always the defenders that were more aggressive in training. But then that is their game, to head and kick the ball – and the opponent!

On the field, nothing significant happened during pre-season. I was never bothered with performances in pre-season. I just wanted to settle in and get myself fit. I used to think if I scored goals in meaningless pre-season games then I might be using up my goals for when the competitive games got underway.

However, something strange happened during pre-season, right out of the blue. My agent received a phone call from Leeds United to ask if I'd be interested in joining them. They'd heard I was already unsettled at Chelsea and Peter Ridsdale, the Leeds United chairman, would give Chelsea their £10 million back to get me. The request was put to me and I told them I was fine at Chelsea and didn't want to leave. Leeds were wasting their time. I was totally committed to Chelsea.

My competitive debut was in a home game against Sunderland. I had two one-on-one opportunities and missed both. We won 4–0 but I was deflated at time-up. I should have scored. I felt embarrassed about the chances I missed that day. I wanted to impress, hit the ground running. I felt fragile as I left the pitch that day.

Looking back, it may have been *the* defining moment of my spell at Chelsea. Had I scored that day, I would have been in a confident frame of mind and the fans would have been onside.

But I did score in our next game against Skonto Riga in a Champions League qualifier. I was pleased to get off the mark. The focus was on me to score goals and, ultimately, I didn't do it often enough at Chelsea. You can talk about systems and formations and the way players were deployed. There was also a rotation system Vialli used and I didn't like that. He would start games with two strikers and then usually sub both of them after sixty-five minutes or so for another two strikers. I didn't find that ideal, but it was the way it worked most weeks and it was the same for everyone.

I was involved in a lot of games and my all-round form was ok. I scored in a 5–0 win against Manchester United and that gave my confidence a big boost. I hoped it would lead to me going on a run of goals but I had no such luck. I don't think I had anybody but myself to blame for what happened to me at Chelsea.

Vialli tried me with different partners. Not even being along-side a world-class player like Zola could make a difference to me. Vialli paired us a few times but it just never worked, really, as we both liked to come to the ball, dropping off from the main striking role. I played alongside Tore André Flo but that never got going either.

George Weah came to Chelsea just after Christmas on loan from AC Milan and I felt we had the foundations of a good part-nership. My game improved and I enjoyed the link-up play for the first time at Chelsea. George was very charismatic and really got me going. George was a nice fellow and we clicked on and off the park. He was really down to earth, good company and liked to enjoy himself. But I wasn't having any fun as a Chelsea footballer.

Looking back, I had lost my confidence and just didn't enjoy going into work. I found it a grind to get out of my bed. It had a negative impact on my family life and I was unbearable to be around. It was the first time in my career I felt major pressure and that I was wilting. I didn't handle it very well. I was snappy and would take my frustrations out when I was with the family.

I desperately wanted to do well and I kept thinking it would all fall into place. It didn't happen. The size of the transfer fee was a burden and it all became horrible for me on a day-to-day basis. There was a lot of negativity towards me and people probably had good reason to be critical, based on my goals record. Strength of character was what I needed at that time. I needed real belief in my own game. It was a flaw in my character.

Some people probably think that because you drive a nice car, live in a nice house, sit on a nice settee and earn a good wage, you don't give a damn about not scoring goals. Trust me, I'd have walked to work every day and slept on the floor every night if it guaranteed me a few goals and the chance to get my Chelsea career up and running. My job was to score goals for Chelsea and I wasn't doing my job properly. It haunted me, to be perfectly honest. I felt very depressed. I was at an all-time low. I probably felt people were against me and didn't want me to do well, but that shouldn't have mattered to me. All the negativity made me paranoid. My mind wasn't in the right place. I was a failure.

I couldn't relax at Chelsea. After a few weeks, I felt tense and tight. My aggression was still there but I didn't feel right. I was hesitating and my hesitation in training and on the pitch killed me. By January or February, rather than taking the bull by the horns and working hard to get into goal-scoring positions by being brave and wanting to be inside the box, I was hiding.

I wasn't prepared to be on the end of chances and miss them. I preferred not be in a position to receive the ball and give me a chance to score. Subconsciously, I thought if I miss a difficult chance, then that's fine. But miss an easy chance and I left myself open to all sorts of criticism. So, there was a clear way to avoid any negativity and that was not to be there to miss chances.

Really, I was on my knees. At the time I didn't realise my faults at Chelsea, but looking back now it's easier to see why things didn't work out. For the first time in my career, when I stepped onto the field, I doubted myself and I was hesitant.

I played a couple of games at centre-half and it was actually a relief to play in that position, an area of the pitch where I didn't have that pressure on my shoulders of trying to score a goal. I played at the back against Everton at Goodison Park and played fairly well. I quite enjoyed it.

But it wasn't overly helpful to me that I felt I didn't have the full backing of some of my team-mates. A couple of players had a go at me in negative interviews, Dan Petrescu being one of them. Then I heard Didier Deschamps talking about me to other French players in his native tongue at half-time during one game. Now, I didn't speak fluent French, but I understood enough to know he was criticising me. I would have preferred it if he had made his comments to my face in English. He could speak English without any problem so there was no excuse for him. It wasn't nice from Deschamps; it was really unhelpful of him. I thought he behaved very badly.

Didier was a nice enough guy and he had a great career as a footballer. I'm not trying to be righteous, and I'm not saying I never criticised people privately when I was in company, but I do understand from my own bad experiences as a player that it's better to offer encouragement. Now, some players do need a kick up the backside but you have to be mindful of what you say to them and how you say it. That's very important. So, for Deschamps to criticise me in that way, wasn't nice and was pretty gutless. I had words with Deschamps about it and told him he should say things to my face or keep his mouth shut. He didn't say anything. But I try not to hold grudges. In football, you can't do that. I spent time with him in the hotel when we signed for Chelsea and he was a nice guy. I was also his partner at cards when we used to play against Wise and Zola.

Deschamps and other detractors should have realised that nobody wanted to be a success at Chelsea more than me, but the transfer fee and the wages were brought up and used against me. I should have been better at accepting criticism but nobody likes to be on the receiving end of it, rightly or wrongly.

After a few months, the Chelsea fans had no patience left and Sam and the boys started to get it as well. Sam was in Harrods with my eldest two boys, Frankie and Ollie, and they had Chelsea shirts on with my name on the back. A woman stopped them and said, 'What have you got Sutton on for? He's useless.' Sam turned to the woman and told her that was the boys' dad she was talking about. To be fair, that was the feeling of many Chelsea fans at the time. That's the way life goes. You enjoy the adulation and the plaudits, but you have to take the reproach when it comes along.

I tried hard but some things got to me. I didn't have confidence and didn't play with a smile on my face. Yet, when I think back, I still wonder what the problem was. Why couldn't I play with so many good players? Why wasn't I a success there? It still annoys me, still rankles me in many ways. I badly wanted to make it work there. I just wasn't good enough at that time. I had to make one or two modifications to my game, but I simply didn't adjust as well as I should have done. I was never a player who played on the shoulder of the last defender. I was someone who could take the ball in, hold off defenders, link the play and lay it off. I'd get in the box to get on the end of crosses and would generally get my fair share of goals. But at Chelsea, it just wasn't happening and I had no one to blame but myself.

I learned from Gianluca in terms of technique and runs to make. He was of a different class and was a terrific coach. He was very well organised. In many ways, he reminded me of Roy Hodgson, albeit he was several years younger. He made the transition from player to manager and made it quite comfortably. The players respected him, which wasn't an easy thing to achieve as he played alongside several of them in the Chelsea team. He spoke very well and you knew what he wanted. He was an intelligent and nice guy.

Tactically, he knew what the game was about. His English was good. One of my biggest regrets in football was that I let him down. He tried his best for me and couldn't have done any more to make me a success at Chelsea. A few things went against me at Stamford Bridge but it wasn't down to Vialli.

He improved my game but it was just unfortunate Chelsea didn't reap the benefits of that. In terms of running off the ball, he really helped me. Even watching him in training every day was a big help. He'd run the channels and take defenders away. It was his timing that was the key. I'd always worked with another striker and it was different from being a lone striker. Running into channels might sound simple but there's much more to it, and sometimes you have to be shown and given an explanation. You are relying on timing but you have to know when to make the run and not go too early. You have to size up where the defenders are standing and choose your moment. It's about making the second run, and then a third run if the second one didn't come off. It was all about awareness and timing. He was outstanding and, more importantly, very good at explaining things.

He also took me for a one-on-one session to improve my volleying technique. I used to try and connect with the ball and hit it as hard as I could. My technique wasn't right. Vialli took time to show me where I was going wrong. He told me to slow down and get my hip up. It wasn't about how quickly I swung my leg; it was about the technique and the actual connection. When you get it right, you hit the ball hard naturally and it gives you a true connection. I practised and practised it. Repetition is important. But repetition can also be a disaster if you're doing it the wrong way and teaching your brain to do it wrongly. I felt I could volley with my left and right foot, albeit I was stronger on my right foot. After my work with Vialli, I still messed up with volleys but I also connected beautifully with a few.

It certainly helped when it came to the volley I scored for Celtic against Juventus in the Champions League at Parkhead in 2001. Juve, ironically, was one of Vialli's former clubs. The goal didn't get us through to the next stage of the tournament, but it helped us win the game and it was one of the most memorable nights of my career. Sure, I might have still scored had I not had that session with Vialli, but in my mind, I trusted myself more as the ball was coming down for me. Something triggers in your brain that makes you believe you're going to connect sweetly. And I did that particular evening. It was just a pity I couldn't score any volleys for Chelsea!

Vialli always encouraged me and I don't have a bad word to say about him. I knew he really wanted me to do well. I could see it in his eyes and felt it when he spoke to me. I felt bad at letting him down. I've always been the type of player that wanted to do well for the manager, especially when they've agreed to sanction a huge transfer fee and shown such faith in signing me.

Vialli left me out of the FA Cup Final team to play Aston Villa at Wembley in the last competitive game of the season. I went to Ray Wilkins and he marked my card the night before the game that I wouldn't be involved, not even on the bench. I hadn't trained as well as I should have for a few weeks prior to that, wasn't applying myself. This probably made Vialli's mind up. I was looking forward to the season coming to an end and leaving the club, although nothing was certain at that stage. But I was always involved when I was fit. I really lost my cool at being left out for the final. I guess the previous nine months just came to a head and I exploded.

I spoke to Vialli after breakfast on the Saturday morning. We stood in a corridor. I told him he was a coward for not telling me to my face that I wouldn't be involved in the final. Then I repeated that insult to him. He tried to explain to me why I was left out. I called him a coward for the third time and he wouldn't accept it anymore. He told me if I said it one more time, he would knock me out. I didn't say it for a fourth time. I shouldn't have said that to him at all, as, over the piece, he was more than fair to me. I regret calling him a coward. It's not something I'm proud of. I was totally unprofessional. I regret it and it was the last conversation we had. I acted like a spoilt brat. It was my fault. My strength of character let me down, nothing else. I paid the ultimate price that day for taking my foot off the pedal in training in the build-up to the final. It was the correct decision to leave me off the bench. To compound it, I behaved selfishly towards Vialli and he certainly didn't deserve it on the day of such a big game. I'm still totally ashamed of my actions that day and Vialli deserved much better.

Chelsea won the game 1–0. Roberto di Matteo scored the winner in the seventy-third minute after a mistake by David James.

It was the last final to be played at the old Wembley. The new stadium was to be built after that and the FA moved the final to Cardiff's Millennium Stadium until the new Wembley was ready. It wasn't a classic final by any stretch of the imagination. That said, I was pleased Chelsea won the game. I stayed and watched and went to the celebrations afterwards. But I wasn't really in the mood for getting involved. The carrying of the Cup, lap of honour, photographs and interviews were not for me. I watched from afar. It was the way I felt. I wasn't that bothered. That was the attitude I had at full-time that afternoon, although I would have preferred a winner's medal with the rest of the lads.

My attitude hadn't been right for many, many weeks. I was drinking far too much. It was a release for me to drink lager. It helped to blank things out and numb the pain. I also got drunk on the flight home from a European game in Turkey. Some of my team-mates and Vialli were appalled. Desailly wrote about it in his book and was critical about me for it. He was quite right. I really let myself down and it was a serious error of judgement. I was an absolute disgrace.

It was a mutual decision that I should move on from Chelsea in the summer. It was a relief, really. I could have sat it out at Chelsea. I signed a six-year contract with them in the summer of 1999 and could have sat there and picked up my money. But I wanted to play football. Money wasn't my motivation at that stage of my career. The time was right to go; I just couldn't stay. It wasn't right for Chelsea and it wasn't right for me.

I was aware negative things were being said about me. Ken Bates was chairman of the club and Chelsea invested a lot of money in me; he had every right to have his say. After I left, he said I was a £10-million disaster and that my attitude towards the end of my time at the club wasn't right. He said I became anxious after my first league game when, in his opinion, I missed two open goals against Sunderland. I did miss two good chances against Sunderland that afternoon but they weren't exactly open goals. How he defined his criticism was up to him. In terms of my attitude, I don't think I covered myself in glory, particularly in the way I conducted myself in training towards the end.

Perhaps that was a defence mechanism from me on the training ground, acting like I wasn't bothered. It was an error of judgement on my part at that time. Was I anxious? Yes, I was. Towards the end, I was still trying but I was so short of confidence.

Ken said it like it was, really. Over the years, people have viewed Ken as a controversial character, but I think what he has said about many different things in the game, including his comments about me, were pretty much spot on.

The former Tory MP David Mellor also felt he had to have his say. He was a friend of Ken's and I'd see them lunching a few times together at Chelsea. Mellor never said anything derogatory to my face but did have his say in the media. It was the same with Ken, come to think of it. They were always amicable to my face. Mellor was a politician who was given a platform to talk about football. In my opinion, his knowledge of the game of football is extremely limited. He was a Chelsea supporter, a punter. What he said was neither here nor there, in my mind. His comments really didn't interest me. There are people who know the game inside out and I value their opinions and will listen to them, although I might not always agree with them.

As much as I wasn't too bothered about Bates and Mellor, I couldn't say the same about Graeme Le Saux. He was my team-mate at Blackburn and was also then transferred to Chelsea. In the build-up to the FA Cup Final against Aston Villa, he gave an interview and made derogatory remarks about me. I thought he was out of order with his comments. Yes, I was touchy at the time and I had been battered all season. I didn't need another kicking from one of my team-mates. It was extremely unhelpful. He was supposed to be an intelligent guy yet when I confronted him about it, he didn't seem to grasp where I was coming from, that I had any right to feel aggrieved. I always thought there was an element of selfishness in Graham as a player and in that moment, I lost respect for him as a person. In my view, he is very self-centred and had a high opinion of himself. He was a good player and had a good career.

As I mentioned earlier, Dan Petrescu also felt he was entitled to criticise me in an interview. I thought he was a bit snide when things weren't going well for me. He gave an interview to a Romanian newspaper and it got back to England that he was critical of me in the article. I confronted him at training one day and he denied it, said he was misquoted. Maybe he was but I had my doubts. Sure, things can be taken out of context, but his explanation didn't wash. Maybe I just didn't want to believe him. He was a good footballer but he didn't like the physical battles. Like Le Saux, he had a high opinion of himself. I wouldn't trust him as far as I could throw him. I was fragile at that time and he should have thought it through more.

We did have some good men in that dressing room. Dennis Wise was the captain. He was a great leader and wanted everyone to do well. I felt he made a positive impact at the club, although I know he wasn't everybody's cup of tea outside of Chelsea. But in my opinion, he was fantastic in the dressing room and a good captain. He tried to knit the dressing room together, bring the different cultures and egos together which couldn't have been an easy job.

Thankfully, despite my poor year at Chelsea, I had excellent options to consider. The fee Chelsea wanted was £6 million – a £4-million hit on me after twelve months. In recent economic times, it's not too bad a loss! I suppose I had some doubt if clubs would spend that amount, but luckily they were judging me on my previous six or seven years at Blackburn and Norwich, rather than my time at Stamford Bridge. Some managers like bringing 'damaged goods' to their club. They feel they have it in them to reinvent a player, get the very best out of him.

I wanted to leave Stamford Bridge and although it would have been nice to stay and turn things around, at the time, to be truthful, I didn't feel I'd be able to do it and I also didn't even want to try. I felt fragile and had struggled to cope. At that time, I was finding out who my friends were and wanted people beside me to be supportive. Subsequently, I realised, I didn't really have many real friends! Some people carry themselves better and hide things well, guys such as Larsson, Shearer and Weah. Is that why they are the players they are? Whether they believe it or not, I think that helps them.

With my state of mind on and off the pitch, some people may have thought it would have been good to turn to a sports psychologist. My personal opinion is that they are a waste of time and definitely not for me. I think you have to work things out for yourself and it's also the job of the manager to get the best out of his players. But if players do want to use sports psychologists, that is entirely up to them and I'd never criticise a player for doing so.

I knew what I could and couldn't do. I wasn't born with physical attributes in terms of running. I wasn't born with sheer pace and athleticism. You're very lucky if you're born with those attributes, but you then still have to marry all of that together and be able to play. I had to look at other ways of being an asset as a footballer and making a living as a professional. So, I made the most of what I had and worked hard to improve my game. I tried to adapt in different ways.

My time at Chelsea was the lowest I felt during my career. It was just a bad experience. I cringe at the way I behaved on some occasions but that was the frame of mind I was in. Gianluca invested the money in me and in that respect I let him down. I felt guilty, not towards Chelsea as a club, but towards the man who signed me. My attitude should have been better. It was right for me to move on. Chelsea didn't merit a cloud hanging over the dressing room in terms of my presence and I just couldn't risk another season of feeling lousy and dejected.

Players can fall out of the game fast and I didn't want to

become a has-been. I was still very driven to succeed but felt a new start and fresh focus would be best for both parties.

A number of clubs made it clear they wanted to sign me and it came down to Spurs, Middlesbrough and Celtic. I knew plenty about Celtic and they were back in the headlines down south after the appointment of Martin O'Neill. I knew Henrik Larsson played for the club and that he was a talented player. I thought my style would suit his play. Even before we'd met face to face, I had a really good feeling about a partnership with Henrik.

Celtic were selling Mark Viduka to Leeds United for around £6 million and that money was used to buy me. I've been led to believe that when Martin O'Neill told Dermot Desmond he wanted to buy me, Dermot expressed reservations. Dermot probably had every right to question paying so much money for me but Martin obviously made a convincing case. He can be very persuasive. Martin's teams had played against me several times and I'd always managed to do well against his players. I scored goals and was a handful for his defenders. In fact, I probably had some of my best games against his teams. He knew what I could do.

Really, taking Chelsea out of the equation, I'd enjoyed a more than decent career at Norwich and Blackburn. I knew I could play football and it was about finding the right environment to do it in. I still had no doubt that I could play. I knew I had it in me to bounce back and Celtic were going to give me the plat-form to do it.

I met Martin in a hotel near Beaconsfield and he shook my hand. He has a very dry sense of humour and the first thing he said to me was: 'What happened to you at Chelsea?' At first I was taken aback by that comment. Then I looked up and saw a mischievous grin on his face. That broke the ice.

He immediately started to cajole me. He told me how much he rated me as a player and that what I'd done over previous seasons had impressed him. He knew plenty about me. I hadn't even

I enjoyed a happy childhood in Norfolk with Mum, Dad, sisters Rachel and Lucy and my older brother Ian.

My dad Mike was a fine footballer who played for Norwich, Chester and Carlisle but a bad knee injury cut his career short.

The ball control that made me a £10 million striker! Here I am honing my skills as a toddler in Norfolk.

Nanny Sutton joins me and Frankie on a visit to Glasgow. She was a huge support to me throughout my life.

Jeremy Goss leads the celebrations after we beat Bayern 2–1 in the Olympic Stadium in 1993.

I joined Blackburn in 1994 as Britain's most expensive player but after spending a night in the cells I feared the £5 million move could have been wrecked.

The awards came thick and fast at Ewood Park as I'm joined by Kenny Dalglish and Alan Shearer in 1995. I felt myself and Alan had an uneasy relationship at times.

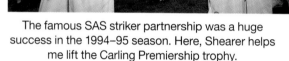

The famous SAS striker partnership was a huge success in the 1994–95 season. Here, Shearer helps me lift the Carling Premiership trophy.

Nothing beats scoring and here I am celebrating a first-half hat-trick against Aston Villa in 1997 with Billy McKinlay.

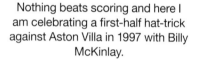

It's a massive regret from my playing career that my only cap for England came in 1997 against Cameroon.

I couldn't wait to get my Chelsea career started after joining them for £10 million in 1999 but sadly the move quickly turned sour.

Henrik and I had a fantastic relationship on and off the pitch and here we are celebrating the fifth goal in our amazing 6–2 win over Rangers in 2000.

Champions League nights at Celtic Park were incredible events and this was an extra special moment for me as I celebrate my goal against Juventus in 2001.

A special goal on a special night as I volley home our fourth goal against Juventus in the Champions League in 2001.

Celebrating another title success with the kids at Parkhead in 2004.

John Robertson was a mentor and a wonderful man to have around the club. Mixed emotions as we enjoy our last game at Celtic together after lifting the Scottish Cup in 2005.

Our incredible run to the 2003 UEFA Cup Final ended in hurt and frustration as we fell 3–2 to Porto in Seville.

Henrik is the first to console me as his Barcelona team beat us 3–1 at Parkhead in the Champions League in 2004.

Dogs are a huge part of our family life and here I am with Fernandez and Antonio sitting in the snow.

I married my wonderful wife Sam in 1995 and we continue to enjoy a fantastic relationship. Here we are on holiday together in Mauritius.

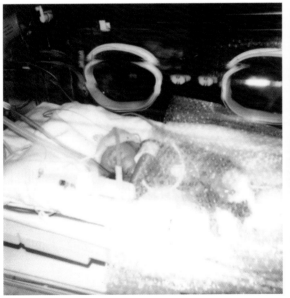

One of the hardest times of my life as I watch James fighting for his life in Yorkhill Hospital.

Frankie and Ollie are stripped for action in their Blackburn kits.

The two St Bernards are almost as big as the boys as we all enjoy a fun day in the snow.

The best team in the world. Sam and I have five wonderful kids and this is us enjoying a dip in the pool in Mauritius.

James at full speed. It's great to follow his development into a strong, active boy.

Frankie and I enjoy a kickabout at Barrowfield in 2004.

My Norwich pal Ruel Fox and I having a celebratory drink on holiday together.

Stiliyan Petrov and his wife Paulina join me, Sam and Henrik Larsson at a charity dinner in Glasgow in 2010.

My first steps in management at Lincoln ended in frustration and recrimination.

signed for Celtic and he was already starting to build me up, trying to get the best out of me to make sure I was ready for Celtic. It was brilliant man-management that set him apart from most managers I'd worked for. I felt great at the end of that meeting, felt full of worth and had an appetite back to be a footballer again.

I grew up supporting Nottingham Forest and Martin was one of my favourite players. He was at the club when they won the two European Cups when Brian Clough was manager. It was a great time to be a Forest supporter.

But all of that didn't guarantee I'd go to Celtic. Middlesbrough made a tremendous effort to get me. Financially, I'd have been better off going to Middlesbrough but, like I say, money wasn't my motivation at that time. This was all about making the right football decision. Bryan Robson was manager and he had big plans for the club. I liked Bryan, had a lot of time for him, and he made a personal effort to get me to The Riverside. But they weren't the strongest Premiership side at that time and I felt going to Scotland was right. Tottenham had also shown a strong interest but things never progressed because I was unsure about staying in London. I never gave them much encouragement.

I went to Middlesbrough on a Saturday to give them a final consideration. They had a fantastic set-up and they made me feel very welcome. The owner Steve Gibson and the chief executive Keith Lamb accompanied Bryan Robson to the meeting. I had Sam and the boys with me; they really made us feel at ease and tried their best to sell the club and the area to us. Such nice people. Their training ground was also incredible.

But, all the time, I had a feeling I was going to go to Celtic. That may sound really rude, after all the effort they made, but I just could not help my feelings. I felt bad for wasting their time, though.

I came up to Glasgow before I signed for Celtic. I drove there from Teesside, visited the stadium and had a look around

Glasgow. I was impressed. Of course I was. Celtic Park is a fantastic arena and as I stood there on a Saturday afternoon in the summer, I tried to picture what it would be like with a full house and how noisy it would be. It wasn't long before I was playing there and we had an intimidating crowd that made some visiting teams quake in their boots.

The thought of joining Celtic had me excited, to be honest. The clubs agreed a fee and I agreed personal terms on a five-year contract. At that time, it was the biggest outlay in Celtic's history and they made a huge financial investment in me, in terms of the fee and salary. I was delighted but also slightly apprehensive, it has to be said. I felt I could get my old form back but, if truth be told, I wasn't absolutely certain. However, I knew I could still play. Dennis Wise phoned me after I joined Celtic to wish me all the best and so did Jody Morris. I like Jody, he is a really nice lad and was a really good prospect then.

When I was unhappy at Chelsea, Sam and the boys didn't like to see me that way. Moving to Scotland was a new start for us and there was probably a part of us that was a little bit unsure about it. But it wasn't a major issue. We were ready for this new period of our lives and we never looked back for the next five years. Glasgow is an exciting city and the people made us feel very welcome.

Yet, the funny thing is, I may well have ended up on the other side of the divide as I almost had the opportunity to sign for Rangers. My name was put to the club when I was to leave Chelsea but word came back that they weren't interested in me.

Trying to resurrect my career in Scotland was a huge gamble. I was making a rod for my own back if it didn't go well. There would have been huge doubt if I couldn't score goals in the SPL and my career would have been threatened. So, it wasn't the easy option to go to Scotland. If anything, it was the move that put the most pressure on me.

I knew some of the Celtic players. The likes of Alan Stubbs and Tommy Johnson were there and I'd played against Alan a number of times when he was at Bolton. I also fancied the challenge of trying to stop Rangers. Rangers were the dominant team and had won the SPL by twenty-one points the previous season. It was up to Celtic to try and close the gap. Martin was so positive and he was such a sought-after manager at that time, having turned down Leeds and Everton not long before, that it reaffirmed my belief that it was right to go to Celtic. Martin hadn't gone there to make up the numbers and accept being second best.

I bought into it but knew it wasn't going to be easy. A few years earlier, Rangers attracted a lot of headlines when they had Paul Gascoigne and Brian Laudrup when Walter Smith was the manager. They then went for it big-style when Dick Advocaat took over in the summer of 1998. I think Sir David Murray bankrolled Advocaat's spending spree to the tune of more than £30 million during his first summer in charge when he bought Giovanni Van Bronckhorst, Arthur Numan, Gabriel Amato, Andrei Kanchelskis, Colin Hendry and a few others.

Rangers won the league during Advocaat's first season in charge. Celtic had Dr Jozef Venglos in charge at that time. After one season with Venglos in charge, a change was made and Kenny Dalglish came in. Kenny appointed John Barnes as head coach. It didn't go well and John lost his job after nine months, losing famously at home to Inverness Caley Thistle in the Scottish Cup, which was the final straw. Rangers went on to win the league comfortably. Martin O'Neill was then appointed manager by Dermot Desmond and the club never looked back for the next five years. Martin brought the good times back to Celtic and a real passion to the club. And we became the dominant force in Scotland once again.

Gianluca Vialli on Chris Sutton

Chris had been a player I had rated for quite some time and he had shown over a number of years the qualities he possesses. I was delighted we managed to sign him from Blackburn Rovers. We paid a lot of money for him, but I wasn't involved in the negotiations between the clubs and the eventual transfer fee. As a manager, a transfer fee was never a problem for me. Perhaps for the player it is different but you have to learn to carry that weight of expectation, that burden, around your neck. A footballer should not be scared of anything like that and should always try to prove any critics wrong.

We had lacked a 'British style' striker in our team. Some of the strikers we had were technically better than Chris but we felt we lacked someone up front that would be there for us when the going got tough, particularly in some away games. In some games we were not able to cope with the physical aspect and we felt Chris could be a big help to us in that area. He had the qualities we felt we lacked and that's why we pursued him. Chris worked hard and I could see he was determined to do well and I actually felt he played well for us and, overall, I was pleased with his performances. It just didn't happen often enough for him.

We tried to marry our European style with a British style and getting that blend was harder than what we thought it would be. Initially, at least, it didn't quite go to plan for us.

He was one of four top-class strikers and I decided to use the Italian system of rotating the players.

Maybe Chris didn't like it that way, I'm not sure. He also had a couple of niggly injuries and that didn't help him. I think he had one or two problems with an ankle.

When George Weah joined us, Chris looked more comfortable and I thought they could have been a good partnership. They were terrific together in a few games. Overall, it just never quite took off for Chris.

The decision to leave Chelsea was mainly down to Chris. Had he decided to stay and fight for his place and try to become a real hit, then I would not have objected. I felt had he stayed for a second season, he would have gone on to become a real success for us. I was sacked a few months into that season but I feel Chris could have stayed.

However, for many different reasons, transfers don't work out and it is hard to point the finger at one single reason as to why this happens. I think most of the criticism towards him was unfair but the press always try to pick someone to carry the can when performances aren't what they should be.

I've often thought that perhaps I could have done more to help him and that the team could have done more to help him. I don't know if I was a good coach for Chris or a not so good coach. Part of my job was to improve my players as individuals and as a collective unit. If Chris felt I improved his game, then I'm happy to hear that.

In terms of the FA Cup Final, I don't have a problem with the conversation we had on the morning of the FA Cup Final. These things happen in football. I felt it was a civilised conversation. I don't hold grudges. He would have been upset with some of the decisions I made, and when you are upset and when you reflect on that, it can affect the way you train, speak and behave. I'd rather not spend too much time talking about this any further.

Chris was a nice person and I was pleased for him that his move to Celtic was a success. Perhaps the style of play used by Celtic was more beneficial to Chris. He scored many, many goals and also played in a number of different positions. He obviously played there with confidence and that is so important.

9

PARADISE BOUND . . .
PARADISE FOUND

My strength as a striker had always been as part of a partnership, in my view. I was best being the focal point, linking up the play and with someone playing off me. I had good awareness of what was around me and I also felt I'd get my fair share of goals. I didn't mind playing on the shoulder of the last defender but Henrik was better at it as he had genuine pace. I would normally go for the flicks off long balls or try to hold it in. I used to try and utilise the gap between our midfielders and strikers, or the hole as it's known in football terms. I tried to give central defenders problems by giving them decisions to make – to follow me and leave a space for Henrik, or stay in position and allow me to either get on a half-turn and try to slide a pass through to Henrik or keep hold of the ball and link the play.

Henrik had pace and he was also a very clever striker. Most of the time, I knew where he was and he knew where I was. When that's the case, I feel you can cause any side problems. I think Andy Cole and Dwight Yorke had that type of partnership at Manchester United. They were outstanding together.

Henrik always wanted to be the top scorer and that was fine by me. I probably wasn't as ruthless as that, in terms of goalscoring. Maybe that's why I didn't go to the very top and why he achieved so much at the highest level. Mentally, he was in a league of his own.

I felt very much at ease in the area of the pitch just in between the midfield and out-and-out centre-forward. I'd be the one who'd drop in and do the defensive shift when required. Invariably, we tried to leave Henrik up as he had the pace.

But Henrik wasn't a selfish striker. If he had the ball and I was in a better position, then he would always pass to me. I felt that when we played together, we were capable of scoring against any side and we usually did.

We both scored in our first game as a partnership to give us a 2–1 win away at Dundee United on the opening weekend of the SPL season. It felt great to get the winner. I went home that night feeling chuffed with myself but I knew there was plenty of hard work ahead of me. I still had a lot of convincing to do.

It was my first home game the following week. It was against Motherwell and I was excited. We won the game. But I was red carded. Never in a million years did I deserve to be sent off that day. Alan Freeland was the referee. He took charge of a number of our games and I felt he was very rarely in control.

That day was the first of many times I felt I received a raw deal from referees in Scotland. It was difficult for referees to make decisions on aerial challenges. It's give and take, six of one and half a dozen of the other. I accepted sometimes I fouled people, through mistiming, and sometimes on purpose, to stop my opponent getting clear contact on the ball. But I can honestly say some referees had a poor understanding of the game and I was penalised far too frequently by the likes of Freeland and Hugh Dallas.

Even worse was when I tried to talk to them about an incident and they told me to shut up and offered no explanation. Keith Cooper, Dermot Gallagher, Graham Poll and Willie Young always tried to explain a decision when questioned and at times responded when I remonstrated by saying I should be far more worried about my own performance than theirs. Some refs were humorous and this always helped the situation.

I always seemed to have more problems when certain referees were in charge. Hugh Dallas was one of these. Maybe it was just the way some referees interpreted the rules of the game and applied them to my playing style. But it seemed to me that Dallas liked to be the centre of attention when it should have been the game and the players that were making the headlines. For me, this often spoiled the game.

The amount of times refs in Scotland awarded free-kicks against me when I had been the victim was quite frightening really. I've no doubt the referees discussed certain players and it appeared as though a few of them didn't judge incidents involving me on individual merit – I think they had pre-conceived ideas.

No one could ever say a referee's job is easy but some decisions made no sense at all to me. Like the one in the 2001 League Cup Final against Kilmarnock at Hampden Park. Dallas was in charge that afternoon and he gave me a straight red for a challenge on Gary Holt on the hour mark. The tackle on Holt wasn't malicious and, as far as I'm concerned, I just used my physical attributes to get my body in front of the player. In Dallas's view the challenge merited a straight red card but to this day I have no idea how he could have made that decision and I still think it was ridiculous. We won the game 3–0, thanks to a fabulous hat-trick from Henrik, but Dallas ruined my day. It was the first trophy we had won under Martin and my first for Celtic. I was delighted for the club and the players but there was also a feeling of rage rippling through me because of Dallas's decision.

I never really got on great with Hugh Dallas. He had the reputation of being the best referee in Scotland and was highly regarded by UEFA, but he and I never gelled and I always wondered if he had some sort of agenda against me. I remember one game against Aberdeen at Pittodrie when I collapsed to the ground with an injury. I felt an excruciating pain in my knee and needed treatment. I had a feeling the 'magic sponge' wasn't going to be good enough for this one. I told Hugh I had a problem and he just told me to get up. I had no idea Hugh was a physiotherapist or a doctor! In the end I received treatment and had to be carried off as I'd torn my anterior ligament. It turned out to be a serious injury and I was out for more than six weeks. Again, Hugh's attitude left me feeling angry.

I wasn't the only Celtic player in our dressing room that had problems with different referees. I would have loved to have spoken out against refs a few times when I played for Celtic but the ramifications would have been serious. The SFA would have hammered me. They did have their moment with me in 2003 after we lost the league to Rangers, but I'll get into that later.

The red card against Motherwell apart, I was happy enough with my start to the season at my new club and we were all doing well. But with all respect to the other sides, Rangers were the marker, the benchmark as Martin O'Neill used to say. Rangers were a cut above all other teams. They were very strong. We were a bit unsure going into the first game against them, really. I think many people in the country didn't give us much of a chance but we managed to beat them 6–2 and in terms of a scoreline, it was an absolute thumping. In terms of performance, it was a good one but we did have some scary moments. However, that afternoon we put down a marker.

We were three up inside twenty minutes. I was lucky enough to score the opening goal inside the first minute. Stiliyan Petrov and Paul Lambert got the other goals. Bobby Petta had a particularly good start to the game and was up against his fellow countryman, Fernando Ricksen. It was Fernando's Old Firm debut and he was taken off by Dick Advocaat after twenty-two minutes. Bobby gave him the absolute runaround. Seeing Rangers making that change maybe gave us a lift, it reinforced the point that we were well on top and Rangers were in real danger of crumbling. That said, I'm sure Bobby would have preferred Ricksen to stay on the field. Bobby, perhaps, had his finest hour in a Celtic jersey that day.

But Rangers got back into it and Claudio Reyna made it 3–1. Just before half-time, they had a goal disallowed for offside. Had that one counted, we would have been a little bit nervous going in at the interval. That was a big moment in the game, no doubt.

After the interval, we quickly got into our stride. Henrik and I were up front and we were enjoying our game against Lorenzo Amoruso and Bert Konterman, who was also making his Old Firm debut that day. To be honest, we gave them a torrid time and I think Amoruso wasn't happy with Konterman as we ran them ragged.

Henrik scored two fabulous goals to put us 5–1 ahead. Billy Dodds made it 5–2 with a penalty and, with a few minutes remaining, I slid home the sixth goal from close range after I got on the end of Stéphane Mahé's cross. Barry Ferguson was red-carded late in the game in what must have been a miserable day for Rangers.

Psychologically, the result gave us a big boost. I'm not saying we left Parkhead feeling we were definitely going to win the league, but we did go home feeling quietly confident that we were going to worry them. After winning the league so comfortably the season before, they may have felt they'd win that game. I'm not saying we were more motivated than them that day but we certainly had a lot to prove. We had a new manager and four or five new players. We had plenty of desire and hunger and that can take you a long way in a game of football. We maybe felt we had everything to prove during that ninety minutes. To a man, we gave our absolute all. If we were going to lose that game, there was a feeling it would have been over our dead bodies.

We won comfortably and, for most of the ninety minutes, I felt we could have scored every time we went up the pitch. We could have scored ten or eleven goals that day, really.

It was an enjoyable game to play in. When we were 5–2 up, the pressure was gone and we could relax. To have that kind of margin over our greatest rivals was a lovely feeling. In terms of games I played in during my career, it was one of the most exciting. When the goals were piling in, the atmosphere was incredible; the fans were clearly having a ball. The last Old Firm game before that was at Ibrox the previous season and Celtic were thumped 4–0. The players and fans must have been hurting that day. So, this was their turn to make the most of it and from where I was standing on the pitch, they lapped up every second.

We went to Ibrox for the next Old Firm game and lost 5–1. It was a real thumping. We were all very dejected after the game. They probably would have felt they were back in the driving seat after that win. We, of course, had other ideas. They had just bought Tore André Flo for a Scottish record fee of £12 million. Flo, of course, was my team-mate at Chelsea. For a variety of reasons, including the mammoth size of the fee and the intensity of being part of one half of the Old Firm, I knew it would be difficult for him. Flo was a nice guy and very quiet. He did very well for Chelsea and was a good finisher. But when he arrived at Rangers, we were big rivals so naturally I hoped he and the other Rangers players performed poorly. It was nothing personal to them as fellow professionals. Ask them about us and they would have felt the same. It was all about winning, all about pummelling Rangers into the floor. You have to be ruthless when it comes to certain things.

Our next game was away to Hibs and the manager was a little bit concerned going into that game. He was keen for us to avoid a defeat, as two losses in a row can damage confidence. It was a windy night in Edinburgh and we came away with a 0–0 draw.

We'd normally have expected to win that game but under the circumstances, a draw was more than acceptable.

From there on in, we steamrollered our way to the SPL title. It was delightful. We scored many late goals and so many things clicked into place. The manager made key signings at different times. Neil Lennon came in before Christmas and he slotted in well, played alongside Lambert. Alan Thompson arrived before him and gave us a lovely balance down the left-hand side with his craft and graft. Johan Mjällby became an out-and-out centre-half and was rock solid. Lubo Moravcík responded positively to some criticism from the manager during pre-season and performed like a magician at points. His feet were like wands.

Didier Agathe was bought from Hibs for £50,000. He was brilliant for us. He had energy and a turn of pace that made me envious. Stiliyan Petrov was superb in the middle of the park and contributed with some important goals. He was the attacking midfielder and always gave me and Henrik an option in the final third of the field. Jackie McNamara filled in a number of positions for us and excelled in them all.

Ramon Vega joined us on loan for the second half of the season from Spurs. Ramon added competition in the centre of defence. He was a powerful player and was supremely confident on and off the park. He threw a party at his flat one evening for the players and their partners and it was good fun. Everyone had a few drinks and I took things a little bit too far. Ramon had this vase – I think it was quite expensive – and I nudged Alan Thompson into it. It wobbled and took an eternity to fall. And fall it did. It smashed and the flowers and water went everywhere. Everybody went quiet and turned to see Thommo standing beside it. I had nipped to the other side of the room. Thommo had a guilty look on his face but was totally innocent. I got away with it. It was one of many nights out and bits of fun we all enjoyed together, which in the end brought us closer as team-mates.

It may all seem simple and straightforward to assemble a title-winning team when you've been given money to spend but it's not. You need to get the blend right, decide on partnerships throughout the team and hope that they gel together. Martin put it all together and his man-management was superb. He also had two brilliant men beside him in John Robertson and Steve Walford. Steve would take training on a day-to-day basis and he made it enjoyable. They made sure we were fit and organised.

At Celtic we'd have young vs old in training and they were competitive games. John Kennedy and Stephen Crainey loved a tackle in those games and they weren't scared to leave a bit on you. Back then, I was a senior professional and used to think, I suppose, that they shouldn't be tackling us so aggressively. But the young lads were quite right to get stuck in. I mean, they'd get criticised for not tackling us but we moaned when they did. It was complete hypocrisy, really. It used to become quite heated. I had a couple of scrapes over the years but nothing extraordinary. A few lads left me in a heap but I was never involved in a punch-up on the training ground. I got punched quite a lot off the training ground, though!

I do remember Olivier Tébily doing me once at training during pre-season at Bisham Abbey. He kept coming through me. Time after time. I eventually had enough and swung my elbow at him, and he ended up on the floor.

John Kennedy was a wholehearted player and some of the times his tackling was very naughty. I'd play up front with Henrik and we used to cringe at some of the tackles that were flying in during the young vs old. I think Henrik used to wear shin-pads on a Friday. Some players train how they play all the time and I certainly think that, in general, it's right to do this. If you are a young player trying to make a name for yourself, you have to try to impress. Some players felt they had to train aggressively for their mental approach. I always felt, as I got older, I didn't want to get injured stupidly with a reckless challenge and didn't want to injure the key men such as Henrik, Stiliyan or Lenny. So I took it easier on the physical side at times. But sometimes after being kicked far too often, I would chuck my toys out of the pram and join in physically. But I hoped injuries wouldn't happen, especially to the big players. It was about judging each situation on its own merits, picking and choosing your times.

I took plenty of hits during games, real tough shifts for ninety minutes, but the most serious injury we had that season was the night Petrov broke his leg against St Johnstone on a midweek night in March. It was cruel on him as he was having such a terrific period. But he still managed to go on and win the PFA Young Player of the Year. Henrik won the PFA Player of the Year. Both were well deserved. Petrov never played again that season but we won that game 2–1. We scored a late goal, which had been a feature of our play in many games that season. We never gave up; we fought to the last whistle. The manager insisted on it and the players wanted it to be that way.

That night, as we got on the bus at McDiarmid Park, we felt the league was in the bag. It would have been catastrophic had we lost it. We did go on to win it and we won it comfortably. Rangers had won it the previous season by twenty-one points and they lapped up every second, quite rightly. It was now our turn to rub their noses in it and we took great satisfaction out of doing that. On the last Old Firm game of the season, we went to Ibrox and won 3–0. Life can sometimes be very sweet.

The final part came at Hampden and we defeated Hibs 3–0 to win the treble. Celtic last won the treble in 1969 so it was an incredible achievement. We were a brave team, we were talented and we were committed. We got what we deserved in that campaign.

On a personal level, it was a huge season for me. After my

disastrous spell at Chelsea the previous season, I couldn't have been any more motivated to do well and achieve something. My first ten months at Celtic saved my career. I couldn't have afforded to have two bad seasons in a row. I may have been playing in Scotland, but I knew eyes were on me from down south and many wanted to see me fail.

Celtic paid £6 million for me and had it not worked out, it may well have ended my career at a high level. I probably would have had to take a couple of steps back to go forward again and I may never have been able to make the transition. I would have been lucky to bounce back from anything going wrong at Celtic.

Looking back, the goal at Dundee United on the opening day of the season really settled me, although I didn't fully realise just how much at the time. It stopped any lingering doubts from plaguing my mind and body. It was a priceless moment for me to get the winner that Sunday afternoon.

That whole campaign gave me many highs at different times. But it wasn't always like that when I played in Scotland. We picked up a few bruises and batterings along the way in later years, most notably in 2003 and 2005.

The manager was keen to strengthen the squad for the 2001–02 season and his most expensive signing was John Hartson for a fee of around £5.5 million from Coventry City. John was a powerful striker, a target man and lethal in and around the penalty box. I'd be lying if I said I didn't wonder what Martin's thinking behind it was, in terms of where it would leave me. We had just won the treble but I did have one or two injury problems and Martin probably felt another big striker with the ability to score goals was required. To be fair, all managers want to sign good players and the right time to do it is from a position of strength. There was also the factor of John having failed a medical at Rangers the previous year when Dick Advocaat fancied signing him. So, you're getting a player who is hungry and probably has extra determination to show your biggest rivals exactly what they missed out on.

I had a little bit of concern but, honestly, I wasn't too worried. I'd played at big clubs and had to compete with really good strikers for a place in the team and I always felt I could live with the best of them. I didn't speak to Martin about it but John Robertson gave me a steer after John Hartson signed and told me there was no need to be concerned. I've never been frightened of competition and I always felt that I'd get into the team. Yes, John was a good goalscorer and we were similar players in some ways, but also very different in other ways. John was a natural finisher and his strength was as a box player. I preferred to link the game more. We were both big and strong but I always felt that when the big games came around, I'd be playing in them. I only ever found myself on the bench when on my return from mid- or long-term injuries.

Barcelona in 2004 was one such game after my hamstring injury and Boavista was another after my broken wrist. I came off the bench at half-time against Barca and scored. Martin encouraged me to declare myself fit, rushed me back a bit. He used to rush me back a fair bit and chuck me in.

We won the SPL title again in 2002 – comfortably. It was unfortunate we couldn't win any cups in that campaign, though. Rangers replaced Advocaat with Alex McLeish in December 2001, but by that time we were on our way to the league championship and we remained focused in the second half of the season to go all the way. But McLeish won two cups with Rangers. They beat us 2–1 in the semi-final of the CIS League Cup and then 3–2 in the Scottish Cup Final. We were twice in the lead that day through John Hartson and Bobo Baldé but it just wasn't to be.

We knew Rangers were resurgent under McLeish but I felt we were still ahead of them. The 2002–03 season was set to be a cracker and it didn't disappoint.

We had so much to play for in 2003. During the month of March, we were in with a chance of winning the treble and the UEFA Cup. By the end of that month, we had lost the League Cup Final to Rangers and we had been knocked out of the Scottish Cup by Inverness. I suffered a blow in the League Cup Final when I broke my wrist. I was going for a high ball and I put my hand down to break my fall. My wrist couldn't take the weight and snapped. Then Bobo landed on top of me. At least big Bobo said sorry!

I was out for a few weeks and missed our 2–0 win at Liverpool that took us into the semi-finals of the UEFA Cup. That was some night. We lost the UEFA Cup Final to Porto but I was back playing again by then.

Later that week, more agony was to follow. In the final league game of the season, we were playing away to Kilmarnock and Rangers were at home to Dunfermline. We were level on points with Rangers but they were top of the table by one goal. They started that afternoon as favourites to win the title, no doubt. But we weren't for giving up our title without an almighty fight. We produced an amazing performance to win 4–0. Rangers won 6–1.

McLeish had won the league by one goal. Just two months earlier, we were on the verge of winning four pieces of silverware and we finished up with nothing. It wasn't fair. Rangers were knocked out of Europe that season at the qualifier stage and it meant they only had the domestic game to focus on. We, on the other hand, played fifteen games in Europe as well.

I was asked to do a television interview right after the game at Rugby Park and I just let rip. I said that it was no surprise Rangers had won the league as I felt Dunfermline had laid down to them that day. The Kilmarnock fans inside Rugby Park also cheered every Rangers goal that day. We knew their allegiances. We knew what we were up against. And Celtic were accused of being paranoid. On more than a few occasions I don't think there was paranoia involved. People were in favour of other clubs more than Celtic, of that I've no doubt. I was angry and pumped up at full-time. Referee Kenny Clark sent me off in the tunnel twice for foul and abusive language while I waited to do television interviews, once on the way out to the pitch for a warm-down and then on the way back in. It proved to be an unfortunate half hour or so but I couldn't help myself. I was in a rage, no other way to describe it. Having a right go at Dunfermline manager Jimmy Calderwood and his players was supposed to make me feel a little bit better. I reckon I only said what a lot of people were thinking.

It's well known Jimmy Calderwood is a Rangers man and he would have wanted Rangers to win the league that day. I don't think that can be denied. But the Dunfermline players took exception to my comments and they had every right to be angry.

It was a massively frustrating season and sometimes you just lose control. I lost the plot during the interview. What we deserved that season and what we got were totally different things.

My comments caused a huge furore afterwards and made headlines all over the place. At that time, I didn't really give a damn. Thinking about it now, I should have kept my mouth shut. It wasn't right for me to question the commitment of other players.

Dunfermline threatened legal action against me. I didn't want that so I tried to defuse the whole situation. I had to do a bit of backing down and a few telephone calls had to be made. I phoned Jimmy Calderwood and the Dunfermline chairman John Yorkston to apologise. John stood up for his club and rightly so. I also phoned the Rangers management to apologise. The SFA still had their day with me and hit me with a six-game ban for my two red cards. I appealed the decision and they reduced it to five.

To lose the league that season was bitterly disappointing. To put so much into that campaign and have no silverware to show for it was totally unfair on us. But despite that, I still had some memorable occasions from that season. Many things had made my move to Celtic worthwhile and some of the highs of 2002–03 added to my pleasure. It would have been good to make it three titles on the trot but it wasn't to be. We lost to Rangers but during the summer my focus was on putting them in their rightful place – behind us – the following season. Thankfully, we managed to do just that.

10

THE CITY OF TWO HALVES

You'd be stupid not to be aware of the rivalry between Celtic and Rangers. It's legendary.

There is, for some people, a hatred towards the other side and there is often a religious element in those feelings. In Glasgow, normally you're either one or the other. You're either Catholic or Protestant and you support Celtic or Rangers. Green or blue. That's the way it is, or certainly the impression I gathered during my time living in Scotland. I did have an idea about this from my time playing in England before I moved to Glasgow, mostly through other players I'd met and spoken to. But ideas and reality are two different things.

The Old Firm are given great coverage on the national news in England and on Sky Television and certain incidents have received plenty of publicity. One I remember well was the incident in 1999 involving Hugh Dallas when he was struck by a coin from a Celtic fan in the stadium and it made him bleed. It was unusual to see that at any level of football. Another was the incident when Paul Gascoigne pretended to play the flute when he warmed up during an Old Firm game. It was an ill-judged act from Paul. Apparently he'd been wound up to do it but he should surely have realised that it wasn't a good idea and was likely to incite trouble.

It was always going to be an exciting environment to come into. The rivalry and passion between the fans make it, for me, easily the most exciting derby in the UK and possibly the world. Rightly or wrongly, there is a real edge to the game, especially between the fans, from the first whistle to the last. The atmosphere is second to none. You can actually feel that the fans don't like each other. And I mean really don't like each other. That's part of what makes it such a spectacle. Those emotions transmit onto the pitch and the players often get caught up in it and sucked right in.

I certainly felt this. When it came to ninety minutes of football against Rangers, I hated them. When I arrived, Rangers had been the dominant force for more than a decade and I wanted to put Rangers in their place. I felt really strongly about this. I came to Scotland to be a winner and to be successful. I had had a bad season the previous year at Chelsea and I wasn't ready for another miserable time.

Off the pitch, I'd met some of the Rangers players socially and they were fine, guys like Craig Moore and Barry Ferguson. I also found most of the Dutch guys to be decent company.

But on the pitch, they were my worst enemies.

I experienced some tasty battles when I was playing against Rangers but it was nothing like what I witnessed in the 2010–11 season. I attended a number of Old Firm games during that period. I was in the stand the night of the Scottish Cup replay which Celtic won 1–0. That was incredible. Neil Lennon and Ally McCoist having to be pulled apart on the touchline. Lenny received a four-game for that and I found that totally unjust. He didn't do anything wrong. As I saw it, McCoist said something to Lenny which made him react. Tensions were understandably high but why did McCoist feel he had to whisper anything in Lenny's ear? What was the point of that? It's almost impossible to unravel incidents like this but to my mind McCoist was the aggressor and Lenny's reaction was understandable and acceptable. If Lenny had done nothing and just walked away and not stood up for himself, then he would have looked weak. McCoist received a two-game ban and it was quashed on appeal but I simply cannot understand that decision by the SFA. Was that really a fair and balanced result given what went on? As far as I'm concerned, the SFA got that one wrong.

In hindsight, I'm sure both would have preferred to react in a different way and I think it's fair to say that you wouldn't have seen Martin O'Neill and Walter Smith acting in such a way. But Neil did very little wrong other than defend himself and his club.

It led to a summit at the Scottish Parliament where both clubs were encouraged to work with the government and the police to improve relations and cut out any sectarian element within their support. I've been told that after Old Firm games, there is an increase in domestic violence and the hospital wards are much busier than normal. That's unacceptable and all parts of society must pull together to prevent as much of this as possible. Footballers should try to behave as responsibly as possible on the pitch. It's very easy to get caught up in the heat of the moment, but they should try their best not to give the moronic so-called fans any excuses to behave unacceptably.

Few people must have suffered more than Lenny during the period of January to May 2011. It was disgraceful what he had to go through – from death threats to nail bombs and bullets being sent in the post. It was shocking. He had to have a panic button installed in his family home and a safe-house for his family to be moved to. When you become manager of Celtic you expect pressure and intense scrutiny, but what he had to go through took it to a whole new level.

If I'd been sent death threats, nail bombs and bullets, I would have walked away. I would not have wanted to live in that environment with constant threats hanging over me and my family. Lenny is very strong mentally, but it must have been a distraction and taken a lot out of him. In my view, Celtic would have won the league had the off-the-field distractions not been there.

People accuse Celtic of being paranoid but they were entitled to feel victimised on a few occasions in 2010–11. When referee Dougie McDonald lied to Lenny after that Dundee United vs Celtic game, he should have been dismissed from his post there and then. But there appeared to be some form of cover-up from within his own circles to protect him. He eventually resigned.

The referees went on strike in 2010 and that was a total farce. There is too much self-protection and not enough accountability. Everybody makes mistakes and refs have a hard job, we know that, but why can't they hold their hands up when they make a poor decision? If they admitted their mistakes, the players and supporters would accept their honesty. By not doing this, they bring extra pressure on themselves. It's stupidity, in my opinion.

After an Old Firm game I'd rarely, if ever, go out. Whether we had won or lost, I was advised the sensible thing to do was to stay indoors and I took that advice on board. Even when it came to my boys' schooling, I sent them to a Roman Catholic school even though I'm not religious in any way. But I'd heard a few horror stories from players who had sent their children to mixed schools in Glasgow. So, I took the safe option. I didn't want to put my boys at risk by sending them to a school where they may have taken stick because their dad played for Celtic. Now, people may have exaggerated in their stories but, nonetheless, I was not for taking a chance. I knew if things were to work out for me and my family in Glasgow, then it was not just going to be about how well I performed on the pitch. More importantly, it was going to hinge on Sam and the boys being happy and feeling at ease in Glasgow. We sent them to St Cadoc's in Newton Mearns and Tommy Burns had kindly helped us with getting them in there as he knew the headmaster. The headmaster was terrific with us and it was a really good school. They made some good friends there and still keep in touch with them.

We lived in Newton Mearns in the early days and then we moved to Thorntonhall. We were all extremely happy there. We enjoyed the city when we ventured into Glasgow. Like my previous clubs, I always got the occasional bit of abuse but nothing too bad – mostly along the lines of, 'Sutton, you're rotten.' I agreed with them – they were normally right! Or else I'd just bite my tongue and walk away. I'd learned to do that by the time I'd joined Celtic.

Yet, when we had a problem with our son James, we got a helluva lot of goodwill messages from Rangers fans. Both sets of fans sent us some touching words. My family and I will never forget that.

That said, any goodwill from the other side goes out of the window when it comes to Old Firm day. All the players used to receive abuse from the Rangers fans when we got off the bus at Ibrox – there was plenty of that kind of thing. It was the same at venues like Tynecastle and Pittodrie. At the smaller grounds, you heard the abuse more clearly and some of it could be quite vile.

I actually liked going to play at Ibrox. The surface was usually good and the atmosphere was always volatile. We had a good record at Ibrox during Martin O'Neill's reign. I played on a winning side there for Celtic on a number of occasions. It's always nice to win derby matches at home, but there was something very sweet about stepping into the lions' den and beating Rangers on their own turf. The away dressing room at Ibrox was situated next to the main road at the front entrance. Rangers fans were aware it was our dressing room window and would shout things in. We'd hear the abuse then, for sure. But when we had beaten Rangers, it gave a level of satisfaction to know how much the Rangers fans were hurting. We'd shout one or two things back at them if we had won. We always enjoyed beating Rangers at 'Castle Greyskull', as we used to call it within the confines of our dressing room.

I think a lot of the players, including myself, thrived on the rivalry between the fans. On many occasions, I brought people up from down south to Celtic Park for Old Firm games and every one of them agreed there is no atmosphere like it in any other stadium in Britain. A few European nights came close, like the night we beat Juventus 4–3 in the Champions League and also when Valencia knocked us out of the UEFA Cup on a penalty shoot-out.

But the Rangers games were very special and I loved playing in them, it certainly got the adrenalin going. The 6–2 game during my first season was such an exciting day in so many different ways but we were brought crashing back down when we lost 5–1 at Ibrox the next time we played them. Looking back on it now, that was a good result in the grand scheme of things, sort of brought us down to earth a bit. It made us get back on track and focus heavily on the job in hand because we hadn't cracked it at that stage. We played Rangers five times in that 2000–01 season and we won four.

We won the league comfortably in 2001 and 2002 but there was a tussle in season 2002–03. There was a real determination at Rangers this season and Alex McLeish had his team doing well. There was a real ding-dong game on 6 October 2002. It finished 3–3 at Celtic Park and Mikel Arteta opened the scoring. Henrik then grabbed a double to put us 2–1 up and then Ronald De Boer levelled it. Shota Arveladze made it 3–2 but I equalised. It was great to get that last goal but we should have won that game comfortably.

Rangers started really well that day and we tried to play too much football, too many passes at the back. We then went long and we started to butcher them, got back into the game. A lot of Old Firm matches were blood and guts. I had some good battles against Lorenzo Amoruso and Craig Moore. I used to relish the physical aspect of that, getting smashed from them and giving as good as I got. Playing against Amoruso was always a good motivation because he gave me the impression he really fancied himself. He was very physical but we always knew we could beat him for pace.

They signed Arteta from Barcelona in the summer of 2002 to enhance their team. He was young and a very good technical player but he lacked a physical presence. I played a few games in midfield against him and I used to think that as I soon as he got the ball, I had to get on top of him and be as physical as possible. I don't think he liked that and he struggled to cope with that side of things. I think that made him look over his shoulder when the ball was coming to him and that was great for us because he had the ability to make Rangers tick. Arteta was perhaps a touch nervous, aware that we wouldn't hesitate to be physical with him so it put him off his stride a little. He is a really good footballer, though, and he has now matured and improved his physicality to be a dominant player in the English Premiership with Everton and that helped him get a move to Arsenal.

I played a few times in midfield in Old Firm games and it was enjoyable. There's a lot of responsibility there; you have to think fast and make sure you get your screening right across the park. You also have to hold your line so that it's difficult for the opposition to play through you.

Barry Ferguson was also in the midfield. He had good skill and was a really talented footballer. Barry had the ability to dominate games and Rangers looked to him for leadership on the pitch. He could be very niggly when he wanted to be. Rangers had many great technical players, such as Claudio Caniggia and Arthur Numan, but we had the upper hand over them physically, that was for sure.

On 7 December 2002, I scored after just nineteen seconds in a game at Ibrox. It's the quickest ever goal in an Old Firm game.

But we went on to lose 3–2. On 8 March 2003, we beat Rangers 1–0. Big John got yet another winning goal in an Old Firm game. It was also important for the fact it was six games since we had beaten them, albeit a few of the games ended in a draw.

Rangers did beat us a few times but I was never ever worried going into a game against them as time went by. I never felt we'd lose to them. When they had their Dutch contingent in season 2000–01, the likes of De Boer, Numan, Mols and Van Bronckhorst, that's when I was a little bit worried. They also had Jörg Albertz, Billy Dodds and Claudio Reyna at that time. That was back in the early days but we were always comfortable after that. I never, ever felt threatened by them after that. If we turned up, they were never going to beat us.

Having lost the league to Rangers in 2003, we were desperate for the first Old Firm game of the following season. It came on 4 October and we won 1–0. We had a few players missing through injury and our squad was depleted. I had to play at centre-half alongside Stan Varga. I was nervous about this, as it was a last minute decision and I didn't have a chance to train with Stan before it. It was a blessing to be nervous, as I didn't want to take any chances that day. Stan and I played well; we were solid. We came under a bit of pressure towards the end of the game but we handled it well. When I look back on that one, it gives me a real amount of satisfaction. I was usually very critical of myself but I was happy enough with my performance that afternoon. I didn't do everything right but, all things considered, it was a good day for me. Big John scored the winner.

The final Old Firm clash of the 2003–04 season came on 8 May 2004. It wasn't a classic but I scored what I consider to be my best career goal and I actually meant it. I scored the winner in injury time in a 1–0 win. It was a chip over Stefan Klos after I'd played a one-two with Henrik and it was my favourite goal against Rangers.

In many games, we had a huge advantage over them in terms of height. We had Bobo, Johan, Joos, Henrik, Big John, Stiliyan and me all in the penalty area and Rangers struggled to cope. On occasions, they had the likes of Michael Ball marking Bobo or Big John and there was a six-inch height difference. Set pieces are so vital and that has become more evident in the game in the past twenty years. In general, we weren't pretty to watch all the time, but we played to our strengths and we scored a helluva lot of goals from set pieces. I'm not being arrogant but we felt we could beat them going into every game.

That said, I'm sure Ronald De Boer went into the games with the same attitude and didn't feel intimidated by us. He would have felt his team had the quality to beat us. I can't ever remember going into an Old Firm game feeling that we were the underdog and that there was more than a fifty-per-cent chance we were going to lose. But I always knew we'd have to battle to get a result.

There was never anything handed to us on a plate because they had guys willing to fight for their jersey, guys like Craig Moore. He loved a battle. He used to be a bit naughty with his tackling, though. Playing against him suited me because I was taller than him and I always believed I'd do well against him. Amoruso was also a good enough player, solid. But he fancied himself and had a real arrogance about him. That was like a red rag to a bull for me. That gave me extra motivation. We also knew Henrik had the beating of him when it came to pace.

On the flip side, I think they had some players that struggled to make the grade there but who would constantly pander to the fans. Nacho Novo was a classic example of that. I was in his company one or twice and he was a nice enough guy, but I couldn't really stand Novo because of his antics. I didn't have a great deal of respect for him because he wasn't like a De Boer or Barry Ferguson, yet he strutted around as if he was every bit as important to the team as they were. That was ludicrous. On the park he'd clap the fans at every opportunity and I couldn't be bothered with that type of player. It used to annoy me. I know it's important to have a rapport with the fans but he took it too far. I'm sure the real Rangers fans could see through that type of behaviour.

Novo wouldn't have got near a Rangers jersey during Advocaat's time at the club. Yet, for all the quality they had at that time, they were powerless to stop us thrashing them 6–2. I know I've mentioned this game before but it feels good to mention it again. Rangers were the dominant side when I arrived in 2000 and we wanted to knock them out of the sky. Put them in their place. I think we achieved that with the 6–2 game.

That ninety minutes stands out more than anything else. It was Martin's first Old Firm game. Also, I even think now, when I look back, that it really was some achievement to score six against Rangers. In terms of my career at Celtic, that game was great. The goals I scored that day were vital. It gave me a huge psychological boost. Got the fans onside from the off and that was important to help me do the job I wanted to for Celtic. A player needs that support, especially goal-scorers who can be a bit fragile when they first join a new club and are desperate to do well.

The previous season, Celtic had finished twenty-one points behind Rangers but we now had real belief. The first twenty minutes were possibly the most frenetic I'd ever encountered. In that game, I was up against Lorenzo Amoruso and Bert Konterman. I found Amoruso to be a good motivation. I didn't him know personally but I just didn't like him. In terms of going out onto the pitch, I wanted to go out there and dominate him, show him who was boss. He was strong and aggressive. But I had it in my mind before that game that I wanted to get out onto the pitch and smash him around. Bert Konterman was his defensive partner that day, but he had just signed so we didn't know too much about him. He struggled a little bit with the physical side of things and I'm not sure he really liked that aspect of the game.

Subsequently, since he retired, I've found that Amoruso isn't the worst guy in the world. But I had that mindset that even though I didn't know any of the Rangers players, I just didn't like them. I think that's the way it had to be when you were out on the pitch playing against them. I just really enjoyed beating them. It was extra special because of the rivalry.

We respected them because they had some very good players but you can't have too much respect for any opposition. Winning personal battles on the pitch was a big part of my game as it was for most players. I used to think about how I was going to get the better of my direct opponent, to out-think, out-muscle and out-manoeuvre him. I couldn't go into that game half-hearted. That was how I went into every game against Rangers.

Considering what had gone on in the previous number of years, we had a pretty good record. I'm certainly proud of the record we had against Rangers during the period I was at Celtic. I think the balance of power shifted back to us. Indeed, Advocaat probably lost his job as Rangers manager because he could not get the better of Martin, despite the fact Sir David Murray was still chucking plenty of money at him to spend. Martin had money to spend but not on the same level as Rangers.

Rangers also built a brand new training complex in 2001 to give them splendid facilities. We were still at Barrowfield at that stage.

We also had that fantastic period of seven straight wins against them. That was a most enjoyable time.

I think we were well ahead of them by that stage and going into the game it was all about keeping the run going. That made it exciting for us and I thoroughly enjoyed any victory against

Rangers. Knowing I'd helped to make hundreds of thousands of people happy was extremely satisfying.

Rangers were at their strongest during my first season in Scotland in 2000. McLeish countered our system in his early period and managed to have a little bit of success. That was one of the reasons why we switched from 3-5-2 to a 4-4-2 at the start of the 2003–04 season. Looking back on the games, other than the 5–1 defeat at Ibrox, I can't remember Rangers ever battering us.

We weren't deluding ourselves by feeling we could beat them. We weren't arrogant. We were just better than them.

People in England criticise the Scottish game but they have no idea. Robbie Savage has added his name to the growing list of detractors. Robbie was outspoken as a player and it was part of his game to noise people on the pitch. To be fair to him, he used to do it well. He was a really good athlete and his game improved as he got older. He made a good career out of the game and is a better footballer than a lot of people gave him credit for. I met him off the pitch and he was actually very quiet. He now does a radio phone-in show and he's definitely not quiet on that. He is very opinionated and that's what the listeners like. I know he has been critical of Scottish football on the programme but he'd have a different opinion if he'd been fortunate enough to get the chance to play for Celtic or Rangers. Until you actually do, then you just have no idea what it means and what it's about.

It's also about what the whole package playing for Celtic brings. Celtic have an unbelievable number of fans around the world. It is truly incredible. They have supporters' clubs all over the world, especially in America, Canada and Australia. We used to play pre-season games in London, against the likes of Fulham and Queens Park Rangers, and we'd have more than 15,000 fans at the game. It really was unbelievable. The Celtic supporters are just amazing. I genuinely believe they are more passionate than any other fans in the world. Now, of course, Manchester United, Real Madrid and Barcelona fans will dispute that. But I just feel Celtic fans are incredible. They treated me well and they still do. Whenever I'm back up in Glasgow, they love to reminisce. They treat former players very well, and I'm proud to have played for their club and to have helped bring success to Celtic Park. Rangers were the dominant side when Martin arrived in the summer of 2000 but we changed things and we won three titles and put Celtic back on the map in European football, which was also very important.

Celtic Football Club is like no other club I've played for. I still feel so much for the club, its fans and the people who work there and my former team-mates. I had the greatest five years of my life in Glasgow playing for Celtic under Martin O'Neill and it's something I will always treasure.

11

FINAL ANALYSIS –
THE ROAD TO SEVILLE

Our run to the UEFA Cup Final in 2003 was memorable. It was a rollercoaster ride from start to finish with more highs than lows as we went all the way to the final in Seville on 21 May. Ultimately, we lost the final to Porto and that defeat still rankles with me to this day. I badly wanted to win that European trophy, create another piece of history for Celtic Football Club.

It all started with a win against Lithuanian minnows FK Suduva. To be honest, we went into that tie still feeling a bit depressed after losing to FC Basel in the Champions League qualifier, but we emerged victorious thanks to a 8–1 victory at Parkhead in the first leg. Henrik scored a hat-trick that night to equal Ally McCoist's record of twenty-one goals scored in European competition with a Scottish club. Stiliyan Petrov, Paul Lambert, John Hartson, Joos Valgaeren and I were the other scorers.

I didn't play in the return game as we had an Old Firm match three days later. The manager rested a few others as well, including Henrik, Neil Lennon and Bobo Baldé. But I didn't travel over for the game, which we won 2–0. David Fernandez and Alan Thompson scored the goals.

We were drawn against Blackburn the next day and it was immediately tagged the 'Battle of Britain'. The Blackburn tie was one that really excited me for obvious reasons. I suppose, in many ways, it was the draw I wanted. On a personal level, going back to play against my old club added to it all. The guys were excited to be playing an English side in a competitive competition. It was the first time any side of Martin O'Neill's had played against an English team in a competitive game and we felt ready for it. I had enjoyed many good times at Blackburn when I was a player and I was looking forward to going back there for the first time since I left Ewood Park three years earlier.

The first leg at Celtic Park finished with a narrow 1–0 victory. The team didn't play anywhere near what we were capable of on the night. In terms of possession, Blackburn absolutely murdered us. To be fair to them, they had some excellent players all over the pitch. The experienced Brad Friedel was their goalkeeper and they had a strike partnership of Andy Cole and Dwight Yorke. They also had Damien Duff on the left wing. He was young at the time and tipped to become one of the best left-sided attacking players in the English game. Duff was coming up through the ranks when I was at Blackburn and was a wonderful prospect. He'd just broken into the first team as I was moving on. He has gone on to have a fantastic career. He moved to Chelsea the following year for a fee around £17 million. Clearly, Blackburn looked to him to get them going, be an out-ball for them, get running at the full-back and get crosses into the box. He was expected to put our players on the back foot. But Didier Agathe played right-back in both games and handled him superbly. Duff just couldn't get away from Didier.

For all the possession Blackburn had, they didn't create too many chances. We just couldn't get a foothold on the game and we had one chance in the first half when Friedel pulled off a wonderful save to deny Stan. We gave Blackburn far too much time and room on the ball. Martin let us know it wasn't acceptable and we improved in the second half. We got at them more and we managed to come away with a 1–0 victory when Henrik popped up to score the winner with six minutes remaining. That was such an important goal. John Hartson came on as a sub and he got on the end of a Thommo corner. Friedel parried the header out but Henrik was there to get it over the line. That was Henrik's twenty-second goal for Celtic in European competition and that made him the record scorer.

Blackburn were managed by Graeme Souness at that time and his history as Rangers' manager was always going to add an extra edge to the tie. Before the first leg, he tried to play it down as some kind of Mickey Mouse encounter and claimed he couldn't care less about the tie, as the only thing that concerned him was keeping his team in the Premiership. I'm not quite sure I believed him on that one. I'm not sure he believed it himself. He wanted to beat Celtic, of course he did. He also stated that Henrik still had to prove himself at the top level. Henrik certainly delivered a reply to him on that front over the two legs.

After we won 1–0 at Celtic Park, Souness came out with the provocative statement saying that the game had been men against boys. In my opinion, my former team-mate Garry Flitcroft rivalled his manager with his ludicrous post-match comments that were also extremely critical of us. We kept our own counsel in the dressing room. To a Celtic player, it was wonderful motivation and we loved it. I personally felt great because if ever I knew we were going to win a game, it was this return leg. We hadn't played well in the first leg, we all knew that and we accepted it. We knew we were better than them, player for player, and now they had given us an unbelievable tool to use against them. We wanted to ram it down their throats. Personally, I felt strange to have these feelings because of my affection for Blackburn and fond memories from my time there. But I still felt the comments about our team deserved to be punished.

Garry was a good player and a decent guy. I was surprised at his comments, to say the least. We didn't need any extra motivation but, naturally, those comments wound us up. Bearing in mind Blackburn lost the game, it didn't make sense for their camp to say such things. But there must have been real confidence within their dressing room that they'd beat us comfortably at their place. It seemed they totally underestimated us, which I found quite incredible, really. They must have known we had some very good players in our team, and that we could play a bit and also handle ourselves. Maybe they thought because we were from the SPL that it would be easy enough for them; I'm not sure. I always enjoyed playing against English sides, whether it be a friendly, a testimonial or a competitive game. I just liked to show people we were a good team and Scottish football deserved credit for having talented players within its set-up.

Had we been playing in the Premiership during that period, we would have been a top four side – without any doubt.

During the period of Martin's time there, the club did pursue their wish to get into the Premiership but too many clubs didn't want us. I would have loved to play in the Premiership with Celtic. We would have been more than capable of beating any side on our day.

I remember getting off the bus at Ewood Park and the Celtic fans were there banging on it, helping to fire us up, not that we needed any assistance on that front. I think the Celtic fans had taken up every seat in the Darwen End and made it feel almost like a home game. There were thousands of Celtic fans there and the atmosphere was electric. It didn't get much better than this. The game took care of itself.

At Ewood Park in the second leg, we showed what we were capable of. It was a rout. Martin changed the tactics for that game and played me deeper. John Hartson and Henrik played up front, Stiliyan and Lenny were the holding midfielders and I played in the hole in behind the front two.

My job on the defensive side was probably more important than the offensive. In the first leg, Blackburn dominated possession and that was mainly down to former Rangers midfielder Tugay. He was a top player. The idea was to not let Tugay get into his stride and dictate the game – which was a tough task.

Tugay made them tick and I was given the job of shackling him. As soon as he got the ball, I was to get on top of him, make it as uncomfortable for him as possible, and not give him time to get his head up and pick passes. In general, I managed to do that.

We scored fairly early. I played a ball round a corner into Henrik's path. A slight slip from Craig Short allowed Henrik some extra time on the ball. Then he was in on goal and in typical Larsson fashion, he sold Brad Friedel and lifted it over him. From then on, we were firmly in the driving seat as they would have had to score three to go through. From our point of view, we just had to work hard and concentrate to see the game through.

We made it 2–0 in the sixty-eighth minute when I made a run to the front post to get on the end of a corner from Stiliyan and I headed neatly past Friedel. I enjoyed the goal but didn't want to celebrate too much. The people of Blackburn had always been good to me and I certainly didn't want to rub their noses in it when they were clearly having such a tough night.

So, we won. And we won comfortably. Truth be told, we could have defeated them by four or five at Ewood. It was a great feeling to knock them out after their ill-judged comments from the first leg. It was an unusual thing for any player or manager to say such inflammatory things when a European tie is only at the halfway stage. First of all, you want the people who have said things to get egg on their face and prove beyond any doubt that what they said was utter nonsense. It's nothing personal towards them – it would be the same if the tables were reversed. But Blackburn was a club always close to my heart and I felt a little tinge of regret for the Rovers fans and people such as Robert Coar, Keith Lee and the Walker family. Blackburn will always be a great club to me.

Souness was a good manager and was successful at Blackburn. He won a major trophy with them. It was very sweet for the Celtic fans to win this tie and was also one up for Scottish football. We wanted to do well for ourselves as a football club but we also wanted to show we could play and show we were a good team. But we were never ones for shouting from the rooftops because, on another day, Blackburn could have beaten us. But there always seemed to be this arrogance down south about Celtic and Rangers not being good enough to mix it in English company. This perception was totally unfounded and incredibly arrogant.

We then came up against Celta Vigo. We won 1–0 at home and lost 2–1 away. Big John got that vital goal over there for us.

In the build-up to the first leg, it was reported in the newspapers that Miguel Lotina, the Vigo coach, said that his team should defeat us as we just ran about like headless chickens. It was like déjà vu. Again, that kind of thing just motivated us and made it nice to ram his stupid comments down his throat. It was such a silly thing to say. People talk about mind-games and I'm not sure whether people take that seriously or not. But comments made by the likes of Souness, Flitcroft and Lotina were used as a tool against them. I'm not sure it made us play better but we went out onto the pitch as concentrated as you can be to get the right result. Celta Vigo had some good technical players – a couple of good wingers – and they played well at Celtic Park, but we deserved just to edge the tie.

We knew it would be difficult to get the result in Spain but we had something to hold on to. After conceding an early goal, we equalised through a superb strike from Big John. He turned his marker at the edge of the box and struck a low shot into the corner of the goal. In the second half, we played a little bit deep defensively. They scored again to lead 2–1 and needed just one more goal to go through, but we managed to see it out fairly comfortably. It was a huge result against a more than decent team.

Celtic is a club that has won the European Cup and not many clubs can lay claim to that. But we knew we couldn't live in the past. When I joined Celtic, the club hadn't performed too well in Europe so the challenge for us was to improve that record and show we could compete. Defeating Celta Vigo was another indication that we were definitely on the right road.

The victory in that tie meant Celtic would be playing in Europe after Christmas for the first time in twenty-three years. We played Stuttgart in the next round in February 2003. The first leg was at Parkhead and we had to play without Henrik, who had fractured his cheekbone. It's fair to say the players were concerned about Henrik's absence going into the game. Big John was also suspended so Shaun Maloney partnered me up front.

Early on in the game, Stuttgart were reduced to ten men when referee Pierluigi Collina booked Marcelo Bordon for bringing down Stiliyan as he ran in on goal. But the German side still took the lead through Kevin Kurányi. Paul Lambert equalised and Shaun put us in front just before half-time. Stiliyan made it 3–1 when he scored from a tight angle to give us a bit of a cushion for the next game.

We went over for the return leg and there was a terrific atmosphere in the Gottlieb Daimler Stadium. Bonnie Tyler sang 'Holding Out for a Hero' on the pitch before kick-off and that got the adrenalin pumping. As ever, the Celtic fans had travelled in huge numbers to support us. Didier was amazing that night and played a part in the first goal, an excellent diving header from Thommo. He then sprinted fifty yards down the right wing and his cut back found me. I gratefully accepted to make it 2–0. It meant Stuttgart had to score five to win the tie. To their credit, Stuttgart never gave up and went 3–2 ahead through goals from Christian Tiffert, Aleksandr Hleb and Michael Mutzel. They put us under incredible pressure in the final few minutes but we held out. It was an outstanding achievement to knock out a side of that calibre with players such as Hleb and Krassi Balakov. In Germany that night, I played a more with-drawn role similar to the one I'd played in the away leg at Blackburn. We had the lead and played accordingly.

It was about this time that going all the way to the final became a reality for us and the word 'Seville' was mentioned on more than a few occasions. But we had to negotiate our way past Liverpool in the quarter-final – another 'Battle of Britain'.

We drew 1–1 at Celtic Park. We battered Liverpool in the first few minutes and when you talk about a whirlwind start, it was definitely one of them. The atmosphere was incredible. Henrik gave us the lead but then they equalised through Emile Heskey. We were disappointed not to have won that night but we didn't rule ourselves out. Although our European record away from home wasn't great we still had performed well in the UEFA competition. We were confident we could get a result, albeit they were now favourites for the tie.

Unfortunately for me, Bobo Baldé broke my wrist at Hampden in the League Cup Final so I missed the return leg at Anfield. I was devastated. Not that I was missed. We deservedly won the game 2–0. I was delighted for the lads, they played ever so well. We scored a goal in each half. Thommo scored a lovely goal from a free-kick, then Big John rattled in an incredible strike from twenty-five yards. We could have won by more, truth be told. To defeat a side with Stevie Gerrard, Michael Owen and

Didi Hamann in it spoke volumes for us and the capabilities we had as a group.

After the game, the players didn't speak first and foremost about the result; they spoke about Martin's pre-match team-talk. By all accounts, it got the hairs on the back of the neck standing up, a real rousing delivery.

I wasn't in the dressing room that night but I could imagine it. When Martin spoke, you listened. He was very good at motivating players. You left the dressing room wanting to win for him and not let him down. He made general, sensible comments. The players responded to him. We were aware of our roles within the team and he kept things simple. In general, I can't really remember him saying things that didn't have foundation. He knew what made players tick and he had a knack for getting the best out of them. He gave you confidence. But you had to earn plaudits from him. He didn't lavish praise on players for the sake of it. But he was complimentary if you performed well. If you didn't play well, he would certainly let you know about it. In terms of me personally, Martin was very fair. That was all I asked. I knew myself if I wasn't playing well. I was always very self-critical.

Beating Liverpool was also good for the players who had played down south, like myself, and then moved to Celtic. Guys such as Lenny and Thommo loved it. And they both played significant parts in that European run.

In terms of a defensive midfielder, there's been few better than Lenny. He was a difficult opponent when we played against each other in England so it was a good to become team-mates at Celtic. He has a tremendous will to win and was really verbal when it came to it. He was never afraid to speak his mind and he sometimes said some strong words. During games and at half-time he was so passionate when it came to sorting things out.

On a personal note, Lenny would sometimes criticise me for not holding the ball up properly, even when he wrapped the ball about eighty miles an hour round my neck. He would then scream at me to get a hold of it. It really got on the nerves of a lot of our players. Some of them never agreed with his comments and he'd annoy a lot of them. He used to annoy me too, but I tried not to get involved with him. I'd mainly be saying to myself, 'Just concentrate on your own game.' If I did have a go at him, I'd try to be jocular and maybe tease him about his weight. I enjoyed a few cracking barneys with Lenny on the pitch. He didn't single any player out; he just used to moan at everybody. So, at least he was consistent.

He was always on the edge and that added to his game. I thought he was a good runner, fit and quick. But he really wasn't in any way attack-minded, although he knew his job to the letter and was very selfless. He wasn't worried about scoring goals. In fact, it amazed me that any midfielder wouldn't be itching to get forward and try and nick a goal here and there. But Neil enjoyed sitting there and protecting the defence. He would drive others on around him and perform really well in big games.

He had to endure a lot from punters because of his background and although he was volatile, underneath it all he is really intelligent and charming. He is a really nice person and has a really good heart. He was great in the dressing room and there was never a dull moment when he was around. He is a true leader in every sense of the word and it was a pleasure to play with him.

Thommo could play wide or come in for one. He had a lovely left foot and great balance and could pick a pass, eye-of-the-needle style. He performed very well in big games and although I know he did get sent off against Rangers a few times, that was mainly down to wearing his heart on his sleeve rather than anything malicious. He also scored big goals and the one I remember most was when he cut inside onto his right foot and bent it around Stefan Klos.

He had a fantastic attitude and was a conscientious trainer. He'd be in the gym most days. He also hit lovely free-kicks and corner-kicks and was right up there with the best when it came to that. I scored quite a few goals from his deliveries. He also put in a terrific defensive shift for the team and loved a tackle. He often played the left wing-back role for Celtic and that was a bloody hard position to play. Alan had the ability to carry that position well and he was well respected and rated by the fans. Like Lenny, he did have the capacity to chuck the toys out of the pram in training. But so did we all.

In the semi-final, we would play Boavista, Porto or Lazio. We were paired with Boavista and were happy enough with that draw. It was the best we could have had in the semi-final stage but weren't taking anything for granted. I missed the first leg. Boavista were a stuffy side but were very resilient, not your typical Portuguese side, like a Porto or Benfica. They took the lead when big Joos scored an own goal. Henrik equalised but then missed a penalty, and a 1–1 draw wasn't a great result in the context of things. We were well fancied to win the first leg but, on the other hand, it wasn't a disaster.

Psychologically, the game was evenly balanced. We had to score and they had to keep a clean sheet. But if they sat in, with the set-piece threat we had, we were confident of scoring against anybody. I came on as a sub in the return leg. It was my first game back after my broken wrist and I played with a plaster cast.

We got the right result and it was terrific. It wasn't a classic game over there. Both sides created a few half-chances but nothing major. The stadium was under construction and that made the atmosphere a little bit strange as no fans were allowed behind one of the goals – the end that Henrik scored the winner at. It didn't really seem like a semi-final, truth be told, but Henrik came up trumps once again for us twelve minutes from time. I had a part in the goal when I played it off the runner into Henrik and it was a strange finish. He is the only player I know who would have scored that goal as most players would have waited for the ball to drop perfectly. But he had such quickness of mind. He had to get his shot off quick and some guys may have taken too long and tried to side-foot it or cut it back onto their right foot. But Henrik struck it, sort of like a toe-scoop, if that makes sense. Their keeper, Ricardo, got a hand to it and the ball seemed to take forever to get over the line. They tried to get back at us but it wasn't frenetic. It was a helluva feeling to win the game and know we were in the UEFA Cup Final.

Bearing in mind that it all started with the big disappointment of losing to FC Basel in the Champions League qualifier, we got things going and beat some good sides to go all the way and meet Porto.

It might sound boring, but all I thought about going into the final against Porto was that the preparation was going to be as good as it could be and that we'd win the game. I tried not to get bogged down with tickets and arrangements for people. It was hard to avoid that but I didn't want any distractions. My family was going to the game, which was great, but it was the match itself that ultimately mattered. Beating Porto was everything.

The run towards the final was terrific. So many highlights. The things I liked about the European games were the dark nights and the floodlights. I loved the night-time games – there was something special about them. And the fans spurred us on, made the club exceptional. Looking back on my career, the fans were great. If I could pick ten of my favourite games in my career then the majority would be the European games for Celtic.

That was one of the many great things about playing for Celtic;

the fans were always there in great numbers, no matter where we played. When you run out at Anfield or Ewood Park and you see and hear 10,000 of your fans getting right into it, then it helps you respond, no doubt. Much better to have that than to play in front of a handful of travelling fans. It was also the same when we played in testimonial games. We had 15,000 down for a game that Manchester United put on for Ryan Giggs. There was nothing to compare to the Celtic fans. They are a special bunch. Even in the testimonial games, your adrenalin would be going through the roof. The older I got, the more I appreciated it. I really loved it.

I enjoyed the build-up to the big games. My routine was repetitive. I always used to eat tons of food the night before the game, stuff like roast dinners, spaghetti bolognese and lasagne, and loads of fruit. I'd then drink loads of coffee on the day of the game – in between frequent visits to the toilet. I don't know if having all that caffeine in my system was good for me or not. I was certainly never sleepy, though.

I used to spend a lot of time in the company of John Robertson and Steve Walford, sitting around chewing the fat. We'd speak a little bit about the game, our opponents and the like. I also used to say to him, 'Listen, Robbo, I don't fancy our chances tonight. I think we're going to get pumped.' It became a ritual. Robbo used to get worried if I didn't say to him on the day of a game that we were going to get pumped. He'd have a concerned look on his face and then it would disappear when I said the words he wanted to hear. He didn't like it if I was ultra-positive.

John was one of my idols. Him and Steve Walford had a huge influence on me and the other players. Both of them liked a drink and a cigarette and a laugh. But they were serious when they needed to be. They made sure the dressing room was a happy place and they were key to the success we achieved at

Celtic. I'm sure Martin would be the first to admit that. People talk about Martin being a great manager, and he is, but both John and Steve also had a positive influence. The three of them worked well as a team. John and Steve were the link between the players and Martin. Martin was a bit more aloof because he was the manager.

John is also a very modest man, bearing in mind the success he had as a player and the fact he scored the winning goal in a European Cup Final for Nottingham Forest. He only used to remind us of it when some of his former Forest team-mates came up to Glasgow to see him. When he had a drink or two, he would say he had a sore back from lifting the European Cup. I don't think anybody ever begrudged him that.

My five years at Celtic were the best of my career and much of that is down to John and Steve. They treated us like adults, treated us normally. If we gave them everything we had, they would recognise that. We'd be given an extra day off here and there, things like that. They treated us the way every footballer wants to be treated. They really trusted the senior players and we never abused that trust.

Steve would take most of the training. Martin and John would analyse from the side. Martin would also sometimes take a session.

If I had to compare Martin to any other manager I worked with, then it would have to be Kenny Dalglish. Both of them backed their players to the hilt. Even after a bad performance, they'd face the media and they would carry the can when they shouldn't have. I think every player would take that. We respected that in the dressing room at Blackburn and Celtic. I didn't agree with everything Martin said but he was very fair. And fairness is all you ask for.

If Martin was unhappy with things, then Robbo and Wally were there to lift the players, get things going again. They were all highly intelligent people and knew their jobs. They were great to work for.

I'd try to get a sleep on the afternoon of a night game and then have a coffee with Robbo and Wally before we got on the coach. Again, this was a ritual we had as we always used to stay at a hotel before home games and away games. It was just about relaxing with them. They are both good people, funny people. We'd be thinking about the game, sometimes too much, and this was a chance to switch off for twenty minutes. Robbo and Wally were good at sensing that and we spoke about different things to help us get away from the game. It was our own little ritual, part of our routine.

Routines, to be honest, are nonsensical in reality. But I, like a lot of sportsmen and sportswomen I know, have them. I mean, you lose games but you rarely change a routine. I'd try to put my strip on the same way and, for our home games, I'd warm up on the same area of the pitch, do my stretching. All silly stuff, really. I never liked heavy, heavy warm-ups. And I didn't like big, structured warm-ups when you were told to do lots of sprints. I felt it was best to save that energy for the game. But I did think it was important to stretch well and make sure I felt nice and loose. As I got older, I also used to try not to do any shooting before games. I remember warming-up for Blackburn at West Ham and in the shooting practice, I hit a screamer from twenty-five yards that rocketed into the top corner. What a strike it was. That gave me a good feeling going into the game, but then I went out and had an absolute shocker. I was rotten. From that moment on, I decided not to do any shooting in the warm-up and it stayed with me for the rest of my career. I just wanted to stretch and make sure I had a feel of the ball, get my touch in. It was important to me to make sure my touch was good because that gave me confidence.

Steve Walford used to leave the players to their own devices, in many respects. He would put on a small, structured warm-up and then let the players get on with it. Some players like to do runs. For instance, Thommo used to like to run across the box and really get his legs going. Bobo was the same with runs and getting his headers in. I was never fast but fitness was a big thing for me. I had to feel fit going out onto the pitch. That's why I just wanted to be loose and stretched. Wally treated us like adults but some other coaches insisted on doing a fixed routine. But every player is different; I was an adult and knew what was best for me.

One game that sticks in my mind because of the warm-up is when we played against Artmedia Bratislava in a Champions League qualifier and it was Gordon Strachan's first game in charge. We trained in the morning, in boiling hot weather, and the players lost a lot of fluids. The warm-up was over the top, which is why it sticks out in my mind. I really doubted the sanity of it all – I thought it was ridiculous. It was a structured warm-up but the players didn't feel good. Whether we lost 5–0 because of that, I don't know. But I know I had doubts about whether or not I would have the energy to last the game. I'm sure many of the players felt the same. As it happened, I was stretchered off with a cheekbone injury after seven minutes.

On the team bus to games, I enjoyed a good laugh, although it was never outrageous stuff. Well, not usually. It was good to switch off and not become too obsessed with the game that was a couple of hours away. Jackie McNamara, Lenny, Thommo and Big John were all up for a laugh but other guys were already in the 'zone', if you want to call it that, and were best left alone.

Joos Valgaeren certainly wanted me to leave him alone at times. Probably at all times! When Joos first came to the club, I shared a room with him. He was a nice guy and superb for us, instrumental in the treble success. He was a tough, uncompromising defender but he didn't really understand my sense of humour.

On the morning of games, I'd wake up and say to Joos I had a bad feeling about the game and that we were going to get pumped. Joos used to get very annoyed at me. He'd shout back, 'Shut up, Sutton.' He never once called me Chris or Sutty – it was always Sutton. It was all part of my ritual. I suppose the Belgians have never been known for their sense of humour. After a short period of time, I ended up rooming on my own.

Joos threatened to half me and so did many of the lads. Jackie, Thommo, Olivier Tébily, Stan Varga, Lenny, Johan, Magnus Hedman and even nice guy Lubo Moravcík – all had had enough of me at one stage or another and wanted a go. Stiliyan threatened to do me in in training one day because he'd had enough.

Bobo Baldé actually did do me one day in the dressing room. Yet, for once, I was actually the innocent party. We were back at Celtic Park after a morning training session and Stiliyan was having a go at Bobo for certain elements of his performance. Bobo told Stiliyan to stop or else he was going to 'sort him out'. But Stiliyan continued with his criticism. Bobo then attacked Stiliyan and I tried to intervene and prevent the altercation from becoming really serious because I genuinely thought Bobo was going to hurt Stiliyan. I tried to pull Bobo away from him but Bobo just picked me up and threw me across the dressing room and I landed in a locker.

Then there was the time when we were on pre-season in New York one summer. I was winding up Magnus Hedman so he punched me in the ribs and stormed out of the cab we were sharing.

I was just having a laugh but sometimes people didn't understand my sense of humour! Basically, I used to like a bit of confrontation. It never bothered me. There's nothing wrong with a good argument. And I've never been one for holding grudges. Most of these instances were wind-ups and quickly forgotten. But it was never my fault! We all pulled in the same direction.

We were definitely all pulling in the same direction on the

night of the UEFA Cup Final. Unfortunately, our best wasn't good enough.

It was a big build-up to the game. I was worried about whether or not I'd be allowed to play. I still had my plaster cast on and I wasn't sure about it. The UEFA rule, I believe, was that it was up to the matchday referee if he was comfortable enough with the support I had on my wrist. Along with the Celtic medical staff, I went to see Lubos Michels of Slovakia on the day before the game to get his opinion and he was absolutely fine about it. I was wary going to meet him and feared the worst. But I was delighted he said I was ok to wear it. It was a big relief.

It was a really warm evening in Seville. I'm not saying that was an advantage to the Porto players but it certainly wouldn't have done them any harm. Ultimately, we lost the game because we weren't good enough on the night. We didn't deserve to win the final and that was extremely disappointing. Yes, they dived and they did waste time. But we knew all of that was coming. It's all part of the game – I accept that – but it wasn't nice to be on the end of all that and we felt aggrieved. However, we can't use any of that as an excuse.

We conceded a goal just before half-time. Derlei scored and it was a crushing blow. Then there was a rammy at half-time going up the tunnel. I think Thommo and Bobo were involved with José Mourinho. I was probably in the dressing room by that point. Believe it or not, I wasn't one for getting involved. I tried my best to keep myself to myself, thinking about my own game. It was the same when arguments were raging on in the dressing room at half-time during games. Some of the lads would be going at it against each other but I was concentrating on making sure I was right for the second half. Don't get me wrong, in a dressing room you do need players, at times, to point the finger and see what comes of it. I would join in a discussion if I felt my point of view would be useful. I think you need to be a right good player to dish it out. I preferred the role of being a counter-puncher in that respect. I didn't mind that role and, to be honest, I quite liked it.

I was more one to offer encouragement. If a player tried a pass and it didn't come off, I'd be at them to keep trying, not to be afraid to try it again. There's nothing worse than a player being on the pitch when he's short of confidence and afraid to try things. Or I'd tell a team-mate to give me the ball earlier, not to hold onto it for too long. That was maybe when I'd give a blast here and there on the pitch. Most of the guys in the Celtic team knew how to play the game, but now and again they just needed to be pointed in the right direction.

Henrik was phenomenal in the final with the goals he scored to get us back into the game at 1–1 and then 2–2. His second goal – a header – was incredible. We made mistakes and Bobo's red card in extra time had a bearing on proceedings. We couldn't hold out and Derlei scored in the 114th minute to make it 3–2. Could I have played better? Yeah, I could have played better. I always analysed my performances and ninety-nine times out of 100 I would be critical. I can't really remember ever coming off the pitch and feeling totally satisfied. I was probably far too picky but that's the way I was. And that's the way I felt in Seville. I don't think there was too much wrong with my performance that evening but I didn't influence the game as much as I would have liked to.

Big John got injured a few weeks before the final so I played up front with Henrik. It's the position I wanted to play in. Yes, I played in deeper roles and I didn't mind the withdrawn role that I sometimes had to play. But I felt playing up top was my best position and it's where I wanted to be. When I played with Henrik, I felt I could be really effective and there were games when it didn't matter who we were playing against – I just felt we could murder defenders when we were both on our game.

We could do little movements, play little balls round corners. I knew where he would go, I knew where he wanted the ball and I knew he wanted to be in and around me. I was limited to what I could do on the pitch, but he knew my limitations and what suited me; he knew my game inside out. When I look back on my time at Celtic, the games I really enjoyed were the ones I played right up top with Henrik.

Porto were a good side and I was up against Ricardo Carvalho and Jorge Costa. They were both good players. Costa was more physical and Carvalho was a lovely defensive footballer. But Henrik got the better of both of them that night. His second goal was truly incredible. To score with a header from that angle and the way he had to adjust his body shape was unbelievable.

Before the game, Martin had said to us all not to let this chance pass us by and to make sure we came off the pitch as winners. Yes, it was a good achievement to reach a European final but we wanted to win it. We didn't go to Seville with the attitude that we'd be satisfied to put on a decent show but not win the Cup.

The post-match party in Seville was a disaster, really. When we got back to the hotel, I felt nothing but disappointment. The players and management were upset. People were crying; my kids were also in tears. We were all so disappointed. We lost to a good side but we could have beaten them. They went on to win the Champions League the following season but I felt we had it in us to beat them that night in Seville. We could beat any side on our day but, unfortunately, they made fewer mistakes than we did.

Technically, they were good and had some talented flair players. Deco was a big influence on the game. Yet, at no point during the game did I feel we were right out of it. It wasn't like when we played Barcelona in the Nou Camp and we got a draw and you think to yourself, 'How the hell did we manage that?' I never felt Porto were much better than us, far from it. When we got back to 2–2, I felt we had a spell in the game that would see us win it. But a man down in extra-time and a goal down left us with the best-case scenario of a penalty shoot-out. It just wasn't to be.

My UEFA Cup medal is in the house, along with the rest of them. It was a great occasion and I do remember it fondly. We knocked out some good sides to get there.

I think the UEFA Cup was taken seriously then. Now, that doesn't seem to happen in the Europa League until the quarter-final or semi-final stage. Personally, I don't like the new format. I prefer the old system of straight knock-out but I know the new system generates money for the clubs and more sponsorship. The Champions League still has the glamour and an edge to it that the Europa League doesn't. That said, there would be nothing wrong with winning it, that's for sure.

My abiding thoughts on the final are still the same. Real disappointment. And I felt sorry for certain people.

I felt for Henrik. His performance that night was brilliant and the important goals he scored for us, not just in the UEFA competition that season but in the big games over and over again, meant that he certainly deserved to win a European trophy. No one was more pleased than me when he won the Champions League with Barcelona in 2006.

I was gutted for Martin, Wally and Robbo, as well. This was really driven home when I saw them after the game, how unselfish they were when they were hurting as much as anybody. But they were all more devastated for us. I could see it in their eyes. With all the hard work they had put into our team, they certainly didn't deserve to lose.

As for the Celtic fans, I can't think of another sporting occasion in my lifetime where a club side has taken so many fans to another country for a final. It's been said that more than 80,000

Celtic fans were in Seville that week. The atmosphere was just incredible. When I was at Celtic, wherever I travelled, the fans turned up in huge numbers but this was exceptional.

Driving to the stadium is something I will never ever forget. They looked so happy and it was a big disappointment we didn't win the trophy for them. It would have been great to help Celtic win another major European trophy.

12

ME, HENRIK AND MARTIN –
A MATCH MADE IN SEVEN

There was an incredible determination to win the title in 2004. The 2003 season was memorable in so many ways but it was very painful at the end when we finished with no trophies. The 2004 season was also to be Henrik's last at Celtic and we wanted his seven-year association to end in the best possible way for him. He got that as we won the SPL and Scottish Cup to complete a well-deserved double.

The games against Rangers were always going to be crucial and we won the four Old Firm league derbies, which was an incredible achievement. It was extremely satisfying to do the whitewash over them.

I played a few positions that season, including centre-half in a 1–0 win against Rangers in the first Old Firm game. I got a lot of satisfaction from the way I played that day. I only found out late that I was going to be playing in that role alongside Stan Varga and I didn't have time to practise. Going to Ibrox to play was always a tough test but I was especially apprehensive going into that one. Maybe, though, it made me concentrate more and, on the day, I made sure I didn't do anything silly and didn't take any chances. I kept it basic, made sure I marked the right side. No stepovers from me that day. I really enjoyed that game.

The final victory against Rangers in that campaign came on

8 May 2004 at Ibrox and I scored an injury-time winner in a 1–0 victory. David Marshall sent the ball long and I got up to flick it on to Henrik. He then gave me the return pass. Stefan Klos was a few yards off his line and I chipped it over him for a goal I was very proud of. It gave me enormous satisfaction. It was lovely to rub Rangers' noses right in it. Absolutely lovely. You had to enjoy those moments when they came around. That's just the way it is.

We won twenty-four games on the spin in the league that season. That was an incredible achievement. We were unstoppable in the domestic game, really. It's such a difficult thing to do, to keep churning out victory after victory. But we managed it and played with some style and conviction.

I played a number of games in midfield and was manoeuvred about a little bit during the course of the campaign. I scored twenty-eight goals and managed to get a couple of hat-tricks that season, including one against Dundee United and then another a week later against Kilmarnock. I felt my form was pretty strong, considering where I was playing. I quite enjoyed my role of drifting into the box with well-timed runs, arriving late, losing my marker and finding a bit of space. In terms of goal-scoring, it was my best season at Celtic, strangely enough.

My consistency was recognised by my fellow professionals and I was voted the 2004 PFA Player of the Year. It was the greatest accolade for me, winning an award voted on by fellow players.

We won the Scottish Cup in May with a 3–1 win over Dunfermline at Hampden. Henrik scored a double and Stiliyan got the other.

I was pleased for Henrik that season. It was nice way for him to bring his career at Celtic to an end. As a player, you want to do well for yourself and your club, but there was a feeling in the dressing room that we also wanted to do well for Henrik, to make sure he left with another SPL medal in his pocket. He, of course, signed for Barcelona; the deal was done and dusted during the summer of 2004 when he was at the European Championships with Sweden. I think Barcelona had registered an interest in him a while before that but I don't know if he had it in the bag for a while or not. Certainly, many, many teams tried to get him and no wonder. The chance to sign Henrik on a Bosman? It was a no-brainer.

Knowing Henrik was going to leave didn't make me happy. I didn't want him to go. I felt the same as the Celtic supporters in that respect. None of the players wanted him to leave. Martin, Robbo and Wally didn't want him to leave. But he'd been at the club for seven years and given excellent service. He wasn't a normal footballer; he could do extraordinary things. The question was asked how would we replace him and the answer was very straightforward in my opinion. We couldn't replace him. Celtic didn't have the spending power to buy someone who could fill his boots. That was a fact.

I didn't feel good about him leaving. I was sorry to see him go. It was always at the back of my mind that he was leaving. And, I suppose, it was quite depressing. Given the number of times the players asked him to stay, he was probably sick of us all. But nobody could begrudge him the move to Barcelona. Any of the other players in the dressing room would have loved a move like that. He had a farewell game against Seville at a packed Parkhead and I felt horrendous that night, to be honest, knowing that was the last time he'd step on that turf and the last time I'd partner him. His departure left a big, big void. I was thrilled for him when he won the Champions League with Barca in 2006 with a win against Arsenal. Like the true great he is, he came off the bench and changed the game.

After his departure, I asked myself what was going to happen to our team and how we would cope without him. We were talking about, arguably, the greatest player the club has ever had. I know Jimmy Johnstone was voted 'The Greatest Ever Celtic Player'. I hadn't seen Jinky play live, just old footage, but he made the game look so easy. I can only say that after playing and training with Henrik for years, he was the greatest footballer I played on a pitch with. He had everything. My stomach actually still sinks when I think about it. I enjoyed playing in the same side as him more than any other footballer.

I'd been fortunate enough to play with good strikers during my career in the English Premiership and I believe Henrik would have scored more goals than any of them. Had he gone to England and played there for a few seasons with one of the top clubs, I'm sure he would have broken goal-scoring records.

When he was thirty-six, he signed for Manchester United for a couple of months and was outstanding. You need to be a top player to go there and he fitted into Sir Alex Ferguson's structure with ease. Sir Alex always seemed to rate Henrik and wanted to sign him on a couple of occasions from Celtic, but Henrik was happy at the club at that time and didn't feel the need to leave until the summer of 2004.

During that close season, Henri Camara was signed by Martin. I'm absolutely sure Martin would have searched high and low to find someone to come in and enhance the strikeforce. But it wouldn't have an easy job trying to do that. Perhaps, in many respects, you had to feel for Camara because it was an impossible job to try to come close to matching Henrik. He was on a hiding to nothing. The other top strikers in Europe would have been out of Celtic's reach financially. When I went back for pre-season, I just felt there was a big void with Henrik not being at the club. But we had to knuckle down and work hard.

We also signed Juninho that summer. He was brought in to play behind the striker to probe and open up defences. He was a top player with Brazil and won medals down south with

Middlesbrough. But it didn't work for him at Celtic. And I know from my own experience at Chelsea that that can happen. Yet, you could see he was a top player; he was wonderful in training. He could see a pass, had a lovely first touch and was a good professional. And he had a fine game in his first Old Firm clash. But it just never kicked on for him.

Juninho had to try to adjust and couldn't quite do it. We all had a bit of adjusting to do with no Henrik. Were we a better team without Henrik? No, we weren't. But we were still effective.

We also lost Johan Mjällby that summer when he signed for Spanish side Levante. Johan had been totally dependable. He was strong, could head the ball and read the game well. So, on top of losing the figurehead of the team in Henrik, we also lost our best defender. We missed Johan a lot. He was another guy we just couldn't replace, certainly not within the club's financial parameters.

We coped fairly well in the 2004–05 season and the loan signing of Craig Bellamy from Newcastle during the January transfer window gave the place a lift. The Celtic fans took to him and he was a lively character in the dressing room. He had blistering pace and an eye for goal. He scored for us in the final Old Firm game of the season when we defeated Rangers 2–1 at Ibrox. That put us five points ahead of them with four games to go. We should never have looked back from that but we lost our next game at home to Hibs. On the final day of the season, we were still two points ahead of McLeish's men when we went to play Motherwell at Fir Park. A victory would have given us the title once again. Rangers were away to Hibs on the same day. Rangers won 1–0 and we lost 2–1. We were 1–0 up at half-time after I gave us a lead. Scott McDonald scored two late goals that day to deflate us. It was devastating. Losing the league in 2003 and 2005 has haunted me at different times.

What made matters worse in 2005 was when news came out that Martin was leaving and would be replaced by Gordon Strachan. Martin's wife, Geraldine, was suffering from cancer and Martin wanted to take time off to be with her. I felt for Martin and his family during that period. The pressure on him to manage Celtic and care for Geraldine must have been incredible. It must have been a horrible period. I really don't know how he managed to cope.

So, we all desperately wanted to win the league for him and his family. It would have been a fitting way to go. But we blew it. Absolutely blew it. I remember he sat in the Fir Park dressing room after the game and held his face in his hands. It was the quietest moment I'd known in our dressing room during all my time at Celtic.

I always found Martin to be very fair, he said things how they were. The majority of the players liked him and respected him. Players wanted to be praised by him and it didn't happen very often, but when he did say something complimentary you treasured it. Martin always had the habit of making me feel special and I know other players felt this. It was his greatest asset.

During my five years working for him, I only crossed him once that I can remember. I played in a reserve game in which Iván De la Peña was on trial for us. Martin came in at half-time and had a right go at me. He felt I wasn't holding the ball up well enough. I answered him back and said something along the lines of he must have been watching a different game to the one I was playing in. Kenny McDowall was in charge of the reserves and he told Kenny to substitute me. I was then summoned to his office. Martin gave me a good dressing down about my previous rant. I kept quiet because I knew he would really destroy me if I tried to justify my comments. But strangely, about fifteen minutes later, when I left his office, I was walking tall again. Martin must be the greatest psychologist of all time. I came out feeling the best player in the world again. He'd taken me to task and then built me back up. The only bad outcome from the meeting was that Martin banned me from playing cricket in the summer. He is Northern Irish and it's not really a cricketing hot bed.

The blow of losing the league was softened ever so slightly when we won the Scottish Cup. We beat Dundee United 1–0 in the final. It was Martin's final game as manager and what he achieved during his five years at the club was magnificent. He won three SPL titles, three Scottish Cups and one League Cup. Celtic were pretty much in the doldrums when he arrived and he lifted the whole place to new heights. The run to the UEFA Cup Final in Seville was truly memorable.

I suppose a frustration for him would have been our inability to win away from home in the Champions League group stages. We beat Ajax 3–1 away from home in a Champions League qualifier in 2001. I scored that evening in the Amsterdam Arena, as did Bobby Petta and Didier Agathe. We lost the return game 1–0 but we were through. It was going to be our first time in the Champions League but we went into it with confidence. We fancied ourselves against any side in Europe. On our night, we felt we could compete with any club. And we did. Many times. But individual mistakes cost us.

We were drawn against Juventus, Porto and Rosenborg. We finished the campaign with nine points after three home wins but it wasn't good enough to take us through to the last sixteen. For all the bad results we had on our travels, we were never humped apart from on one occasion in our first season, when Porto destroyed us 3–0 in Portugal.

We managed a run in Europe during the 2003–04 season. Because we finished runners-up in the SPL, we had to play two qualifiers to get into the Champions League. Our first game was against FBK Kaunas. We won the first leg 4–0 in Lithuania. Henrik, Shaun Maloney, Liam Miller and I scored the goals. But it was after the game that the real drama occurred.

We were due to fly home immediately after the game, which was the norm on European away nights. But there was a problem with our aircraft and the pilot decided we shouldn't fly out as the aeroplane needed some repair work. So we had to go back to the hotel and stay over. There was a little bit of panic as word reached us that had we taken off, we would have been goners. We were hurtling down the runway, ready to take off, and the pilot slammed the breaks on. There was a problem with the speed gauges. Had we continued, we would have been in serious trouble.

John Robertson doesn't like flying and he turned whiter than white as the brakes slammed on. I just felt lucky we didn't take off and tried not to think too much about it. We went back to the hotel to stay over and had a few beers at the bar to settle us down.

I was rooming with Thommo. Now, the two single beds were very close together and Thommo fell out of his bed in the middle of the night. He was a little bit disorientated and still more than half asleep, apparently, and ended up climbing into my bed beside me. Bearing in mind I was starkers and so was he, it wasn't the best feeling in the world! I jumped out of bed and screamed at him. He just got out of my bed in a bit of a daze and went back to his own bed. We remain friends to this day but it's not an incident we like to talk about!

We won the return leg 1–0 and then we were drawn against MTK Hungaria. We defeated them 4–0 over there. Stiliyan, Didier, Henrik and I scored. Henrik's goal was his thirty-first in European competition for Celtic and it made him the highest-ever scorer for a British side in Europe. The return was comfortable and we won 1–0. I scored the only goal.

We were in the Champions League and drawn against Bayern Munich, Lyon and Anderlecht. We were very comfortable in Bayern's old Olympic Stadium. Thommo put us ahead and it felt good. I played in midfield that night and Owen Hargreaves was in the middle of the park for them. I had to try to stop him from getting on the ball too often and not allow him to dictate play. Then we lost two goals. The second goal was heartbreaking. Magnus Hedman held his hands up after the game and said he shouldn't have made the mistake, that it was an error of judgement. That's fair enough, these things happen, but it was a big disappointment to lose that night. At no point during the game did Bayern pummel us; they weren't opening us up at will. I'd won in Munich with Norwich and I thought it was going to be the same again with Celtic.

We also had Anderlecht in our section that season and we should have beaten them over there. Stan Varga had a chance to score but we couldn't do it. Anderlecht had a man sent off and we still couldn't score. They beat us 1–0.

That campaign went from bad to worse and we lost over in Lyon. We conceded soft goals. I scored to make it 2–2 with ten minutes to go and we thought we'd get a draw, at least, but they had some very good players and scored a winner. Had the winning goal been a fantastic volley or one of their players dribbling past three or four of our lads, then fair enough. But we conceded a penalty when Bobo Baldé was penalised for a handball and that made it harder to take.

In the end, however, you get what you deserve. It's easy to be critical and point the finger at players and say it was his fault or his fault, especially as mistakes are always highlighted and discussed. And both defenders and goalkeepers are often the fall guys because even if you're not scoring, at least you can salvage something from a game provided you're not also shipping goals at the back. And defensive mistakes cost games. But, after a defeat like that one, I'd still be critical of my own performance when I felt I could have played better.

Football is difficult to understand, really. The fact that we couldn't win away from home in Europe didn't get to me psychologically. At the end of the day, home or away, you're playing against the same players, on a grass pitch with a football. When you are the home team, you do feel you have to be more attack-minded, more aggressive in a way. But we felt we could win home and away, and why shouldn't we? There really shouldn't have been that much of a difference except in the way we approached the game psychologically and tactically.

One of Martin's phrases was that we had to see games through – he was big on that. Too often we didn't do that and that left him tearing his hair out at times. He was distraught after some European games. He knew we were so close but we only had ourselves to blame. It's about knowing the importance of holding onto a game, running the ball into corners, taking your time with throw-ins, killing the pace. As Martin said, it's about seeing games through.

We finished third in the group with seven points – all gained at home – and that got us entry into the UEFA Cup. We knocked out FK Teplice in the last thirty-two and then the mighty Barcelona in the last sixteen. But we didn't have enough to get past Villarreal in the next round. Not many sides can actually say they deserved to knock Barcelona out of a European competition and we'd fall into that category. We battled hard and we were organised. I didn't play in the home game through injury but we won 1–0 through a goal from Thommo. There was a fight in the tunnel at half-time and Rab Douglas was sent off. David Marshall came on for him and was just brilliant.

I played in the return game and we managed to do enough to get through. Did we really expect to go there and get a good result? Well, in all honesty, no, I don't think so. We were controlled and resolute but I don't remember getting into their half too often. It was a backs-to-the-wall job. But it was enjoyable. In the end, Marshall had an extraordinary night and to do it at just nineteen years old was truly heroic. He was brilliant. John Kennedy was also terrific. For a young lad, he was always physically strong and able to tackle properly. It was an enormous result to beat Barcelona. There is a huge gulf in terms of player budgets between the clubs and when you think that they had Ronaldinho and the like, it really does make that result one to be proud of.

We knew it wouldn't be easy against Villarreal, but some people thought it would be a formality and we'd go all the way to the final. Sure, we were a fairly experienced team and a well-seasoned side, but it was a lot to ask us to continue to win so many European ties when you consider how many games we had played in Europe the previous season when we got to Seville and to carry that on. We didn't have a massive squad so injuries, suspensions and tiredness caught up with us. Also, I suppose, that bit of luck you need to win big games ran out. In the end, they defeated us 3–1 on aggregate and deserved to win the tie.

The 2004–05 Champions League was bitterly disappointing for us. We were in a 'Group of Death' having been drawn with Henrik's Barcelona, AC Milan and Shakhtar Donetsk. It was a formidable line-up but, as a professional player, it was the sort of challenge that you relished.

Barcelona came to our place and we hadn't lost a home tie in Europe for more than three years. But Barca were a cut above with Ronaldinho and Deco in the team. They gave us a bit of a chasing in the first half and led 1–0. I was just back from injury and came off the bench at half-time. Marshall then saved a Ronaldinho penalty. I felt I played well and I levelled the scoring. We were then in the ascendancy and looked like getting another goal. Frank Rijkaard then put Henrik on for Ronaldinho. Henrik received an excellent reception from Celtic fans that night.

Giuly put Barca ahead and then Henrik made it 3–1 with a lob. It was strange to see him scoring against us but probably expected. Our next two games were away from home and we lost 3–1 in Milan and 3–0 in Donetsk. We beat Shakhtar 1–0 at our place and then drew 1–1 at the Nou Camp, which was a great result when you think how things had gone at home. We finished the campaign with a 0–0 draw at home to Milan. We were bottom of the group and out of Europe. It was a sore one.

We were very proud of our home record over four seasons in the Champions League under Martin. The only team to beat us at home in ninety minutes was Barcelona.

When I look back on my career, I really loved the night-time games in Europe. I was lucky to play in such great matches and I cherish the memories. There was something about playing under the floodlights in front of 60,000 Celtic fans. Really, the hairs on the back of the neck stood up when you were walking down the tunnel. And then to hear the Champions League theme tune followed by 'You'll Never Walk Alone' was incredible.

For me, there were a couple of games that stood out from the rest, including the tie against Juventus and the UEFA Cup home tie against Valencia in 2001 when we lost to them on a penalty shoot-out. Both nights had a fantastic atmosphere thanks to the Celtic supporters.

Personally, I felt the way I played against Juventus was one of the best performances of my career. We knew we had to win that night and we did, 4–3. But it wasn't enough. Lubo Moravcík started for us that night and he played brilliantly. His fellow countryman Pavel Nedved played in the centre of midfield for Juventus that evening and I think Lubo nutmegged him in the first half. That was a great moment. Losing to them over there, in the manner we did (a dubious penalty decision in the last minute), gave us extra motivation to beat them at Parkhead. That was the game of our campaign. The bottom line was we had some very good players, players that knew what to do. We didn't feel inferior to Nedved and Del Piero. We weren't intimidated by any side. The Champions League was an incredible experience and if ever I felt privileged to be a footballer, then it was most definitely on such occasions.

I was never one for exchanging jerseys after games when we had lost. I know some players will ask a certain player during the warm-up for their jersey at full-time. I find that pathetic. I only liked to get an opposition jersey if we won. If we lost, I wasn't interested. Maybe I was being stroppy. Henrik's was the only jersey I really wanted when he played for Barcelona against us at Parkhead and I got it. We lost that game but I made an exception that night. If we lost games I'd sometimes not even shake hands and would run up the tunnel as quickly as possible. I was quite pathetic, really, when it came to that. I was too busy sulking. I mean, you are there to win a game of football. That's all that should matter. When we lost to Lyon with a late goal and when we lost to Porto in the UEFA Cup Final, the last thing on my mind was getting the jersey of another player. I didn't get a Porto jersey in 2003. I wasn't interested.

The UEFA Cup Final defeat was the sorest, of course. Anderlecht was painful, too, because we played very poorly. For all the difficulty we had trying to win away from home in the Champions League, we beat Blackburn and Liverpool away in the UEFA Cup and drew twice in the Nou Camp, which was quite incredible.

I'm sure Martin treasured some of those European nights. But there were to be no more as he was leaving the club. I knew things were never going to be the same without him, Robbo and Wally. And how right I was.

Martin O'Neill on Chris Sutton

One of the first things I had to deal with when I took over as Celtic manager was Mark Viduka's situation. Mark was a fine player but a bit temperamental. But, then again, who isn't? I think he'd had a bit of a fall-out with the club from the Inverness Caley Thistle defeat in the Scottish Cup tie a few months earlier. There may well have been some other problems with the football club but I'm not sure about that. Celtic indicated to me that there had been strong interest in Mark from Leeds United and one or two clubs in Spain. I thought it best to speak to Mark directly to find out his thoughts. He was in Australia and I telephoned him. If he wanted to stay then I would have been delighted as he had forged a very good partnership with Henrik Larsson. But he made it absolutely clear that he didn't want to come back and play for Celtic. I told Mark that was fine and that we would all get on with our lives. Mark joined Leeds United for £6 million.

Chris Sutton was the player, perhaps the only player, that I thought could immediately replace Viduka and make Celtic competitive. He had been brilliant for Blackburn Rovers in their Championship-winning season, forming a splendid on-field partnership with the prolific goal-scorer Alan Shearer, and as a result, moved to Chelsea in a £10-million deal.

For one reason or another, things didn't work out for him at Stamford Bridge and as a consequence, he lost a little self confidence. But the lad could still play the game and I thought this might be the best opportunity to take him away from there for a reasonable fee. Celtic negotiated a deal with Chelsea, essentially paying out the £6 million received from the sale of Viduka. This gave me the chance to speak to Chris so John Robertson and I met him at a hotel on the outskirts of London. He seemed quite a shy lad, although very intelligent and articulate, with a

strong desire to get his career back on track. And, most important, a keen interest in resurrecting that very career north of the
border with Celtic, despite the clamour of other Premiership
clubs for his services.

He struck an immediate rapport with John Robertson, a friendship that has remained to this day, and the conversations went
well. Despite this, John and I were far from certain about the
eventual outcome.

Chris can be a strange lad on occasion – I suppose anyone
who lives with goats, hens, cows, ducks, horses, dogs and cats,
possibly all in the same house, could be considered a little eccen-
tric – and in truth, John and I didn't really know him then. We
left him to ruminate on matters for a while. If I had known then
just what an impact he would make at the club over the next
few seasons, I wouldn't have allowed him to leave the hotel
room before he had signed for Celtic. Thankfully, this he did
some short time later.

Chris was earning some very good money at Chelsea, and
although he personally wasn't looking for any financial gain
from the transfer, it was still a huge outlay for the club, being a
combination of transfer deal and five-year contract. The club's
owner, Dermot Desmond, may well have had a few concerns
about the transfer, but he gave it his complete backing and Chris
became, perhaps, his most favourite player in the seasons ahead.

The player arrived at Celtic Park to embark on a new, exciting
and altogether magnificent chapter of his career. His ability to
play with his back to goal was as good as any other striker in
Europe and his partnership with the fantastic Henrik Larsson
over the next few years was to prove sublimely unique.

From the opening game of the 2000–01 SPL campaign on an
early Sunday evening at Tannadice, when both players scored
in a vital victory over Dundee United, to the end of Henrik's
time at the club in 2004, they were supreme.

And when John Hartson signed to add even more goal power to the club, it was the talismanic Sutton, with the talent to play in just about every outfield position, who dropped seamlessly into a deeper lying position for the benefit of the team in general. Henrik often stated that Sutton enriched his game. Few who saw them play together would argue.

Chris went on to play many more fine games for the football club. But one evening in particular seems to stick in the memory. His performance against Juventus in the Champions League at Celtic Park was absolutely breathtaking. We won 4–3, Chris scoring a fantastic volley. He was unplayable that night against Italy's finest and, if any vindication was needed to show that he was indeed a brilliant player, then that was indeed his proof.

The win gave us nine points in the Group but not enough to carry us through to the next stage, Porto's late winner at home to Rosenborg taking them through instead. Ironically, we would meet them again in the months ahead – in Seville.

I didn't know until later that Chris, when growing up, had been a Nottingham Forest supporter, with John Robertson being a particular favourite. And quite rightly so, John being absolutely outstanding in that team. This may well have had some influence in Chris's friendship with John. I never discouraged Steve and John forging relationships with some of the players, although I tended to keep just a little distance apart. There's no doubt there was a great camaraderie within that group of Celtic players and it stood them in great stead over the seasons.

It was a genuine pleasure to work with Chris, despite his protestations to Steve Walford, the coach, that training was not to his liking – every day for five years.

13

STRICKEN BY STRACHAN

Gordon Strachan was appointed as Martin O'Neill's successor. It was never going to be easy for any manager to come and follow Martin as Martin had spent five years building the club up to being No. 1 in the country again. I liked Martin and the Celtic fans adored him. So, taking all of that into account, I didn't envy Gordon.

Gordon had played for Aberdeen, Manchester United, Leeds United and Scotland. He had a highly successful career in Scotland and England as a midfielder. As a manager, he started out as player-manager of Coventry and then moved to Southampton. During his time at both clubs, he carved out a more than decent reputation for himself. I had played against Gordon and came up against his teams, but didn't know him personally. As a player, he was very confident. He was good and seemed to be very sure of himself. Not cocky or arrogant, but he had a confident personality and he was able to back it with his ability.

As a person, I suppose what I knew of him came mainly from his appearances on television as a pundit. He was known for having decent one-liners. I found him amusing the times I watched and listened to him on the box. I was willing to get behind Gordon and I wanted to stay at Celtic. My family was very happy in Glasgow and I didn't want to disrupt things.

But there were signs from quite early into Gordon's time at Celtic that all might not work out well for me. First of all, he wanted to play me as a holding midfielder. Now, with the greatest of respect to the other strikers at Celtic at that time, I think I was more than capable of leading the line up front. Playing me as a defensive midfielder wasn't a problem, as I had played many different positions, but I think I would have been of more benefit to the team if I had been deployed as a striker.

Some interviews were given by the Celtic players to the media and the inference was they were being critical of the way Martin handled the team and the fitness of the squad when he was in charge. A few of the boys may have been saying training was better, stuff like that. I didn't like that. I found it totally disrespectful. Surely there has to be loyalty? I was disappointed with certain players for doing this. It all just left a bad taste in my mouth.

On the contrary, I found Gordon's pre-season training monotonous and boring. Some of the players left over from Martin's time said that the training under Gordon was better and we were more organised. Now, I'm not trying to put a spin on things, but that was utter nonsense. Things weren't better under Strachan. And, training aside, the fact was that we didn't have the players we had before and we weren't as good a team. Gordon, of course, had to work with the squad he inherited, get the best out of us and work on getting in the new players he wanted to move the team on as he saw fit. That was his job. But when it came to training and fitness, Gordon had a different way to it all from Martin.

That didn't mean to say Gordon's way was better. I always believed that a good pro was the best judge of his own fitness and knew what he needed to do to top himself up, if it was required. I used to be more confident going into games when I knew I had the fitness to perform at a high level of intensity. I felt good knowing I'd be able to run for ninety minutes and make life difficult for the opposing players for the entire ninety minutes. I used to do extra training and gym work to get to that level and

I knew what I needed to do to achieve that. At Celtic, the likes of Thommo, Lenny, Johan and Stiliyan were exactly the same.

Martin was comfortable enough letting the senior players decide on their fitness. At pre-season he'd always make sure we had a good base to build on for the rest of the season. He then put the responsibility on the shoulders of the players. Treated us like adults, really. In terms of fitness, there's a fine line between doing too much and too little on the training pitch and, as far as I'm concerned, Martin got the balance spot on.

Gordon's first competitive game as manager was in a Champions League qualifier away to Artmedia Bratislava. The Slovakian champions were far from household names for Celtic fans in the summer of 2005, but now it's a club they'll never forget. We were battered 5–0. It was a shambles. A total embarrassment. Considering, under Martin, we'd defeated the likes of Barcelona and Juventus, this was an unexpected scoreline to say the least. This kind of thing on the European stage just shouldn't have happened to Celtic.

I came off injured during the game when the score was 0-0. Neil Lennon accidentally put his knee into my face and fractured my right cheekbone in four places. I was taken to a hospital in Bratislava and given morphine to ease the pain, calm me down, whatever you like, because it was an incredibly painful injury. When I returned to the stadium to get on the team bus we took pelters. I was in a dazed state but my injury didn't concern the fans after such a shocking result. As I boarded the bus I still heard the shouts of 'Sutton, you're finished,' and 'Your legs have gone, Sutton.' I took a fair bit of abuse. I'll never forget that whole evening. Between the score, the injury, the pain and the insults, it was a horrible experience.

What I wasn't to know at that time, however, was that the injury was the beginning of the end of my Celtic career. Further down the line, it also brought an end to my whole career.

I went in for an operation the following morning. The surgeon had to drill into the right-hand side of my head to put in a plate to help with the cheekbone repair and he was pleased enough with the result of his work. However, after the operation I developed blurred vision in my right eye. My cheekbone got better, right enough, and although the pain was bad it was just about bearable. The way I was treated by Strachan wasn't.

I was out with the cheekbone injury for two months. During that time, Strachan never once spoke to me. I never once received a phone call. Due to the seriousness of the injury I was very depressed but as far as I'm concerned he showed no interest. Most managers would have made some kind of effort. I do think it's common courtesy to ask after one of your players when they have been sidelined with a fairly serious injury. In my opinion, he treated me appallingly and, to be honest, that hurt. When you're injured for a while, you inevitably start to question your place in the team and a little encouragement and reassurance would have been appreciated. I suppose it's all down to managerial style.

With this injury, the first time he tried to speak to me was when I was having lunch in the players' canteen at Celtic Park. I think I was sitting with Neil Lennon. Gordon wandered past me and tried to crack a joke with me. I didn't laugh. I blanked him totally. I didn't think his brand of humour was funny that day. Even if I had found it amusing I still wouldn't have laughed. He wasn't happy with me not joining in. His assistant, Garry Pendrey, was with him. Maybe Gordon felt belittled by me in front of one of his members of staff. At that stage in our relationship, I couldn't have cared less what he thought.

I knew that he wasn't best pleased with me for ignoring him and it came as no surprise when later that day I was asked to go and see him in his office. I made my way there and there was no small talk on my arrival. We got straight down to it.

He asked me why I didn't speak to him and what my problem

was with him. I told him I didn't have a problem with him but I did say that I was disappointed he'd blanked for me for two months when I had an injury. I told him I thought he could at least have had the decency to phone me to ask how I was doing. He said that he did phone me and left me a voicemail and I said I had never received a call from him. He insisted that he had made the call. I insisted that he hadn't. It was a bit like a pantomime. This went on and on and I eventually stood up to leave the room. I told him that if he said he had left a message then fair enough, he had left one. But I still maintain I did not receive it.

We managed to move on from there but I was sensing that there was an underlying problem. It may seem a small point, that the manager didn't take the time to speak to one of his senior pros when he had a long-term injury, but feeling like I did, it was important to me. Had he at least spoken to me then I would have felt valued and it would have made the whole recovery process easier to bear. And surely it's just good man management?

Looking at it now, and putting it bluntly, I'm not sure that I was part of his long-term plans. Managers are entitled to their opinions and, of course, they live or die by what they do which means they need to take tough decisions, but if he did want me away from the club then I don't know why. I think I was still performing at the highest level and I believe I had a lot to offer the team and the supporters.

I was definitely starting to feel out of the loop at this time, and not just because of the injury and the lack of contact. It was more of a general feeling of unease. Between any player and their manager there needs to be a bond of trust and I was starting to feel that any bonds we'd had were loosening. In reality it had got to the point where I had a real problem with the management team of Strachan, Garry Pendrey and the goalkeeping coach Jim Blyth and although I was determined to carry on and do my best for the club, I felt I couldn't trust them as far as I could throw them.

Having been at Celtic under the previous and very successful management team of Martin O'Neill, John Robertson and Steve Walford, the new team didn't have the same appeal for me and it was hard getting used to the new set-up. I felt that the whole vibe at the club had deteriorated, that we weren't as together as we had been and that some of the excitement had gone. The thing is, you compare people to the previous regime and I just preferred Martin, John Robertson and Steve Walford. Bad vibes were around the place under Gordon and his coaching staff and, in my opinion, they created them. I did try to give the new regime the benefit of the doubt and try to believe them, but over a period of time I lost faith because of different things that happened.

Following the injury, the manager put me back in the team and played me at centre forward. I was delighted with that. My form was pretty decent and I felt I was making a good contribution to the team. We were making progress after losing to Artmedia Bratislava and our stuttering start in the SPL when we drew our first game in the league 4–4 away to Motherwell and also lost the first Old Firm game of the season at Ibrox. Having missed the opening period of the season it was good to be back in the team and to see our performances and results improving.

Strachan had signed Artur Boruc and he was showing he was a top goalkeeper. He also brought Shunsuke Nakamura to the club and he was a fine player. He was lovely on the ball and very good from set pieces. There was no doubt he'd be an asset to the football club and, with these signings, my own form for the team and our improved results I was starting to feel that things under Gordon Strachan might really be starting to go in the right direction. I felt more settled, was happy to go to training and was looking forward to getting stuck in to the rest of the season and making sure Celtic would be winning silverware.

Then, during the month of November, Gordon and myself had a couple of conversations about my contract situation. He made it clear he wanted me to stay for longer at the club and sign a one-year extension, to keep me at Celtic until the summer of 2007. With that being the case my contract extension should have been straightforward as there was a clause written into my current deal that stated if the club wanted to offer me an extension then my wages would remain the same. I was more than happy to sign under those circumstances but as it turned out that was the start of the real trouble. From a positive start to the contract talks, things began to stall and it then went from being positive to him not being forthcoming about the contract.

I asked him about the contract extension again in early December and he said it was all in hand. But he then came to me just before Christmas and said that there was still a deal on the table but it would not be on the same money. It was to be based heavily on first-team appearances. Gordon said the club felt this was the best thing to do because of my injury record. Now, if they were basing that offer on the fact that I was out for a while with my cheekbone injury then that was very unfair. There was nothing I could have done to prevent the injury in Bratislava. I said the new terms the club wanted to offer were a non-starter as the terms were already agreed in my previous contract, there in black and white. I was angry and felt let down. In this new contract they wanted me to sign, it meant I would be taking a drastic cut in my money. Gordon said he would go back to the Celtic board of directors and see about it. From that day on he never gave me another definitive answer.

I knew where I was in the pecking order, in terms of playing as a striker in the team. I felt I deserved a place and I wasn't deluded. It's not like I was competing with Pele or Larsson or Diego Maradona for a place in the team. I could do the job.

The other problem at that time was that I had a niggling

adductor injury which was getting me down. It wasn't hugely serious but I had missed the odd day of training here and there and it was getting me down a bit. With a big injury, in some ways it was easier. You knew what the recovery period was, what you could and had to do to regain fitness and, as long as there were no setbacks, you knew you'd be back to full fitness and ready to go. Niggling injuries that come and go are much harder to deal with sometimes. You never know when they will flare up.

It may be that this was on the manager's mind during the contract negotiations and it may be that this contributed to them stalling. I don't know. What I do know is that the contract extension should have been straightforward if the manager had wanted it. It's true that I was getting a bit older, but my injury record was pretty good, I'd played a lot of games for the club and I knew that the adductor injury would be sorted out in due course.

On top of this, I was starting to feel really let down by Gordon and disappointed by the whole contract business. I also felt that Gordon was trying to avoid me and it became difficult to pin him down. He kept fobbing me off and I thought this was disrespectful.

I'd been managing the adductor injury as best I could but I now thought it was the time not to risk further injury. I had to protect myself and my career. I wasn't 100-per-cent fit but I had been putting my neck on the block for Celtic in games and now it all now appeared to be one way. I decided I didn't want to risk myself any more by playing for him with an injury. It just didn't make any sense for me. I was thirty-two years old and, aside from the odd niggle, I still felt I was fit and had a lot to offer Celtic, for a few more years.

I decided to ask Gordon about the contract one last time. I got the same answer – the contract on offer was a contract heavily weighted towards appearances. It was then I knew I had to go and I was given permission to speak to other clubs which was my entitlement as I was out of contract at Celtic six months later, in the summer of 2006.

As I've already said, managers have a job to do and it's not an easy job. Their job is constantly under scrutiny and always on the line so it has be their call about what players they want in the team. I had loved my time at Celtic and was convinced that had Martin been in charge the new contract would have been a formality. With Gordon, however, everything had changed.

With any new contract for a player, it's usually the manager who tells the board what they want to do. No doubt there are then various discussions and a deal either gets done or it doesn't. I had no conversations directly with the Celtic board so I can't say what their view on the contract extension was. From my point of view it was Gordon who was speaking to them and it was his responsibility to relay information to me about the contract extension. All I heard, however, was that the club could only offer an extension on reduced terms rather than on the terms already set out in my existing deal. I just felt that if the manager had wanted me badly enough he'd have fought tooth and nail to make sure I got the deal that was in my contract. And he should have known that there was no way I'd have accepted a lesser deal. Maybe it was simply that he had other plans for the team, other players in mind but, if so, why start discussing a contract extension in the first place? Why not just let the contract run out the following summer and release me? If it had been the board that objected to the extension then I believe the manager should have told me that straight, that he wanted to keep me but couldn't. At least then I'd have known where I stood.

It has to be said that my relationship with Strachan wasn't as good as it should have been. I simply couldn't help comparing Strachan and O'Neill as man managers, as people and as bosses. Martin is without doubt one of the best managers I have ever played for, with a management style that gets the best out of his players and seems to make him universally respected. He's been at the top of the game making a huge success of some fairly ordinary teams languishing towards the bottom of the league by motivating and inspiring, applying the right tactics and getting results.

But managers come in all different characters and, for me, Gordon Strachan was not one of my favourites. He hadn't inspired the same level of trust as Martin had, I found him more difficult to deal with as a character and I ended up feeling that he was largely responsible for me leaving Parkhead. Whether he was or not, or whether there were other factors involved behind the scenes, I never found out, but I held Strachan mainly responsible for me leaving.

Had Martin been in charge I would have been given the contract that had been agreed. I just didn't trust anything Strachan said. I can't criticise Peter Lawwell or the board for what happened as I never had a conversation with them about my deal. But Gordon spoke to them about it. Now, Gordon could have given me the 'heads up' on what was happening, told me that the board weren't for sanctioning the deal I had in place. What I can categorically say is that I didn't want to leave. I'd have been happy to play for the rest of my career at Celtic.

The situation that had developed over the contract and the bad taste it left made me feel that there was no way I could keep playing for Strachan. He would have driven me nuts. In the end, during my final few weeks at Celtic, I was sad and depressed. I just couldn't stand it under him and his assistant manager. I was angry and I just needed to get out. I felt let down and I blame him totally for that. Rightly or wrongly, I couldn't stand him any longer and I couldn't trust him.

If he didn't want to keep me at the club then he should just have said it to my face. Told me straight. At the end of the day these things happen all the time, players come and go. I would have preferred it if he had been completely straight with me. I would have respected him if he treated me that way. It's just not the way I think you should do business and nor is it the way I think people should be treated. We're all adults and I think it's easier to take any setbacks if you know what the truth is.

Having to leave Celtic was not the outcome I wanted. I wanted to stay. My family wanted to carry on living in Glasgow. Ultimately I believe it was Strachan's decision for me to go. I didn't think too much of him, really.

I was glad to get away from him, to be honest. In my mind Strachan wanted to dismantle what Martin had built up during the previous few seasons and I didn't enjoy it at all under him. I felt he didn't treat me well, not that I was looking for any special treatment. I just wanted to be treated like an adult and to know where I stood. I was prepared to give Gordon and his staff a chance. I did give him a chance and I just felt he threw it back at me. So, we agreed I would go if I could find a club during the January transfer window.

You could, of course, argue that even the reduced deal was good money, that maybe I should have been grateful to accept it and to stay at Celtic. But as far as I'm concerned a deal is a deal. If the manager and the club wanted to extend my contract then there was only one option and that was to honour the deal that was in place. Either that or sell me or let me leave the following summer. Trying to get me to re-sign on a lesser deal was simply never an option whatever Strachan or anyone else thought. The style of man management I respect is when you're told exactly what the situation is from the outset and you can then make your own decisions based on clear information. That didn't happen in this case as far as I'm concerned and it is still a big disappointment to me.

The contract I was offered was with the basic weekly wage

reduced by between fifty and sixty per cent. The money, though, wasn't the point. The point was that it was written into my previous contract that I'd get a certain amount of money. It was the principle of it all and how he dealt with it. Now, let's turn this one around. Had I said to Gordon that I was happy to sign but not on the terms we had agreed earlier and I now wanted an extra £18,000 per week to do so, would that have been fair of me? No, it wouldn't. It would have been bang out of order. The club would have felt betrayed and would rightly have made me out to be greedy and unfair. As a matter of principle, I would never have done that.

The day I left Celtic I packed my boots into my bag and left by a side door. After five and half years at the club I felt it wasn't a nice way to end my time there. But that's the way it goes.

A consolation for me was that I had several good offers from Premiership clubs to consider. Everton, Fulham, Portsmouth and Birmingham all made contact. David Moyes put forward a good case for Everton. That definitely appealed as David is a great manager and a man I respect. I met Steve Bruce and he'd impressed me when I'd played against him years earlier. Now, as a manager, he impressed me as a man. That was important after everything I'd been through under Strachan. Birmingham were by no means a club anywhere near the size of Celtic but he sold it all to me. I was now going back to play Premiership football after a six-year absence. But I wanted to remain at Celtic.

I think many of my team-mates at Celtic were disappointed with the way I had been treated in the final few weeks. They were sad to see me go. Many of them also felt Strachan just wanted to change everything and remove as much of Martin's presence as possible. Managers need to make their own mark, of course, but there was much about the legacy that Martin O'Neill left behind that was worth keeping.

It was a wrench to leave but I had little choice. At that moment

I went on instinct and I did make the right decision to leave. I've never really been calculated about things but I wanted to get away from Strachan and wasn't going to be treated like a fool.

When I looked at the some of the players Strachan signed after I left it made me feel a little bit better not to be a part of his dressing-room and his set-up. Steven Pressley was signed from Hearts on a free transfer. I played against Steven at under-21 level for England against Scotland at the Toulon tournament in France. I actually thought he was a decent enough guy and decent enough player. But then I think he developed into an odd character when I played against him for Celtic and he was at Hearts. It was his demeanour and manner, really, and I used to think it was all a front. He liked to be vocal in the tunnel before games. He was the same on the park. But he used to shout ridiculous things. I'd listen to some of his comments and think 'what a buffoon'. There was one occasion at Tynecastle and he started shouting in the tunnel at five to three and I could even see the Hearts youth-team players laughing at him. The young lads were standing at the back of the tunnel, not involved in the game but helping with some of the matchday duties, and they didn't appear to have much respect for him. He's maybe a nice guy off the pitch. He then went on to join Celtic and I know some of the players at Celtic raised their eyebrows when Strachan signed him. I used to like playing against him as I didn't think he was particularly capable. He may well have been a good organiser, I don't know. To be honest, in many ways I was glad to be away from Celtic when Strachan brought guys like him to the club.

On the other hand, Roy Keane came to Celtic a few weeks before I left. He was a really good guy and settled in well. A ferocious competitor. He was aggressive and a brilliant footballer. He always had plenty to say at the start of his career. I didn't know him back then. But from afar I didn't like him because he played for Manchester United. He was one of the players that stood between me and Blackburn being successful.

Keane was one of those players I'd have loved to have stood next to in a tunnel, knowing he was in your team. I didn't get to really see him in action for Celtic on and off the pitch. He was known to be opinionated off the park and he was bloody horrible on the park. If you look back through the history of the Premier League then he'd have to be right up the top of the list.

I don't know the ins and outs of his time with Celtic but he only stayed five months and then retired from the game. From the outside looking in, it seemed really strange to me what happened to him. I thought he'd be a great signing but there seemed to be a few odd things going on. Now, I have to say I didn't pay a great deal of attention to what was going on at the club after I left because Strachan had sickened me. I just didn't want to know what he would do next. I didn't have any bitterness towards the club, just towards Strachan and his backroom team. However, I thought Keane would have been an integral part of the first team and I think the way his career ended at Celtic wasn't fitting for such a top footballer. I felt it just didn't seem appropriate to treat him that way, naming him as a sub for games and giving him a few minutes here and there. It was a really strange situation and I never understood why it was allowed to happen. But, of course, it was none of my business. I was away from Celtic by then.

I came into contact with Gordon Strachan again a couple of months after I left Parkhead when I bumped into him in a hotel in Birmingham where I was staying. Sam was down that day with three of our boys. They were distraught at the time I left Glasgow and were all still upset when we came face to face with him once again. Despite everything that had gone on at the end of my time at Celtic, he chatted to me as if we were good friends. It was also the first time he'd ever met Sam but as he chatted away to her I could see she was ready for telling him what she really thought. I was gobsmacked at the way he chatted to both of us and I wondered if he was from another planet. Maybe he was simply oblivious to it all and didn't know what a wrench it was for me and my family to leave Celtic and Glasgow.

14

DEJA BLUES

Birmingham were second bottom of the Premiership when I joined them. I knew it was going to be a battle for the club to remain in the Premiership but I felt good about the challenge. It appealed to me and so did playing for Steve Bruce. Playing under Steve was the main reason I joined.

The first home game I played in was a 5–0 win over Portsmouth. I felt I played quite well. Steve played me up front alongside Emile Heskey. As much I was enjoying myself at the club, I was still having problems with my adductors. The injury had been niggling away at me, causing me discomfort since my latter days at Celtic. I tried to battle through it and Steve was good at letting me come in and out of training when the injury dictated. I wanted to do more for the team, be more of an asset on the pitch, but I struggled with this injury.

Results weren't going our way and it became clear this was going to take an extraordinary effort to avoid relegation. Muzzy Izzet was at the club and was a very good player, but he was struggling with a knee injury. Nicky Butt was there and had wonderful experience. He was a great player and also a really good guy. But he wasn't going to be able to get Birmingham out of the relegation zone on his own. It was also good to have Heskey there as he had a fine pedigree.

This was my first taste of Premiership football since 2000 and I didn't find there was much of a change. The standard hadn't improved or gone backwards to any noticeable extent. Any side can beat any other on its day, really. I found the Premiership to be over-hyped, maybe at times not as good as some believed. But Birmingham struggled and we didn't get the necessary points for a reason – we just didn't have enough quality players.

I scored one goal in eleven appearances. It came in a 3–1 defeat to Aston Villa in the Midlands derby clash. We ended up third bottom of the Premiership and were relegated. That prompted a few comments from Birmingham owner, David Sullivan. He was clearly frustrated at being relegated to the Championship. It meant losing millions and millions of pounds. I came into Sullivan's line of fire and he left a bit on me. He stated I wasn't worth the money they had given me because I didn't play enough games. I wasn't overly impressed with what he had to say – after all, he had agreed to pay me the money in the first place. No one was more frustrated than me about my injuries. But the unwelcome remarks from Sullivan didn't sour my thoughts on the club.

Sullivan later sold Birmingham and bought West Ham. The Hammers were relegated in 2010–11 and there appeared to be similarities between how he acted when Birmingham were relegated and with West Ham. He was obviously upset and decided to air that disappointment in public. A few people came into Sullivan's line of fire but I thought it would have been better to keep his counsel.

However, for the most part, I was well treated at Birmingham. The club's chief executive Karren Brady was very helpful to me and my family, made sure the boys got into a good school. She couldn't do enough for us, really. I felt for Steve more than anyone. He was a good manager and a good man and I wanted him to keep the club in the Premiership. In general, I was sad to see Birmingham go down. It wasn't a pleasant feeling but once it's done, it's done. There's nothing you can do about it.

I really liked Steve and I wanted to perform well for him. He was similar to Martin O'Neill in many ways, very fair and he spoke very well. He was also straight down the middle and you always knew where you stood. If you weren't pulling your weight, he'd let you know. He was a winner as a player and could be a nasty customer on the pitch when he needed to be. He was very fair as a manager and had a great desire to win.

Eric Black was his assistant and they worked extremely well together. I rated Eric highly as a coach. It was just a pity I wasn't able to make more of a contribution. My injury problems curtailed my appearances for Birmingham and I was frustrated I couldn't be out on the pitch more to help Steve and my team-mates.

I felt Steve was very unlucky to be relegated that season. Steve had a lot of fire-fighting to do there as they had become a bit of a yo-yo club in between the Premiership and the Championship. Birmingham were relegated and inevitably the knives were out for a few people to have a dig at him. One of these people, surprisingly, was the club captain at that time, Kenny Cunningham. Kenny was very critical of him and I thought it was wrong to have a cheap shot. As usual when things go wrong, some people start pointing fingers and it's the fault of everybody else. It seems to be a pattern that occurs at most clubs when the going gets tough. I personally always found Kenny to be a good guy but his attack on Steve was unnecessary and unjust. I found Steve to be totally trustworthy and that made a pleasant change after my dealings with my previous manager.

I left Birmingham that summer. I spoke to Steve before I left and he wished me well. He told me once I had sorted my injury problems then I was to let him know if I felt like rejoining Birmingham. I appreciated that offer. I was determined to get my injury situation sorted out because I felt I had plenty still to offer the game at a high level.

I then took the decision to have an operation on my adductors and the operation was a success on both sides. In hindsight, I should have gone under the knife to correct the situation a lot sooner. I knew it would take around three months to get back towards fitness. After a few weeks I started rehab and I received some help from Tim Shepherd, my former physio at Norwich. It was very good of him to help me.

As I edged closer to fitness, a few clubs made it known they'd be interested in signing me. Discussions had taken place with Norwich when I was leaving Celtic. I still had a house in the area and a move back there would certainly have suited the family from a geographical point of view. Norwich weren't doing particularly well in the Championship at the time and Nigel Worthington was the manager. The feedback I received was that he'd consider taking me if one or two of his players picked up injuries. Now, without being arrogant, I was trying to do Norwich a favour. I had Premiership sides interested in me but I would have liked to be able to help out at my hometown club. Norwich weren't doing well and Worthington wasn't for having me. I thought I could have gone there and helped the club out, try to improve things from the unfortunate predicament they found themselves in.

It wasn't even as though it was down to wages because we didn't get as far as discussing personal terms. The wages wouldn't have been a problem as I'm sure we would have been able to come to some agreement. Only Nigel knows the exact reasons for not signing me. I found it all pretty disappointing, to be perfectly honest. I would have loved to go back and play for Norwich and maybe if he'd signed me, he would have kept his job.

The family had moved back to Norfolk in the summer of 2006 and that made Norwich an option once again after I left Birmingham. There was speculation in the local media that I was on my way back to Carrow Road but I never felt it was going to happen. Fulham made me an offer and Martin was now back in football, this time at Aston Villa. Martin phoned me and asked if I'd join him at Villa. I think I said to him he must be desperate to want to sign me! But it definitely appealed to me. Of course it did. My only concern, however, was making sure I had fully recovered from my adductor injuries and was fully fit. I had put myself under pressure at Birmingham and Celtic by trying to train and play with the injuries, and it wouldn't have been fair to myself or my new club to do that again. It was important in my mind to be pain-free when I joined Villa.

15

IT'S OVER –
IN THE BLINK OF AN EYE

I trained on my own during the summer, self-policed myself. When I felt ready to step up my training schedule and join in on games, I closed in on a decision about where I wanted to play my football. I chose Aston Villa and signed for them in October 2006. I fancied working for Martin again. Aston Villa is a huge club and I had the best years of my career under him at Celtic. I also had tremendous respect for his backroom staff, John Robertson and Steve Walford, and enjoyed the thought of working with them. Also, because I was in the latter stages of my career and with the injuries I'd had, I knew the way Martin and his staff would treat me. Travelling from my home in Norfolk was going to be an issue. It was more than a three-hour drive from my house to the training ground and I found the journey to be quite hard. Being stuck on a motorway isn't my idea of fun. I would travel to Birmingham on the Monday and if we had a midweek game I'd stay right through until the Saturday. It was hard on me and hard on Sam and the boys.

If our schedule permitted, Martin would give me an extra day off here and there and trust me to do my own thing. I worked hard when I had to train on my own. I wouldn't have messed him around. He was like that at Celtic and I found the training at Aston Villa to be similar to the way it was at Celtic. If players had little niggles he would let them judge what was best to do when it came to training.

I played a few reserve games and my fitness improved. I then got into the first team. Martin had inherited a squad that had just avoided relegation the previous season under David O'Leary. He had a tough job on his hands because the players and club had under-performed the previous year. The players were low on confidence and Martin had his work cut out. But he is a fantastic manager and soon started to get things moving in the right direction without making any drastic changes. He was a brilliant motivator and started to get a bit of momentum going. He brought in Stiliyan Petrov from Celtic for £7 million. He played me as a central striker and I played with Gabby Agbonlahor alongside me. Gabby had great potential but was very raw at that stage. He was learning the game but had great pace. I also played alongside Juan Pablo Angel. He was a more rounded player than Gabby at that time but lacked his pace.

I was under no illusions about the fact that I was a short-term fix. I was thirty-four and hadn't built my hopes up that my move to Villa would be for two or three years. But I was at an age and a situation where if I was playing well enough and still performing at the highest level, then I would carry on.

I felt I produced decent performances and scored the winning goal in a 1–0 win over Everton. I was delighted to score again in the Premiership. I felt good about myself, especially considering I had one or two concerns after the adductor operations. With every passing game I played, my confidence grew.

Martin was really getting things going at Villa. The players wanted to play for him and he was building up the kind of mentality within the dressing room that we had had at Celtic.

I played against Manchester United at Villa Park in a league game on 23 December 2006. A long ball came forward, Nemanja Vidic and I both went for an aerial challenge and I got a blow to the side of my head. I'm unsure if it came from his elbow or his head. I went down and when I got up I felt dazed. I went in at half-time but still didn't feel quite right. I didn't know whether I was concussed or not but the vision in my right eye was hazy.

We struggled to live with Manchester United in the first half and I didn't feel I was contributing as well as I should have been. I was up against Vidic and Rio Ferdinand, two exceptional defenders and a good partnership, up there with the best ever in the Premiership. So, it was in my mind that maybe, subconsciously, I was using the challenge from Vidic as an excuse for not being at the level I wanted to be at. I was really motivated to cause the pair of them problems in the second half so I played the rest of the game. I wanted to do better but we were well beaten 3–0. After the game, I knew my right eye wasn't as it should be. Again, I thought I may have been concussed so I spoke to the medical staff and they told me to keep them informed as we had a game seventy-two hours later.

Sadly, that game against Manchester United was to be my last ever as a footballer. I never played again.

We were playing Tottenham in London on Boxing Day and I reported to the hotel in London on Christmas Day night. I told the club doctor, Roddy MacDonald, that my right eye was still blurred and that I had doubts I'd be available for selection. I don't think Martin was overly pleased but I had already voiced my doubts immediately after the Manchester United game.

Roddy didn't want to take any chances and he arranged an examination with an eye specialist at Wellington Hopsital in London. I left the team hotel and headed straight there. The first set of results endorsed my own fears. I had problems with my vision in my right eye and it was suggested by the doctors that I shouldn't play the following day.

Being told I wasn't able to play against Tottenham wasn't the news I wanted to hear. I desperately wanted to be given the all clear. During the following few weeks, I went for more tests with different specialists and I was advised to stop playing. I was told it was the sensible thing to do. It was a massive shock.

After the initial injury against Manchester United, I thought there would be a little bit of trauma and it would improve within a day or two, maybe a week at most. But my eye didn't get any better. As the time went by, I started to get worried. Seeing the specialists and hearing their diagnosis of the damage, I had to reluctantly accept their recommendation to stop playing. Had I been twenty-four, I would have seriously considered ignoring their advice. But at thirty-four? No. It wasn't worth the risk. Had it been ten years earlier then it would have been a different decision. I still wanted to play but my eye wasn't going to get any better. The idea of wearing Petr Cech style helmet was mentioned but it was far-fetched. It would have been fine for a goalkeeper but not for an outfield player.

As the weeks ticked by, I started to become anxious. I went to see three different specialists for their opinions and the common theme was that playing on would be a big risk. The eye wasn't showing any sign of improvement and I was told it probably wouldn't. An operation wasn't a possibility. Tests continued for three months and towards the start of April, there was no improvement in my eye and the specialist thought there was no chance of it getting back to normal. On a visit to the third specialist, I got some very direct advice. He didn't hedge his bets and he told me to stop playing. On the night of that Manchester United game, not for a second did I think my eye injury would bring about the end of my career.

But the end of my career wasn't all down to that Vidic challenge, it had started during/after the operation I had had to repair a quadruple fracture on my cheek when I played for Celtic. I had thrown myself to block a shot from distance and Neil Lennon was attempting to do the same thing. As I looked up, Neil came running across and his knee went through the side of my face. It was some knee. I was stretchered off after eight minutes. It turned out to be a bad night all round for Celtic, who lost 5–0 in Strachan's first game in charge. For the record, we were doing all right for the first eight minutes! I went to a hospital in Bratislava to find out the extent of the damage, then flew back with the team to Glasgow and had an operation to repair my cheek the next day. A plate was inserted in my cheek. Before the operation, my vision was fine. When I awoke after the operation, my vision was blurred in my right eye. The operation involved insertions in the side of my head and at the side of my eye. It was a delicate procedure and I think the initial damage was done then.

Lenny came to see me at the house and was upset with me for hurting his knee! He said he'd been having treatment on it. Typical Neil.

Deep down I knew it was the end but kept hoping I would wake up one morning and my eye would be better. I eventually announced my retirement. I don't blame Vidic or Lenny for what happened – it's part of the game. I was fortunate to play at the top level for the best part of sixteen years. But, being greedy, I wanted to carry on.

Injury is part of sport. I don't think any player goes out to seriously injure another. But there is so much pressure in the game that sometimes things spill over in the desire to win or in the disappointment of losing. It's a physical game, an emotional game and all players are extremely competitive. Once the game finishes, in my experience, every player is the same and wouldn't wish serious injury on a fellow professional. Vidic never phoned me to ask how I was and I didn't expect him to. If players were to phone opponents every time they caught one another, then they would spend every Saturday night on the phone apologising. I caught players with my arms and elbows on many occasions but I never purposely tried to cause an opponent any serious damage.

It was sad for my playing career to end that way but I was fortunate to have enjoyed a very good career at a high level. I would have preferred to go on for a few years, the way Teddy Sheringham did and the likes of Ryan Giggs playing on as they get close to forty. I missed football. I missed being in a dressing room on a day-to-day basis. I missed training. I missed the fun. I missed the buzz of running out of the tunnel at a packed stadium. I missed a manager's half-time team-talk. I missed the adrenalin rush. I missed the verbal abuse. I missed the feeling of winning. Nothing else is like it. Nothing compares to it.

The one silver lining from my career ending was that I hadn't really had a break from the game for almost twenty years. It was nice to have time off and have a summer holiday not thinking about the game. I was always thinking about the new season, what we'd be doing for pre-season and making sure I had a decent level of fitness when starting back. Family holidays must have been a nightmare for Sam and the kids. I always had one eye on pre-season and making sure I was fit enough.

Initially when I retired, I wasn't at a loose end. I had a wife and five sons to spend time with and I enjoyed that. We also have plenty of animals, including horses and dogs and cats.

Being out of football also gave me the chance to pursue other sports, like golf and cricket, although I had to wear a helmet at cricket as a heavy knock around my eye could cost me my sight. I took up shooting and would go away for the day with friends to do that. I had to learn to shoot left-handed because of the damage to my right eye but it's a good pursuit. It has also given me the privilege of meeting people who wear ridiculous salmon-pink trousers and matching velvet slippers.

I got enjoyment from all the other sports and pastimes but nothing compares to playing football at the highest level. You can't beat the feeling of achieving something in an important game, particularly scoring a goal like my volley against Juventus, the winning goal against Rangers in the last minute when I chipped Stefan Klos, the opening twenty minutes of my Old Firm debut when we beat Rangers 6–2, and scoring against Ajax in the Amsterdam Arena in a Champions League qualifier. I was never going to get that feeling again and it wasn't easy to come to terms with.

I enjoyed playing golf but if I had a six-footer to hole and I missed it, then so what. There was no intense pressure. I missed the professional competitiveness, the edge, the pressure. I tried to find different things that would give me the same thrill. At times I didn't think I fully appreciated what I had. But, to be honest, I found everything else to come up well short of playing.

I never wanted to go down the road of starting a business, owning a pub, that kind of thing. I wouldn't know where to start. I've earned relatively well in the game and didn't want to invest money into something I've no expertise in.

So, I suppose I hoped to get back into football and had to wait to be offered a role within a club. It was never going to be easy but after a couple of years of being out of the game, I decided to think seriously about it and apply for jobs. I wanted back into football, in the form of management.

16

MY TEAM OF WINNERS

I was lucky enough to play with and against some of Europe's and the world's greatest players. Having seen so much talent on the pitch, it's a daunting task to assess who's best and who I would pick for my ideal team. I could have picked at least two line-ups for each side comfortably. So to pick a Dream Team and an Opponents' XI is one of the biggest challenges I've had in writing this book. I can't include every good player I shared a pitch with and I hope I don't offend anyone. It speaks volumes for the people I played with that the likes of Gianfranco Zola, Alan Shearer, Martin Dahlin, Efan Ekoku and Kevin Gallacher can't get into my line-up as any of the strikers. In their own way, they all possessed natural talent and knew how to play up front. Playing as a defender is slightly easier, I feel, but I still had total respect for the ability and professionalism of Tony Gale, Ian Pearce, Colin Hendry, Henning Berg and Martin Laursen. As a striker, I relied on service and had the good fortune of being supplied with goal-scoring opportunities from talented wide men such as Alan Thompson, Stuart Ripley and Jason Wilcox.

I've also selected eleven of my toughest opponents. Having played as a centre-forward, central defender and central midfielder, I can assess the many different players I came up against. Some of them made my life as a footballer really difficult and that's why I selected them. I'm sure it would have been an interesting game between my dream team and toughest opponents. I do have to point out that I have selected a front two in my opponents line-up and have gone for two guys with outstanding individual talent. However, I was sorely tempted to go for a proven partnership and was close to choosing Dwight Yorke and Andrew Cole. They were, quite simply, the masters of twin-strike play. They were brilliant to watch and marvel at. They had a telepathic understanding and knew one another's game inside out. Both were great goal-scorers and played a pivotal part in Manchester United's many successes, including the Champions League win in 1999.

But here is my Dream Team selection and, needless to say, I have not selected myself in the dream team. I'd prefer to give the guys a chance of winning!

CHRIS SUTTON'S DREAM TEAM
4-4-2 FORMATION

TIM FLOWERS

Tim was a brilliant shot-stopper with a great attitude and he had a big personality. I played against him a few times when I was at Norwich and he was at Southampton. At that point, he was THE up-and-coming keeper in the country. We then became teammates at Blackburn. The day that defined Tim was our second-last game of the season for Blackburn against Newcastle and we won 1–0 in the Championship-winning season. Tim's perform-ance made sure we were still top of the league going into the last day of the season against Liverpool at Anfield. It was the best goalkeeping performance I've ever witnessed to this day. We had 30,545 fans inside Ewood Park that night – our highest attendance of the season – and he gave every one of them a treat. Mind you, his post-match interview didn't live up to his perform-ance on the pitch. I think he mentioned the word 'bottle' about fifteen times. He was just excited, I think. It was a response to Sir Alex Ferguson who had questioned our mental strength a few days earlier in terms of winning the league.

It was unfortunate he wasn't capped more than eleven times for England – but he was up against David Seaman and Seaman was well established. Tim had good knowledge of the game and was an intelligent guy. He was a conscientious trainer and would batter himself every day. The last time I saw him, he looked as though he'd had about eight hip operations. I admire people like that, players that push themselves every day because when he made a fantastic save on a match day, it was down to his hard work during the week. He was an example to everybody in terms of his application, commitment and dedication.

DIDIER AGATHE

The right side of defence isn't Didier's favourite position – he would have preferred to play up one. But one game sticks out for me that makes me comfortable putting him in that role. He played against Ronaldinho when he was at the height of his powers at Barcelona and didn't give the player a sniff that night. Didier turned in a brilliant defensive display. Ronaldinho used to make top players look stupid, he was that good. But Didier kept him totally subdued all night. He also had some incredible games in Europe against the likes of Ajax, Juventus and Stuttgart. That's the level where the best players are judged.

Didier's pace was a massive asset although I used to think, when he went on a dribble, at times he looked like he'd gone up a cul-de-sac. But more often than not, he had this amazing ability to nick the ball away from his opponent at the last second. It's fair to say he didn't have a very good left foot and I used to say to him that I thought it was artificial.

He was raw when Martin O'Neill signed him from Hibs for around £50,000 but he was a brilliant signing and was a big influence on the success we had. He'll be best remembered as a wing-back and used to cover the ground at some speed. He's the fastest player I've ever played with. I used to like his trick – which was to stand beside someone and boot the ball twenty yards up the pitch and then beat them in a foot race. It was extremely effective.

Yet, he wasn't a good trainer. He had some nightmares on the training ground day-to-day. He never really looked like a footballer – in fact, you would have thought he was a baker or a waiter who had won a training day with us. But he produced when it mattered because he was intelligent, adaptable and could read the game well. He was also a really nice guy off the pitch and had a good sense of humour.

JOHAN MJÄLLBY

Johan played many times for Sweden and adapted his game to be a central defender after arriving at Celtic as a midfielder. He was solid, aggressive, knew where to stand, never got flustered and knew what to do. He made it hard for the opposition to score and made sure the striker he was up against had an uncomfortable ninety minutes. He was an absolute winner. His desire was second to none and he was a fantastic reader of the game and made good decisions. Before games, you just left him to his own devices; he likes to be quiet and get himself into the 'zone'.

No matter the level of game we played in, whether it was a big European clash or an SPL game, I can't really recall anyone getting the better of him. He was extremely dependable and physically strong, without being blessed with too much pace. He made sure he got his distances right and rarely got caught out. He was another one with an 'over my dead body' attitude.

He was a good guy off the pitch, as well. I played against top central defenders such as Tony Adams and Steve Bould, and I feel Johan deserves to be up there with them all. Johan may think I've only included him because I'm scared of him but that's not totally true. Yes, he once threatened to rip my head off in a hotel dining room on the day of a game when we both ordered poached eggs and toast for our pre-match meal. A waiter brought one dish out and I tried to claim it. Johan said he had also ordered poached eggs and wasn't happy that I attempted to have mine first. After him threatening to rip my head off, I decided not to confront him. The eggs looked a bit undercooked anyway.

A real nice guy who had a six-pack to die for.

MARCEL DESAILLY

His record speaks for itself. He is a French World Cup winner and won the Champions League with AC Milan and various other trophies in one of the best club sides Europe has ever seen. He actually headered me off the ball in a game between Blackburn and Chelsea. His nickname was 'The Rock' and he lived up to it. He had all the attributes of a top player – strong, quick, very good in the air and technically sound. He was also a great reader of the game. It was a fantastic experience playing with him at Chelsea.

JACKIE McNAMARA

I played with some good left-sided defenders such as Mark Bowen and Graeme Le Saux but Jackie just nicks it. Jackie was stronger on his right foot but was also very dependable on the left-hand side. He was reliable and made good decisions. He read the game very well – an intelligent footballer who always got forward at the right times. He was similar to myself in that he could play in most positions, all the way across the back and across the midfield. He could play them all very well.

It took him a while to get into Martin O'Neill's starting side but when he did, he became a mainstay. He wasn't a flash player, he was selfless and his attitude overall was of the highest standard. He was a good user of the ball and master of the scissor-tackle. An intelligent guy, bit of a pretty boy, good-looking lad, butter wouldn't melt and all that stuff, but he was very aggressive. In fact, he could be really horrible when he needed to be. I fell out with him once or twice. I caught him at the wrong moment one time during a training session and he threatened to snap me in two. I kept my mouth shut after that. He was very quick-witted and cynical in a funny way off the pitch.

RUEL FOX

Ruel – along with Ian Crook – was the main reason why I progressed in the game. For me, Ruel should have played for England. I can't think of many players who had his all-round ability. He was very tricky and had pace. He had a fantastic football brain. He was a wide player but liked to come inside, pass and play round corners and link up. He could really rip full-backs, was a good crosser of the ball and scored his fair share of goals. He had brilliant skills and great feet.

He taught me about linking up the game. Ruel and Ian helped me develop and identify my strengths. They were willing to adapt to help me when I was a young player at Norwich. I appreciated that. On his day, he was as good a player down the right-hand side as you could ever get. When he was sold to Newcastle, that was, in my mind, the beginning of the end for me at Norwich. It never felt the same without him. I felt, with Ruel in the team, we could have kept going places, that's how highly I rated him. He had a dry sense of humour off the pitch and was another who'd cut you in two.

STILIYAN PETROV

I played with many terrific central midfielders such as Lennon, Lambert, McKinlay, Sherwood and Wise, so it was always going to be a difficult area to choose. When you talk about quality midfielders, then Stiliyan is the man. He used to play a more attacking role at Celtic with Lennon holding. He used to bomb forward and was a great support player for me and Henrik. It was my favourite time in football, playing when Stiliyan and Henrik were on form with our link-up play. We played well together and I knew his game. He also knew how to play to my strengths. When I first arrived at Celtic I didn't know Stiliyan, but after chatting to some people it seemed he was a chubby, Bulgarian right-back who used to have to get the bus to training because he was on such a low wage! He was a good passer of the ball, and was fantastic at getting on the half-turn and then having the power to drive away from players. His awareness, with and without the ball, was fantastic, as was the timing of his runs. He scored many crucial goals for Celtic in Europe and against Rangers.

He signed for Aston Villa when I was there and he found it difficult in the initial period because, for me, not enough of his team-mates were on his wavelength. The Villa fans got on his back but like a lot of fans, they didn't understand the game. He'd be two moves ahead of some of the guys he had to play with and that cost him. Some guys would be on the back-foot and Stiliyan would be playing passes around corners. They'd be used to players taking a touch, while he'd be passing first time and moving. I felt angry with what was happening but it showed the measure of Stiliyan that he had to adapt his game to suit them. He now plays the holding role at Villa, which he makes look extremely easy. For me, he's wasted playing in that position. He has a great football brain, makes good decisions when in possession and great runs off the ball. He was very confident on the pitch. When I played with him in the latter stages of my Celtic career, he was good at calming players down and progressed from a kid into a leader.

IAN CROOK

Chippy's passing ability was second to none, probably the best I played with. He used to smoke forty cigarettes a day, yet was fit enough as soon as he crossed the white line. When you looked at him you'd think you could blow him over, but he was streetwise. He was brought up at Tottenham with the likes of Glenn Hoddle, Mickey Hazard and Ossie Ardiles. With the competition for places so fierce at White Hart Lane, he moved to Norwich. It was certainly Norwich's gain and he helped my career develop. He was the best passer of a ball I played with and when I look at the players in the game today, I still haven't seen anyone better than him. His long and short passing was always brilliantly weighted and precise.

We had a free-kick routine and I scored a few goals because of it. Even though I was a young, raw teenager when I started, Ian gave me an appreciation of the game in terms of the timing of my runs and he had the skill to execute the pass. He tried to help me and other young guys out at the club. He wanted to see the kids progress and was really enthusiastic.

His nickname was 'Chippy' because he used to chip everything. He really was sensational. Just a pity he wasn't taller, faster, had a better engine or was better in the air. He was brilliant from dead-ball situations and seemed to be two yards ahead of every other player on the pitch with his awareness. A real players' player and someone I looked up to.

LUBOMÍR MORAVCÍK

I have played with many great wide players, such as Alan Thompson and Jason Wilcox. Jason was phenomenal when we won the league with Blackburn in 1995. Thommo had a lovely left foot, could pick the eye of a needle pass and also performed particularly well in big games. So, bearing all of that in mind, this was a really tough decision. But Lubo had it all. I couldn't leave a player of his quality out of the side. His right foot was unbelievable and his left foot was equally sublime. He was a brilliant footballer who beat people and scored amazing goals. Technically, he was as good as any footballer I've ever seen. He was thirty-five or thirty-six by the time I played with him at Celtic and even then he was still incredible. He had exceptional deliveries from dead-balls. I only wish I had played with him at Celtic when he was a few years younger so he didn't have to retire in 2002. We missed his ability when he left.

GEORGE WEAH

I only played with George for a short period, but when he arrived on loan from AC Milan he gave me a real lift. I wasn't having a great time at Chelsea, but he was the one player I felt could get the best out of me and link up with me. My game got better with George. He knew I was on a bit of a downer and he tried to help me. I started to enjoy my football more when he came. He had incredible skill and was unbelievable when we used to play little keep-ball sessions before training.

The goal he scored for AC Milan when he ran the length of the pitch was sensational. He was the top man in Serie A when that league was the best in Europe and every side had strong defences. If you talk about a man with absolute presence then this is it. He must have been intimidating to play against and when it came to the crunch, he had it in his locker to be nasty and horrible.

Off the park, when he walked into a room, he had an amazing stature. He was twice World Footballer of the Year and that says it all. He was strong, good in the air and could dribble. When he arrived at Chelsea, he'd maybe lost a little bit of pace but was so intelligent. He was also a lovely person. On a night out, he was great company. Overall, I was so impressed with George that I named one of my pigs after him.

HENRIK LARSSON

The greatest footballer I played with. A focused player and a brilliant professional. Another one who had to be left alone before a game. He was extremely focused, the same as Johan. He had attention to detail and his only thought was just about going out to annihilate the opposition. I admired that and it impressed me. When I stood with Henrik in the tunnel, I felt we had a chance of winning the game, regardless of how good the opposition was supposed to be. I never ever got the impression he was nervous, he was just preparing himself and was totally anti-social on the day of a game. Footballl-wise, Henrik was the best and I was very lucky to have been able to play with him for four years during the peak of our careers. He could drop deep, play on the shoulder, play up front on his own, finish with both feet, was good in the air and could chip.

The goal that stands out for me was the chip over Stefan Klos when we beat Rangers 6–2 at Parkhead. He beat Lorenzo Amoruso and then nutmegged Bert Konterman to give himself a one-on-one. I don't know any other player, and I mean this, that would have had the audacity to chip Klos from there, especially when the ball was actually running away from him. Most strikers would just have smashed it or placed it either side of the keeper, made sure it was on target. To score a goal like that, in that situation, showed incredible confidence and talent.

He was a player that made a difference in tight games. He was brilliant for my game. It used to make me laugh when people asked if he was good enough to play in the English Premiership. He moved to Barcelona and was phenomenal, helped them win the Champions League in 2006. He then had a terrific time at Manchester United. I was lucky to have played with him and so many other world-class strikers.

TOUGHEST OPPONENTS XI

PETER SCHMEICHEL

He was up there with the greatest goalkeepers the Premiership has ever seen. A brilliant shot-stopper and also unorthodox at times, he used to make some incredible saves and was good at collecting cross balls. He was also a good kicker of the ball who managed to fill his goal very well and had a major presence on the park. He had real attitude and because of that, he used to rub lots of people up the wrong way. He did annoy me on occa-

MY TEAM OF WINNERS

sions but that's football. When I was at Blackburn I was desperate to beat him, didn't want him to win anything. However, he was a fantastic all-round goalkeeper.

LEE DIXON

He just edges Gary Neville. Dixon was a nasty piece of work when he wanted to be. He was a very capable, tough-tackling and dependable defender. He was a major part of that brilliant back four Arsenal had under George Graham. It was very rare any opponent got the better of him. He, along with the other Arsenal defenders, used to have an uncanny knack of making decisions for the referee! It was a nightmare for opposition teams as they had to be at least 120 yards onside so as to not be flagged offside. He had a distinguished career and won many trophies.

TONY ADAMS

A brilliant leader and organiser. He got the very best out of the players around him. He would be my captain. I'd have loved to have him in my team every week. He wasn't the quickest but he was a brilliant defender, which was more important than anything else. He was exceptionally aggressive, strong in the air and a brutal tackler. But, above all, he was a brilliant reader of the game.

When I played against him, the tackle from behind was still allowed and he, along with Steve Bould and Martin Keown, certainly didn't disappoint when it came to that. Balls would come up to me and I'd try to get my body in front of him and hold it in. I'd then count in my head, one . . . two . . . thr . . . and

WHACK. I'd get it. Also a nice man. He took time out to speak to me when I was part of the England under-21 squad and he was a senior international player. I really appreciated that and it's something I've never forgotten.

ROBERTO AYALA

I only played against him once but that was enough to leave a lasting impression on me. I had an incredibly physical battle with him in a Celtic vs Valencia UEFA Cup tie at Parkhead. He and Manuel Pellegrini were the central defensive pairing and he had fantastic spring for someone of his size. He read the game very well and was accomplished on the ball. Ayala was an Argentinian internationalist and he loved to jump for high balls using his knee for leverage, more often than not right into my lower back. It was extremely painful. I can't remember ever being as angry during a game as I was with him. I used it as a motivational tool for that night, a contest that sticks in my memory for that reason and the fact we battled with them for 120 minutes and then lost on penalty kicks.

ARTHUR NUMAN

A talented Dutch international whose only fault was that he played for Rangers! A brilliant all-round footballer. Arthur was a fantastic passer of the ball, very good going forward and an exceptional crosser of a football. First and foremost, he was a fantastic defender and a great reader of the game. I was also impressed with his superb temperament – he never seemed to get flustered. He had some fantastic battles against Didier Agathe in Old Firm games.

DAVID BECKHAM

Choosing a wide-right midfielder was an extremely tough deci-sion bearing in mind the calibre of player I played against, such as Ronaldo, Seedorf and Ronaldinho. I opted for Beckham because his record speaks for itself. He is a fantastic passer of the ball and probably the greatest ever crosser of a football. He has also taken some wonderful free kicks, under enormous pressure, such as the one he scored for England against Greece at Old Trafford. He also has a fantastic engine.

I clashed with him at Old Trafford in a testimonial for Ryan Giggs in August 2001. He liked to tackle and could be niggly at times. One of his tackles led to our little altercation. He liked to leave his foot in and caught me on the back of the calf, out on the touchline. I was still standing so he then wellied me. I suppose it was more of a skirmish but it led to me giving him a slap. He has played important parts in success stories at some massive clubs and he is an ultimate professional. I have total respect for the career he has had.

ROY KEANE

A fantastic player who led by example. Had an incredible engine and an unbelievable will to win. A tough-tackling, inspirational leader. He could do everything and also came up with some impor-tant goals. To be honest, as was the case with Beckham, I didn't like Roy when he played for Manchester United and I was at Blackburn. It was all down to the rivalry. But Keane wasn't there to be liked. He joined Celtic towards the end of his career just I was leaving Parkhead. I didn't get the chance to play alongside him for Celtic and I would have loved the opportunity to do that.

XAVI

The player who makes things tick in arguably the world's greatest-ever club side. Paul Scholes would run him close for this midfield position. However, Xavi gets the nod. When he plays, he looks like he's having a kickabout in the back garden because he appears to be so relaxed and makes it look so easy. He always has time on the ball and is a lovely passer, both long and short. He also always plays with his head up and his vision makes him stand out as a player. Opposing players try to get close to him but seldom do.

RYAN GIGGS

For me, the greatest Premier League player of all time. Unstoppable on the left-hand side when running at pace with the ball. He has great skill and change of direction. He beats players with ease and makes it look effortless. Over the years, he's had a fantastic end product and scored some incredible goals. The one that stands out in my mind was his fantastic solo goal against Arsenal at Villa Park in the FA Cup semi-final replay in 1999. Has won everything in the game, time and time again, and still has a wonderful desire to go on and on.

IAN WRIGHT

He was brilliant, unstoppable on his day. He and Robbie Fowler were the strikers I believed could score any type of goal. Ian was just a natural finisher. He had great awareness, always knew where the goal was and where the keeper was standing. I had first-hand experience of trying to contain him and he was horrible to play against. I remember playing for Norwich against Arsenal and he destroyed us. He was clever, quick and could beat players. He was a late developer and always had an infectious attitude. He was a real personality. To my mind, he was very unfortunate not to be capped more by England.

ERIC CANTONA

A genius. Probably the best there ever was. What a buy he was by Sir Alex Ferguson from Leeds United. Another Manchester United player who had that great aura about him. He was so clever and could do everything on the park. He was impossible to contain when he was on his game. He supposedly had a dodgy temperament and was arrogant, but that made him the player he was. It must have been inspirational to play with him. He had incredible vision and could do things other players could only dream of. A consistent goal-scorer and scorer of great goals. Maybe even the coolest penalty taker of all time. I played against him when I was a young centre-half at Norwich and he destroyed me. He pulled me all over the place and took me into areas I just didn't want to go. United won the game easily. It was a lesson learned for me that day.

I could have added many more players but I had to be brave and ruthless – as all managers need to be at certain times. It would be some game if those two teams came up against each other. I'd have paid money to watch that one.

17

MANAGING EXPECTATIONS

It was fair to say football management never really crossed my mind while I was playing. I only ever thought about what I was going to do on the pitch and how I was going to approach the game. It was all about preparation. It was just about the here and now for me, really. Subconsciously I thought my playing career would never end. Retiring at thirty-four gave me something to think about though. I wasn't totally sure what my next move would be. I had had eighteen years in one job, the only line of work I knew, and I wasn't going to be able to find anything that could compare with playing. John Robertson always told me to play for as long as I could, as there was nothing like pulling on your boots and playing in a competitive game.

My friend Billy McKinlay convinced me to start taking my coaching qualifications, so at least I would have the option if I did eventually want to pursue a career in football coaching and management. It was obviously sensible to give myself that option. I was sceptical about going on some coaching courses, maybe a bit arrogant in wondering what I could possibly learn after playing at the level I had played at. But I found them to be very beneficial. I felt at the time my knowledge of the game was very good. But the courses helped me understand that the most important thing is how to get the information across. I also learned a lot in terms of organisation and communication. But what benefited me as much as anything was watching some of the coaches and managers at work. In order to help with education and preparation for getting into that side of the game, I went along to clubs like Fulham, Norwich and Aston Villa, just watching and learning. As an egotistical player, I took it for granted that managing and coaching was an absolute breeze and that there wasn't much to it. That's the way most players felt, I'd imagine.

It soon became apparent that, in the main, I was lucky to play under some really talented people and that it certainly wasn't the easy job I'd thought. In 2009, the Inverness Caledonian Thistle manager's job became available and I showed an interest in that. But I didn't hear anything back from the club. Then in September 2009, myself and Ian Pearce, a good friend of mine and former team-mate at Blackburn Rovers, decided we'd have a crack at the Lincoln City job that had become available. Peter Jackson, the previous manager, had been sacked after losing nine out of his first twelve games in charge. We turned up for our first interview at the Belton Woods Hotel just outside Grantham. More than seventy people applied for the job and we thought it would be good experience to see how the interview process worked. To be honest, we weren't expecting much more than having a blether with the Lincoln hierarchy. We certainly weren't expecting to be asked back for a second interview. But we were.

After the second interview, we were offered the job that same evening. The process was a good experience in itself and I felt we were well prepared and organised. We also felt we knew the game quite well. It's always very interesting to see the reaction managers get when somebody is given a job for the first time.

'They lack experience' is the usual cry from some but my reply to that would be very simple – how do you gain experience if you're never given the opportunity? But we were very honoured and proud to take our first step into management.

Having said that, Ian and I went into the job with our eyes wide open. We didn't have any experience of playing football at Division 2 level. But the game is the same and the rules are the same no matter the level you are involved. Nothing changes in that respect. The contacts we had and the hard work we'd put in on the training ground meant we didn't see this as an impossible job. We were extremely excited and positive about going in there. We'd also taken the job after just twelve games of the season gone and we had more than three quarters of the campaign to go to avoid relegation. That was the target given to us on our appointment. Having said all of that, it was going to be hard work.

Football, in my opinion, is all about players. The better players you have the more chance you have of winning games, make no mistake about that. With the greatest of respect to the footballers that play at Division 2 level, they are there for a reason, mainly being that they aren't good enough to play at Division 1 level or in the Championship and the Premier League, albeit some will progress. However, many players at that level have deficiencies in their game, whether that's something technical in terms of ability or to do with athleticism. Some guys are journeymen professionals and some other players are kids who hope to be able to step up to the next level.

Money was tight and wages, in football terms, weren't good in most cases. Buying players was virtually impossible with the budgets we had and you needed to adhere to them. A lot of clubs have ended up in financial difficulty and entered administration, and ultimately have been deducted points as a result. I didn't want to go down that road. Our budget was very tight and was virtually spent by the time I arrived. We had to generate our own money to spend in the market. We had to do that by wheeling and dealing. We also knew that a good run in the Cup would be important and would help increase our budget for bringing in players. The FA Cup was always going to be important to us in that respect.

It was tough but it was the same for most clubs in Division 2. I had taken a team that was low in confidence – losing three out of every four games didn't breed belief. But as is quite often the case when a new manager takes over we got an immediate reaction. We won our first two games: 1–0 at home to Aldershot and by the same scoreline away to Macclesfield. Whether both victories were deserved or not was another matter. But it was massive psychologically to get the six points. I found during my year at Lincoln that most teams in the division were of fairly similar standard and could beat one another on any given day. We were no different, but we were conceding too many goals and not scoring enough. I know it sounds simple but that was our starting point – defend better and be more clinical in front of goal. And while it seemed simple enough to understand what the problem was, finding a solution was always going to prove to be more difficult.

It was a fantastic learning curve for Ian and me. Getting better players in was the obvious solution but as the budget was used up when we arrived, there was no room for manoeuvre. But we were promised revenue from the FA Cup. We were more desperate than most lower-league clubs and non-league clubs for income being in the position we were in and we badly wanted a decent run. The board had promised they'd put every penny we produced from the Cup back into the playing budget.

Lincoln City had an appalling record in the FA Cup and had struggled to get past the first round in the previous few years. We had a couple of tricky away ties to negotiate and we managed to defeat AFC Telford 3–1. We then came up against Northwich. That game was televised as they had been the Cup-competition giant killers at that point, having just beaten Charlton Athletic. We beat Northwich 3–1 to set up a tie away to Premier League side Bolton Wanderers. It was the first time in ten years Lincoln City had qualified for the third round proper.

Although we lost the game 4–0 at the Reebok Stadium, the boys did themselves proud. It was 0–0 at half-time but we conceded two quick goals just after the break and went on to concede two more. There was a gulf between the players, but our lads had a right go and we were very proud of their display. The support that day was exceptional and I think around 3,000 Lincoln fans travelled to the North West, which was incredible.

The money we generated from the FA Cup was going to be very important to us. However, unfortunately, to use a footballing term, the goalposts were moved and I'll get to that later.

The footballing side I enjoyed and we tried to get the players on board from the first moment I walked through the door. I wanted them to buy into my training methods and to start to believe in themselves individually and collectively. I always believed as a player you had to enjoy your working environment. We worked hard with the lads in training, tried to educate them, tried to make them better footballers and more confident. We put on different sessions and tried to keep it interesting. There's nothing worse than being bored at training, going home after your work and feeling you got absolutely nothing out of it.

The manager is crucial to this. As I said previously, I was very lucky to play under some greats who made it seem so easy and logical. Managers who knew how to treat you well and make you believe in yourself are, in my opinion, priceless. If you have players wanting to play for the manager, then it will assist you in trying to be successful. I tried to emulate this. It was important the team and the club were united and moved forward on the pitch. By that I mean the first team, the youth set-up and at boardroom level.

The youth set-up was and is so important at that level. You need to be producing your own. That is what safeguards the future. Lincoln didn't have many players coming through the youth ranks and we tried to put a plan in place that would try to increase the chances of kids breaking through with our training methods. But the bottom line is, you get better results if you have better players. It is far easier to progress through the ranks at Division 2 level as a youth team player than it is at Championship and Premiership level, that's for sure. Lincoln didn't really have a reputation of being a developing club but it's a massive help financially to produce from within. From a playing perspective, a young apprentice should see that if he knuckles down, listens and works hard, then the pathway into the first team at a club such as Lincoln shouldn't be an impossibility. Far from it. It should be very real and always within touching distance for them.

In my year in charge, we encountered obstacles in terms of trying to implement our ideas. We were swimming against the tide. We were certainly undermined trying to make changes for the good of the football team.

We managed to stay in Division 2 with a bit to spare, three games to go if memory serves me correctly. It certainly wasn't all straightforward but we got there in the end. The group of players I inherited gave me everything. What they lacked in terms of confidence and quality they made up for in terms of endeavour.

One or two stepped out of line on the discipline side but nothing too serious. I was a player myself and made mistakes, so it wasn't difficult to sort things out and explain how the disciplinary system at the club worked. Young men make mistakes in most jobs and football is no different. I wasn't a dictator. That's not my style. I wanted a level of conduct from them, but also wanted them to feel relaxed and look forward to coming into work every morning. The bottom line is you want the players onside and you want a harmonious dressing room. It's a competitive environment, players all competing for a jersey. In general,

I think the players did enjoy their time under me. It was about making things as comfortable as possible. We had a small squad so we couldn't afford to hack them off.

We had some very good players who helped make my job that little bit easier. Scott Kerr was club captain and a really good leader. I had a lot of time and respect for him. In the early days, Scott wasn't getting into the starting line-up but he never felt sorry for himself. He just got his head down and worked harder. Scott played a big part in the group and us staying up in the division with his leadership qualities on and off the park.

The biggest part of us staying up was our use of the loan system. With the help of various loans from Aston Villa, Fulham and Leeds, the quality of our performance improved. The Villa boys – Nathan Baker, Eric Lichaj and Chris Herd – really lifted the other guys, as did Matthew Saunders and Adam Watts from Fulham. You could see they had been taught really good habits at their respective clubs, as they were always doing extra work after training, really looking after themselves, doing lots of stretching and going to the gym. The excellent attitudes rubbed off on the rest of the players at the club. They could see players from a higher level not taking their football for granted and continuing to work hard, and it inspired some of the guys. Not all of the players took it on board, unfortunately. But that's life. The smarter ones always work harder.

These guys lifted the level on the pitch. And in Davide Somma we had a genuine goal threat. In all honesty, he was the main reason why we stayed in the division. Somma was rated highly at Leeds by Simon Grayson and Gwyn Williams and he was on loan at Chesterfield when I went to watch him playing in a game against Crewe. He missed a penalty that night and pulled his hamstring, but you could see that he knew what to do, had a decent awareness and was bright and intelligent. We were fortunate to be able to sign him on loan and his goals proved to be the difference for us.

He was a bit raw when he first arrived but he knew how to finish – right foot, left foot, he was very natural in front of goal. And he scored some tremendous goals. Davide worked exceptionally hard on his game, and we worked with him on the timing of his runs and his understanding. By his own admission, he was by no means the finished article but by the time he left, he was really getting there and it was very pleasing to see him scoring goals for Leeds the following season in the Championship. It just shows how quickly things can change in football. It was all down to the player's work ethic and drive. He was conscientious and wanted to improve. He wasn't scared of hard work and his attitude was fantastic. He was very strong mentally and one of his biggest strengths was that he wasn't frightened to miss a chance. He wanted to improve and was relentless in his training.

The end of the season should have signalled a well-earned break. But recruiting players for the next season occupied all my time. It was very difficult trying to get the players we wanted. The goalscorers were the hardest to attract and were usually snapped up very quickly. We were in desperate need of someone with an eye for goal, but it was hard to get anyone to come and play at the level we were at. It was also difficult to pay them the kind of wage they were looking for and, ultimately, deserved. I found that despite many, many attempts for different players, I just couldn't get what I was looking for. We tried to get Somma back but Leeds wanted him to stay and fight for a first-team place at Elland Road. Still, I was relatively happy with the squad we had assembled, although Messi and Rooney would have been nice.

Ian and I spoke at the end of the season about our performances and contributions during the previous campaign. We discussed what we were pleased with and where we felt we could have done better. We wanted to improve and not repeat any mistakes we may have made. We were very proud of the achievement of keeping Lincoln City in Division 2 despite many problems we'd encountered in our relationship with the chief executive, Dave Roberts, which gave us great cause for concern.

After a meeting on the Thursday night before the first league game of the season at Rotherham, we met Dave and Bob Dorrian, the chairman, at Café Bleu in Newark. It was during that meeting we found out we weren't getting the money we generated from the previous season in our FA Cup run. Yet we were promised the money. It was a major blow to our plans. There was also another and arguably even more serious issue about money from our FA Cup run that I think should have been paid to the players but for various reasons never was. With all this going on at the club, our trust had gone.

In the car on the way back to Grantham, I told Ian that we should leave the club immediately. I felt what was said in that restaurant was totally unacceptable. We were totally flabbergasted with the way the club was acting and the effect this would inevitably have on our plans. We'd both had our reservations from the previous season but I now felt that things were on a slippery slope because the club were not going to deliver what we'd agreed.

By this time I had totally lost trust in Dave Roberts. I should have left the club there and then but Ian convinced me to stay on. He felt we owed it to the players and the supporters to try and build on the achievement of staying up. He said it was our first job in management and we should to keep at it for as long as possible. I agreed, albeit reluctantly. However, in the pit of my stomach I knew we weren't for Sincil Bank much longer. Too many things had happened and the meeting at Newark was the final straw. It had left a sour taste in my mouth and the relationship between myself and the chief executive was beyond repair.

My relationship with Bob Dorrian was always fine but it was

different with Dave. It was becoming impossible to stay. I believed my position was untenable.

Ian was a brilliant guy to work with and was always playing devil's advocate but behind closed doors he was also becoming disenchanted with what we were having to deal with. Ian was getting as frustrated as me. On the day of the Burton game I told Ian I was going to speak to Bob after the game and tell him that I believed I had no option but to leave the club. Ian was a bit unsure about leaving and said maybe I should reconsider. Ian felt the same as me about certain issues but wasn't quite at the tipping point. However, when we arrived at the ground and read the programme notes written by one of the directors, Kevin Cooke, who was critical of our players, Ian was as infuriated as me. He was furious and told me that I was spot on with what we had discussed earlier.

Bob Dorrian came into my office after the game, as he always did whether we won, lost or drew. He commented on the performance of the team and said we were unlucky not to win but a 0–0 draw wasn't the worst result. We continued to chat about the game. I then threw Bob a programme across the desk and asked him what he thought of the notes written by Cooke. Bob agreed that it was disgraceful and wholly unacceptable.

I then went through my year in charge and the problems I'd encountered, some far more serious than others. I asked him how he would feel if he was in my shoes. Bob said he would not be very happy. I said that under the circumstances I didn't want to work at the club any longer. Bob said if that was truly the way I felt it would be better for both parties if I left. He said he totally understood the way I felt. I said that I couldn't speak for Ian, only myself. Ian was party to the whole conversation. Bob asked me if I would reconsider but my mind was made up. Bob said that he would be sorry to see me go but accepted what I had to say. Ian then told Bob that he would be leaving with me. Ian's words were, 'We came as a pair, we will leave as a pair.' Knowing Ian as well as I did, his loyalty didn't surprise me.

Bob then asked how we would want a statement worded in terms of the way my time at the club ended. Bob said the club would put a statement out in the media saying it was mutual consent. I said I wasn't bothered how a statement was worded. I trusted Bob so I was happy to leave it to him. That was naive of me. Hindsight is a wonderful thing! I should have got the English LMA involved to make sure everything contractually was tidied up, but not for one moment did I think anything untoward would come of it.

The irony was that Ian suggested in order to protect the club and keep our own counsel, it might be better to say we left for personal reasons. We didn't want to cause Bob or the club any embarrassment; we didn't want to bad mouth the club. Bob said he appreciated that and gave us his word that he would not say a bad word about us, and that personal reasons would be better as it would eliminate people asking questions. I then said to Bob that I hoped there wouldn't be any trouble in us receiving the payments that we were owed up to date. Bob said that wouldn't be a problem. I stood up and said I was sorry for him that things had turned out as they had, but I was left with no choice due to the position I'd been put in. Bob seemed a bit emotional and said he was sorry it had come to this. We shook hands, wished each other good luck and promised each other that we would stay in touch.

I'd have stayed if I thought my position was not impossible. If I had felt things were heading in the right direction, and my relationship with certain people was good and I could trust them, then I would have carried on. But problems had been brewing for a while. There was interference, broken promises and incompetence. Enough was enough, really.

And I wouldn't miss the living arrangements. I stayed in a flat with Ian in Grantham, close to the A1 for the road back down to London for him. We had no curtains in the place and used to hang up our suit-carriers as curtains. We had a little portable television and a couple of rocking chairs in the living room. We used to rock on them like a couple of mad men. It was no fun, really.

It meant a lot of commuting for me, time spent in the car, and I didn't get to spend as much time with my family as I would have liked. Sam and the boys remained in Norfolk. But I knew it was never going to be easy. I didn't go into management expecting every day to be a wonderful experience. In many ways I realised I had to be ruthless if I wanted to do well. Managers can end up married to the job.

In terms of my backroom staff, we had a good group, even if it was quite small. Ian was good for me. We had a first team coach, Scott Lindsey and I had a goalkeeping coach, Paul Musselwhite. He was a good guy and I had a lot of time for him. He was also still a good goalkeeper. We had our kitman Matt Carmichael who did a great job. Some clubs have to take home their kit and wash it but we were fine in that department. We'd also get DVDs of the game and we would spend time breaking things down and putting packages together for the players. I feel it's important when players are making mistakes that you point it out to them and try to show them how to improve, what's going to make them better footballers. I was sad at leaving the players behind as so many of them had given their all for me the previous season.

A week after I left, I met the vice-chairman, Chris Travers, in a pub in Norfolk for some lunch. He wanted to discuss why I had taken the decision to part company with the club and how I felt it could move forward. I had a good relationship with Chris and Bob and they were two people who had the club's best interests at heart. We had a nice lunch and shook hands after. During that discussion, Chris asked if I would come back to Lincoln as manager. I declined the offer.

I stayed in touch with Bob and Chris. I would sometimes text or phone them before games to wish them luck. I invited them both as my guests, with their partners, to a Charity Dinner Celtic put on for me in Glasgow on 7 November 2010. It was to raise money for Yorkhill Children's Hospital. They came to Glasgow and enjoyed the hospitality. We shook hands and had a nice catch-up. Yet, it then all took an incredible twist, a sequence of events that left me flabbergasted.

The first thing that shocked me was receiving a letter from the club's solicitor saying that they were suing me for breach of contract. It arrived a couple of days before Christmas 2010 and was a real bolt from the blue. I was still in touch with Bob and he told me that the board's decision on this action was unanimous. I found that incredible. I just didn't get it. I found the whole thing to be in poor taste.

The League Managers Association have been representing me on this but as yet nothing further has happened.

At the end of the 2010–11 season Lincoln City were relegated to the Conference League. I was saddened to see that happen. Bob was then interviewed by the media about what the financial repercussions of this would be for a club like Lincoln. During that interview he was critical of me and the signings I had made the previous summer. I phoned Bob up about his comments and he backtracked and told me that had I remained in charge then the club would not have been relegated.

There's a lot more I could say about the whole situation but most of it wouldn't do anyone any good. What I can say, though, is that when I left the club I shook hands with Bob and told him I would not reveal the extent of the reasons why I left the club and that I'd defy anyone going on working under such circumstances. Trust was a big thing for me and that's why I found some things totally unacceptable.

The chief executive, Dave Roberts, was not a guy I really wanted to work under. Roberts came away with some ridiculous suggestions to raise money for the club. In the summer of 2010 when Neil Lennon kindly agreed to send down a Celtic side to play against us in a pre-season friendly, the club organised an Open Day around the stadium for families and supporters. Roberts spoke to me about the Open Day and suggested we should have a 'sponge-throwing stall' with me standing in the stocks and fans charged fifty pence to try and hit me on the face with a wet sponge. At first I thought he was kidding but then I realised he was deadly serious. I had to laugh. Was he for real? It would have taken 100 sponges for us to raise fifty quid. I told him I'd be too busy preparing the team for the game to get involved in something like that so close to kick-off.

At Lincoln, we also inherited a backroom staff guy and within a few weeks it became clear that myself and Ian could not work with him. We asked for Roberts and the board to remove the guy from his position so it could free up a wage to bring in someone I felt could do that particular job. But they were hesitant and seemed to think that if they didn't deal with the issue then it would just go away. Roberts kept coming back to me to ask if there was any way possible I could work with the guy and I told him time and time again that it wasn't possible to do so. Then, after three months, the board hit me with the sledgehammer news that they couldn't rid of the guy because he was on a different contract and they were unable to terminate his deal.

Had they not left me with no choice other than to walk away, we could have built on what we achieved in May 2010 by keeping the club in Division 2.

I was criticised by Bob after I had gone and Lincoln were relegated at the end of the season. I found that very disappointing and unjustified. When the team was seven points off a play-off spot in January I received no credit for that. But when they went down four months later to the Conference League, Bob put some of the blame at my door. They took just one point from their final ten games. Steve Tilson had thirty-seven games to keep them up when he took over from me. I had only thirty-four games when I took over from Peter Jackson.

Leaving Lincoln was the right decision at that time. The way Bob and the board have behaved towards us subsequently, in terms of trying to sue me and blaming me partially for the relegation, means I'm glad to be away from them. I don't want to work for people like that. In many ways I wasted a year of my life, but all experiences are valuable and it was certainly an experience.

Out of respect for Lincoln City and the club's fans, I hope we can draw a line under this whole saga and all move on. In the end, certain issues led to our parting, some more serious than others. But Lincoln is a good club and gave me an opportunity to get into management. It was certainly an experience I've learned a lot from. It was a period in my life I will not forget in a hurry. What I learned there must certainly stand me in good stead.

As a manager you are planning ahead every hour of every day, for every week. I had to make hundreds of decisions every day and I wrestled with a lot of them in my mind, whether I'd called something right or not. Sometimes it threatened to eat me up. I had to switch off from it whenever I could, but it wasn't always easy.

Playing is easier than being manager. It's much, much easier. There are so many things you have to contend with when you're a manager. I had to deal with things at Lincoln I didn't think I would have to. I wasn't afraid of hard work and doing my bit, helping out wherever and whenever I could, but there were some things I didn't expect to be in my remit.

We'd stayed up in my first season and that was a good achievement. When we came in our main aim was to stay in the league and we managed to do that. We were asked to keep Lincoln up, that was our remit. Has the experience at Lincoln totally soured me? Not at all. I still want to get back into that side of the game and if something comes my way then I will consider it.

I wish Lincoln all the best and hope the club returns to the football league where they belong.

Ian Pearce on Chris Sutton

We were grateful to be given the chance of an interview with Lincoln City and we prepared ourselves well. We were then asked back for a second chat and offered the job that same evening. I was thrilled and surprised. I was looking forward to the opportunity of working with Chris.

When we arrived, the players had an unacceptable level of fitness. We had to put them through a mini pre-season schedule, as well as try and get them organised and into our way of wanting to play. We were keen to get them into a pattern of play but some players at that level need to be told six, seven and eight times how to do things. Even then they still might not grasp it.

That was more frustrating for Chris than it was for me as, when he was a player, he could follow the instructions of a manager immediately. He knew exactly what was required of him. That's why he played at such a high level and was the best striker I played with.

To be fair to the players, they gave their all and that was the most important thing. But halfway through the season, I had my doubts whether we'd be able to avoid relegation.

But we got there, with games to spare. We kept our side of the bargain, which was to make sure Lincoln City stayed in Division 2.

However, rather than being allowed to build on what we had achieved the previous season, obstacles were put in our way by certain people at the club. It really ripped the heart out of us because we had been excited about the new season. Promises were broken and the trust was gone. The plans they were putting in place and one or two things they wanted to do to the players didn't sit comfortably with Chris and myself. It festered away and after that meeting in Newark, Chris said he thought we should leave.

I tried to talk him round, I suppose. Told him to dig in for the players and see it out for them. Then we read the programme notes from a director on the night of the Burton Albion game. The comments he made were very negative. That was the final nail in the coffin.

We were busting our nuts for the football club, making sacrifices. Chris got players to come to the club that would normally not have looked twice at a club like Lincoln. But some people in authority were undermining us. Unfortunately, it left us with only one choice.

Chris told Bob he was left with no choice but to leave because of certain issues which had occurred. Bob said if that was the way Chris felt, it was best for both parties if we parted company. I echoed everything Chris said. I was also going. Bob then phoned me the next day and asked if I would be interested in taking over from Chris. I mean, really. If I was unhappy with things as assistant manager, what made him think I'd accept the same things as manager? We came as a pair and we left as a pair. I would never have accepted that job.

Putting the issues and lies from the people in authority to one side, I actually enjoyed the experience of being involved as an assistant manager to Chris at Lincoln. Chris made it that way for me. He was a pleasure to work with and I learned many things from him. It wasn't always easy but he handled things exceptionally well. The football side of things went well and we had fun. I hope we will get the chance to work together again in the future. I know Chris has something very good to offer the game of football and I would like to be a part of it.

18

THE PURSUIT OF PERFECTION –

A LIFE OF MAKING DECISIONS

Paranoid. Opinionated. Arrogant. Self-doubting. Silly boy. Manic. Stubborn. Strange.

These are words used in this book by some of my former managers to describe me. Thank God Glenn Hoddle didn't contribute!

On these pages, I've tried to be as open as possible and I couldn't argue with a single adjective used to describe me at different stages of my career.

Well, maybe just one. Paranoid? I know what paranoid means but, for the avoidance of doubt, here's the definition from the Oxford Dictionary – Paranoid: delusions of persecution.

To say I was paranoid would be to suggest it was unwarranted for me to feel victimised. To me, I wasn't suffering from paranoia in terms of how I felt a certain person acted towards me. It was all real. But I can understand why some people would think I was paranoid. But it's just a word, isn't it?

Balanced. Intelligent. Sublime. Influential. Determined. Versatile. Friendly. Humorous. Shy.

Other adjectives used by some of my former managers to describe me and I thank them wholeheartedly for their kind words. In different ways, they were all good for me.

I did give a few of them cause for concern and I regret that. When I look back, I'm bitterly disappointed with the way I behaved at certain times. I made some really poor decisions, some terrible errors of judgement.

I deeply regret the anguish I must have put my parents through for a period of time when I moved out of the house after I joined Norwich on the YTS scheme. I'm not proud of my behaviour off the pitch during that period. My performances on the pitch belied my attitude off the pitch. My thought process at that stage was that I was just loving everything and I was a bighead. Coming from the background I had – I was brought up well, to be respectful and show manners – when I left home at sixteen, I just didn't know what hit me. I felt intimidated, out of my comfort zone, mixing with boys who were far more street-wise than I was. I had to stand up for myself and join in.

Football is a game for the working man. A lot of it is banter. If I was reading a book in the dressing room, or doing a cross-word in one of the broadsheet newspapers, I'd have to put up with a bit of ridicule. But I never took it personally. It was banter, as far as I was concerned. I mean, I criticise grown men I play cricket with who play on PlayStations. I say to them, if you read a book you might become cleverer. But people shouldn't be judged for playing on a computer. I shouldn't be judged for reading a book. I think books are better than films. In a book, you can actually feel what somebody is writing, get a proper insight into their mind and soul, but in films you can feel things but you can't get inside their head.

I could look after myself when it came to banter, and I could be quite scathing when I wanted to be and needed to be. My former team-mates at every club will no doubt vouch for that. And I'm sure some players I've played against would also say

I could be scathing towards them on the pitch. But a lot of what I said on and off the pitch was just my way of being humorous. I rarely meant to be nasty.

I loved the banter in the dressing room, especially at Celtic. We all got on, in general. There were big characters inside that dressing room and you had to be sharp and on your toes to survive. You had to be prepared to take flak. I miss the dressing room, I really do. It was an exciting environment to be in and it was also educational.

Despite my early misgivings about life at Norwich City as an apprentice, I began to thrive on it and became a Jack the Lad as I started to make a name for myself at Carrow Road. I enjoyed the attention and adulation.

I went to Blackburn and I didn't like being criticised by the media for my performances. The shoe was on the other foot for me; that was the first time I had really been criticised and it didn't sit well. Who would like criticism? I was young and I didn't cope with it. I just saw things as black and white back in those days. After a few years and with a Premiership title under my belt, it got to the stage at Blackburn where I was in a comfort zone and didn't have to leave. I could have sat there on my money but I decided to go to Chelsea, where once again I was out of my comfort zone.

It didn't go well there for me. I was absolutely pummelled by the press. A lot of the stuff that was written about me was brutal. I don't feel I'm exaggerating to say they butchered me on a regular basis. I felt they had it in for me and it wasn't a pleasant situation I found myself in. But in my early years as a footballer, I courted the press and you can't have it all ways. The spell at Chelsea was the lowest point of my career. It made it even more unbearable when Sam and the kids started to be verbally abused when they were out and about in London. It was awful for Sam and my sons to be abused in that way. That hurt me more than anything. At times I felt like walking away from football. I contemplated quitting because I didn't like it when my family got dragged into things.

I blame myself totally for not performing well enough on the pitch. It was down to me. And I bitterly regret speaking to Gianluca Vialli the way I did on the morning of the FA Cup Final. He was a really good man.

One situation I didn't regret was the way I handled leaving Celtic under Gordon Strachan. I felt totally justified and vindicated. I don't regret the way I dealt with all of that in the slightest. The only thing I regret was having to leave the club, not Strachan.

The positive to come out of it was that I ended up back in the English Premiership with Birmingham and Aston Villa. It was just a pity I only got another year or so, when I would have loved to play a lot longer back in that league.

I had a great career with many ups and downs. To win the Premiership with Blackburn and three SPL titles with Celtic was just phenomenal. To play for my home club Norwich in Europe was fantastic and to win the Golden Boot award is something I'm very proud of. I'm lucky to have so many great memories.

Although I've been self-deprecating and negative about myself in many of these pages, I did know what I was good at. And I worked hard throughout my career, from an early age. I took myself off to do the weights with Chris Roberts when I was a teenager at Norwich when nobody else was doing it. That was off my own back. I was dedicated and wanted to succeed.

As a youngster, I didn't think I was outstanding. I felt in my own company I was good and could handle myself. I owe most things to my dad, especially. Had he not been an influence on me when I was twelve, thirteen, fourteen and fifteen, in terms of building up a base for my fitness, then I would not have become a footballer. I'm certain of that. My biggest strength, I thought, was my awareness. I could read the game well. Being able to understand things and take them on board. Knowing what I could do well. Knowing my weaknesses and place in the pecking order was a strength to me because it made me work harder. I knew my limitations but it was a plus point to recognise my weaknesses; it meant I tried to play the game to my own strengths and my opponents' weaknesses. Being in good physical shape made my state of mind strong, gave me confidence. I used my physicality to my advantage.

I was never frightened of hard work. I worked hard at Norwich on my fitness and first touch. I worked hard at Blackburn and Celtic. I knew I wasn't as naturally talented a striker as someone like Shearer or Larsson or Ian Wright, because I was limited with some of my qualities. But, in the end, I was good at what I did and I knew I was good at what I did. I relied a lot on the people I played with and I never lost sight of that.

At Norwich, I progressed and blossomed because of the players around me like Ruel Fox, Ian Crook and Efan Ekoku. We all worked well together. These more experienced guys helped my game because I was young and raw. They gave me good guidance and created so many good chances on the park. They helped kick me on. They helped my understanding of the game. I was very aggressive and I was never worried about a battle. I thrived on the physical side of the game. It's just a pity I didn't know how to play the centre-forward role properly at a young age. It was more off the cuff. I now understand when to run and where to run. I know the game better now – that comes with experience. I wish I knew then what I do now.

A major regret in the game was refusing to play for the England B team – even if I felt at the time it was for the right reasons. It was a poor decision from me even though I felt I should have been in the full squad. Glenn Hoddle did nothing wrong. I should have abided by his decision.

I also wish my playing career hadn't ended when I was

thirty-four. I would have loved to play on for longer. But I had some fabulous times and have some wonderful memories.

Being my own worst critic spurred me on. I wanted to achieve the highest possible standards. After games I always thought what I could have done better. That may well have been a strength in my make up or it may have been a weakness in my make up but I was never really satisfied with myself. Even in the Juventus game, arguably my best ever game for the club, when we beat them 4–3 at Celtic Park in the Champions League, I can remember being really tired near the end of the game. When a cross ball came in, I tried to head the ball but I had cramp in my calves and I just didn't have enough spring left in my legs. I just couldn't get over the ball enough and the header looped over the bar. Yet I was disappointed in myself for not getting a hat-trick as I'd scored two by that stage in the game. I was striving for perfection all the time.

There was no better feeling, I thought, than playing in big games, against a really tough team, and winning your personal battle against your direct opponent. When I was at Norwich and we won 4–0 at Leeds United, I was up against David O'Leary and I felt I ran him ragged. For me to play that way against a man of his experience and calibre, who'd had such an outstanding playing career, was very satisfying. And when Valencia came to Celtic and they defeated us in the UEFA Cup, Roberto Ayala kicked lumps out of me because I was causing him problems.

Beating Arsenal 3–1 at Highbury with Blackburn in 1997–98 was also very memorable. We never usually got any change out of them but I competed really well against a really good defence. I didn't score but it was a satisfying performance for me personally and for the team.

The night Henrik came back to Parkhead with Barcelona, I was on the bench but came on at half-time. For a period in that game, I felt I was causing them problems. I wasn't dribbling past players but I knew that Carles Puyol wasn't coping well with my physicality. I used to like physical confrontation on the park. It was a big part of my game.

In an Old Firm game at Ibrox, I remember Dick Advocaat coming out of the dug-out and really screaming at the referee to sort me out as I was always backing into Lorenzo Amoruso. Amoruso was a strong player and you had to deal with that as best you could. But I knew Advocaat was only screaming for one reason and that was because he was concerned.

I think I've been extraordinarily lucky to have played with Weah, Larsson, Zola and Shearer. They were all great players but playing with Larsson was the biggest highlight. People would give their right arm to play alongside these guys. And that's just four of the top ones. I also loved playing with Ekoku, Gallacher, Hartson and Dahlin. I was very lucky in that respect. I wasn't as talented as the four top ones but I did know how to bring the best out of them. I have no doubt that, other than Zola who also liked to come to the ball, I helped the likes of Shearer and Larsson and was a good foil for them. I was effective without them and played very well as part of a two-man strikeforce.

I used to have to sacrifice myself for the sake of the team and I think I put my team-mates before myself on many occasions. As a striker, it didn't bother me if I finished the season as top scorer at the club or not; it may have been the difference between me and the great strikers such as Larsson and Shearer. Yet, it was nice when it did happen for me, at Norwich and Blackburn, but it never happened at Celtic. That was totally fine. I didn't have an ego when it came to that. When I played at Celtic, I felt invincible in games when Henrik was beside me and Petrov was bombing on. Special, special times in my career.

I enjoyed my time in Scotland. I was at an age where I appreciated it all far, far more. I enjoyed the success, the goals and the friendships. After the year I had had at Chelsea, it was just what I needed.

My playing career helped me get into management, got me my start at Lincoln City. My year at Sincil Bank wasn't a wholly enjoyable experience but it was definitely beneficial. People say nothing surprises you in football. I've always been quite cynical and certain things that happened to me at Lincoln and after I left the club have confirmed that.

The experience of keeping them in the league the first season and all the stuff that went on, positives and negatives, have left me feeling that I'm now in a better position to manage again. It hasn't soured my viewpoint on wanting to get back into management. I was let down by people at the club when they failed to keep their side of the bargain on many things and a lot of rubbish has been talked by people at that club. I hope to be given another opportunity in football. If I like the look of the job, feel I can help the particular football club, then I'll go for it. I know I have something to offer.

Most recently, my life has been dominated by my children and animals at our family home in Norfolk. I like animals. That's why we have ten dogs, eight horses, chickens and cats. Animals don't let you down – they are very loyal!

I'm busy with my five sons and, as I write this, we have another baby on the way. My life is different now from what it was when I played the game and managed at Lincoln. But I'm busy all the time, never a spare moment. I'm playing cricket again at a decent level but I'm totally out of my depth. I play golf badly and I go shooting. I enjoy the other sports but they don't mean as much to me as the football.

The shooting is great fun. I've met nice people in that environment such as Andrew Fischer, Will Esse, Robert Gurney, Ian Mason, Galton Blackiston, David Milner and Charlie Buchan. As a man brought up in a working-class environment, I'm very lucky to be mixing in such circles, some real hierarchy! A couple of them, who shall remain nameless, who've always been particularly good amateur village sportsmen, give me a particularly hard time about my limitations at shooting, golf and cricket. I met some of these people for the first time at a parents' night at the school and didn't feel appropriately dressed. I thought it was fancy dress night as most of the dads were all wearing either red or salmon-pink trousers!

In this book I've owned up to many of my weaknesses and frailties. Pity others haven't followed suit. On one shoot at a grouse moor, my friend Ian Mason was shooting particularly badly and missed a few. He complained of an eye infection. Typical!

On a more serious note and getting back to my career, decisions I made in football shaped my career. Some good, some bad. The way I handled the England situation was a bad decision. Moving to Scotland to play for Celtic was a great decision.

I also made one decision in March 2011 that was major. Earlier this year, a mole developed on my face and I decided to get it checked out. It was cancerous. I had it removed and it was sent away to be tested. The results showed an early sign of skin cancer. It certainly gave me a fright. Over the years, I wasn't bothered about protecting my skin. It still concerns me that I got the condition due to sun damage over the years. Clearly, I wasn't giving my skin enough protection and wasn't applying enough sun cream. Thankfully, I caught that one early enough for the surgeons to deal with it.

It gave me a real fright, though, and it was a warning to me never to take my health for granted. Doctors always say that if you are concerned about something, then go and get it checked out. I'm glad I confronted the mole on my face rather than pretending it didn't exist and hoping it would go away.

My condition was the tip of the iceberg compared to big John

Hartson. Thankfully, John found out about his testicular cancer just in time for it to be treated, although it had spread to other parts of his body. I was delighted for him and his family that he made a recovery. He was a strong player on the pitch and, having beaten cancer, is clearly as strong a character off it. Unfortunately, Tommy Burns died of skin cancer in May 2008. It was a tragedy. Tommy was a lovely man and very passionate about Celtic.

Usually, I would wait and wait and wait until going to get something checked out. Had I left the mole on my face for a year instead of going to see about it within a few weeks, then who knows what the doctors might have been telling me. The news, so far, has been all good but it's something they will keep an eye on, as I'm susceptible to it because I haven't been careful enough over the years protecting my skin. I got my mole removed but it could have been much worse for me. It was a lesson learned and thankfully we caught it in time. I'm much more aware about covering up now.

At the start of my book, I spoke about decisions and how making them shapes all of our lives. Sam's decision to rush James to hospital saved his life. I thank her for that. My boys and I owe so much to Sam and I want to thank her again for her support and understanding.

We talk about making decisions in life and getting my mole checked out was undoubtedly one of my better ones. With my playing career at an end, I feel I have learned a lot and I hope to continue to make choices that will enhance my life and that of my family. Decisions.

CHRIS SUTTON CAREER STATS

Full name: Christopher Roy Sutton
Date of birth: 10 March 1973
Place of birth: Nottingham, England
Height: 6 ft 3 in
Playing position: Forward

YEARS	CLUB	APPEARANCES	GOALS
1991–94	Norwich City	128	43
1994–99	Blackburn Rovers	161	59
1999–2000	Chelsea	39	3
2000–06	Celtic	199	86
2006	Birmingham City	10	1
2006–07	Aston Villa	8	1

INTERNATIONAL

1992–94	England Under-21	13	1
1994	England B	2	–
1997	England	1	–

MANAGEMENT

2009–10 Lincoln City